Ocean to Plate

KUSUMA COORAY

Ocean to Plate

COOKING FISH
with HAWAI'I'S
KUSUMA COORAY

A Latitude 20 Book
UNIVERSITY OF HAWAI'I PRESS
HONOLULU

19 18 17 16 15 14   6 5 4 3 2 1

Library of Congress Cataloging-in-Publication Data

Cooray, Kusuma, author.

Ocean to plate : cooking fish with Hawai'i's Kusuma
Cooray / Kusuma Cooray.

pages cm

"A latitude 20 book."

Includes bibliographical references and index.

ISBN 978-0-8248-3890-4 (pbk. : alk. paper)

1. Cooking (Fish)—Hawaii. I. Title.

TX747.C768 2014

641.3'92—dc23

2014007479

Designed by Mardee Melton
Printed by Regent Publishing Services

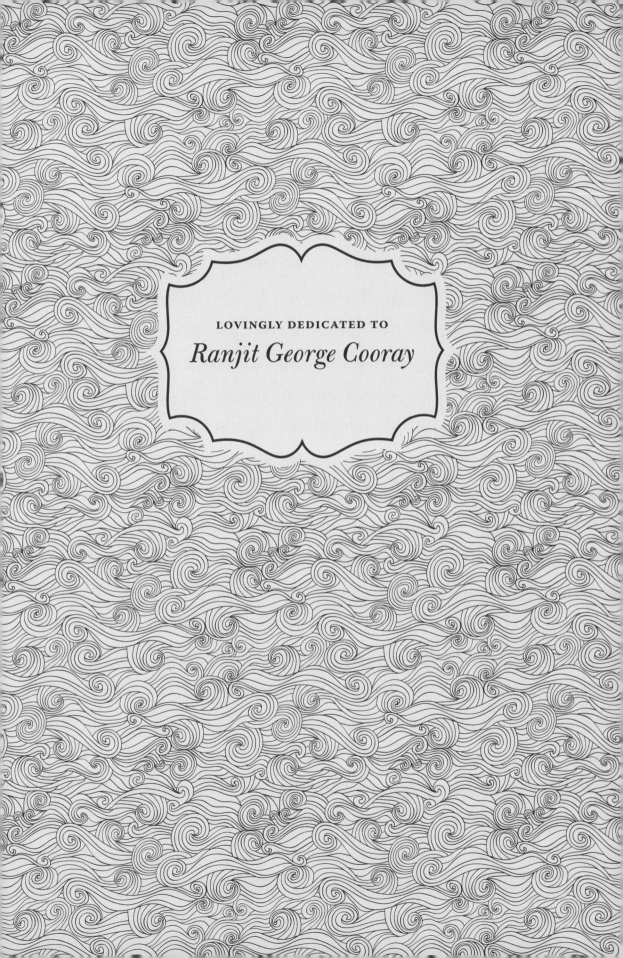

LOVINGLY DEDICATED TO

Ranjit George Cooray

Contents

Foreword

I ka moana no ka i'a, liuliu 'ia na pono lawai'a.
While the fish are still in the sea, get your gear ready.

I HAVE KNOWN AND WORKED WITH Chef Kusuma Cooray for over twenty-five years as she has been a mainstay in the Culinary Institute of the Pacific within our community colleges. She has shared with me the rich culture and culinary traditions of her home country, Sri Lanka. These traditions were beautifully illustrated in *Burst of Flavor*, her first cookbook published by the University of Hawai'i Press. I have enjoyed many a meal with Chef Cooray as she has hosted dinners honoring dignitaries visiting the university, as a fellow member of the Chaine des Rotisseurs, or on the many occasions where she has simply shared her talents with grateful supporters of the university who have a love for good food. Mostly, though, I have watched as she has taught generations of future chefs the techniques, the artistry, the creativity, the passion, and the discipline that she possesses and that the students must learn to be successful as culinarians.

I grew up in the Midwest and I can assure you that seafood, particularly fresh seafood, was not a regular part of our dining. However, the traditions of preparing fish are deeply imbedded in an island community, and since coming to Hawai'i some four decades ago, my eyes and my taste buds have been opened to the joy of good fish, well prepared. Now with this second book, you have the opportunity to be one of Chef Cooray's students, to learn how to ensure that your fish are indeed "well prepared." As the 'Ōlelo No'eau or Hawaiian proverb above notes, you must also prepare yourself. So gather your skillets, your spices and flavorings, your imagination, and the knowledge that Chef Cooray shares with you. I know that you will enjoy the results.

JOHN MORTON
Vice President for Community Colleges
University of Hawai'i

Acknowledgments

THIS BOOK WAS PUT TOGETHER WITH the help of many. First I must express my admiration for some of the greatest figures in the world of food: the late Julia Child, James Beard, and Louis Szathmary; and Anne Willan, Dianna Kennedy, André Soltner, and Jacques Pepin. Knowing them all personally and their work has been an inspiration to me.

Thanks to the University of Hawai'i Press for giving me the opportunity to write this book on fish, one of my favorite foods, and especially to Masako Ikeda of UHP, who invited me to write this book, and laid the initial groundwork for it. Thank you also to Nadine Little, acquisitions editor, for her constant support, and to Cheri Dunn, managing editor, for her assistance and encouragement. As my copy editor, Joanne Sandstrom gave life to my work; thank you.

My sincere thanks to Larry Vogel who insisted on and made it possible for my visit to Japan's Tsukiji Fish Market. Visiting Brooks Takenaka, manager of the United Fishing Agency, Honolulu, was exciting, and observing the fish auction was unforgettable. I thank him for sharing this wealth of knowledge about the industry with me. It helped me to get to a good start on my writing.

The Ishimoto Fish Market in Honolulu's Chinatown was always the place to go for fresh fish. Charlene and Chad Ishimoto always had good advice for me, and I ended up getting the best of the best. Fish from the Ishimoto Fish Market ended up dressed and photographed for this book.

I express my gratitude to Dr. John Morton, vice president for Community Colleges, University of Hawai'i; Dr. Leon Richards, chancellor of Kapi'olani Community College; Ron Takahashi, chair of the Culinary Arts Department at Kapi'olani Community College and Dr. Carl Hefner, chair of the Department of Social Sciences at Kapi'olani Community College, for their enthusiastic support.

I am honored to have had Dr. Alan Friedlander, University of Hawai'i, Department of Zoology, the expert on fisheries, work with me and advise me on the "What Fish Is This?" fish glossary. In the process of working with Dr. Friedlander, I acquired much knowledge in the scientific world of fish. I appreciate his patience and understanding.

Lisa van der Spoel did the drawings and the metric calculations for the book. Lisa, thank you for your dedication and the hard work you put in.

Rico Gatdula of HawaiiProPhoto lent his expertise to capture my cuisine in sixty tantalizing pictures for this book. Rico, thank you from the bottom of my heart for your patience during the long days and long hours you put in to make this book so special.

Thanks to Kristy Kiesel, our computer expert. She was a pillar of strength I could lean on during the hectic last three years of producing the book, and to Sally Yamaguchi, our Culinary Office manager, who was always there for me.

Finally, I greatly appreciate the good wishes from friends and family from many parts of the world.

Introduction

I GREW UP IN THE TOWN OF MORATUWA in Sri Lanka only three hundred yards (274 m) away from the Indian Ocean. When I was a child, we never bought fish from the market. The fishermen and fisherwomen brought the fish fresh and glistening to our back doorstep, and we could take our pick. I still remember the beautiful wahoo, known as ono in Hawai'i, and my excitement knowing that we would be eating a fat center chunk braised in a creamy sauce and seasoned with stone-ground mustard seeds and thick coconut milk that evening. Like the rest of my family and neighbors, I had a passion for fresh fish. No one could surpass us at cooking it either—with our special Sri Lankan style of spicing! Even today, my town of Moratuwa is famous for its fish dishes such as Curried Wahoo Steak, Devilled Sword Fish, Wahoo with Onion and Mustard Sauce, and Fried Anchovies.

I have lived and cooked in four distinctly different environments—Sri Lanka, England, mainland United States, and Hawai'i—and my culinary career has spanned the world, from private chef to executive chef to professor at Hawai'i's renowned Culinary Institute of the Pacific. For this volume, I draw on a lifetime of experience in preparing and serving fish and focus on Hawai'i's finest choices.

I grew up in a comfortable home with loving parents and four siblings. My mother's world was to feed her family and of course she had plenty of help. Food was a big part of our lives. There were always discussions about what we were going to have for our next day's meals or Sunday lunch, which was always special. Growing up in this environment molded me into a food lover and a serious culinary student. I was only nine years old when I started my "apprenticeship" in my own home kitchen under the watchful eye of the kitchen helpers. In this kitchen, I saw a bewildering array of fish, both whole and cut up, from different species and for a multitude of different preparations. I was allowed to gut the small fish like silvery white anchovies and to wash whole and cut-up fish. I learned that a pinch of turmeric rubbed into fish before washing helps to take away any strong fishy smell and, in addition, gives a golden blush to the fish. Before I was twelve years old, I could cook a simple yet delicious fish meal for my family. I was never squeamish with fish, and my specialty became fish cookery. I could identify a good number of fish varieties and knew the basic principles of handling and cooking fresh fish. I could cook even a whole fish with the head on. Later I learned that the French always left the fish heads on when they cooked fish whole, so that one would know the identity of the fish.

Home was where my culinary education began and my desire to become a professional chef grew. I had the desire to travel and experience the tastes and the grandeur of French food I had only read about. I realized there are many similarities in the respective cuisines. Like the French, our cuisine does not depend on artificial flavors and flavor enhancers. Our herbs are fresh and our fish is the freshest as fresh can be, just like theirs. One difference is that we have a unique way of spicing, a technique few chefs in the West take time to master. I not only wanted to taste the foods of the world, but I also wanted to share our cuisines with the world.

I had the good fortune of studying at the Cordon Bleu in London and Laverene in Paris. To complete my culinary studies I apprenticed with Master Chef Maurice Cazalis at his restaurant Henri IVth in Chartres. This was an unbelievable experience, a dream come true. I saw French cooking at its best. I discovered new ingredients and techniques, new flavors and textures. It was in France I first tasted sole. The French made sole in many styles, but the best was their simplest, sole à la meunière. The large fillet of sole was browned to a luxurious deep golden hue, simply dressed with freshly chopped parsley and shiny browned butter. The flesh of the freshly cooked sole melted in my mouth, an unforgettable taste. I learned that Scottish salmon was velvety and juicy, and with sips of Champagne the taste sensation was unreal. Wine-poached fish, satiny sauces like fish velouté, fish quenelles as light as feathers, and enticing garnishes such as golden fleurons, tender asparagus tips cooked in butter, and tiny tomatoes stuffed with fish mousse were fascinating to me. These taste sensations still live with me. My culinary studies and my personal experiences enhanced my knowledge of cooking and gave me confidence. I saw my childhood training as a foundation that I stood on. My food culture was a big part of me, and soon I realized I had a cooking style of my own, and a unique one.

Further good fortune brought me to Hawai'i, a melting pot of high-energy East and West influences, where I met and married a studious young man who was also a food lover. We made a good team and studied Hawai'i's fish together. We visited the fish auction and the fish markets. In multiethnic Hawai'i, Asia Pacific cuisines evolved with seafood as a central focus. My first taste of ocean-fresh raw fish here was thinly sliced red snapper sashimi gracefully lying on a haystack of shredded radish and wisps of pickled red ginger. We ate these morsels after dipping them in soy sauce and Japanese horseradish. Soon we started enjoying Hawaiian and other ethnic foods. Our plans to make our home in Hawai'i became real when fate stepped in.

I was offered a job with the fabulous Doris Duke and ended up as her corporate chef. She loved my special style of cooking. I traveled to many cities in mainland America—Los Angeles; Newport, Rhode Island; New York; and Sommerville, New Jersey—to the Duke residences. This unique experience added to my repertoire, and the memories remained. In Newport, Rhode Island, I attended my first clambake. Maine lobsters were the sweetest I had ever tasted anywhere. These sea-fresh memories intermingle with others on America's Atlantic coast—plucking periwinkles from rocks on the shore bordering Doris Duke's Rhode Island mansion, Rough Point, or cooking a freshly caught, plump black bass from the lake in her gardens in New Jersey.

After the dream job with Duke, I took the position of executive chef of The Willows Restaurant in Honolulu. I began to entice numerous diners with the fragrances of Asian spices in foods we served. It was a rewarding job.

Presently I am attached to the University of Hawai'i's Culinary Institute of the Pacific where I teach Continental Cuisine. At this great institution we train Hawai'i's young men and women to take their places in the hospitality industry.

The structure of this book has been carefully designed not only to introduce the cook to a broad variety of international fish recipes, but also to teach the best application of cooking techniques to what can be a challenging food. This book will help you learn how to shop effectively at the fish market; how to know when to buy or not to buy a fish; and, of course, how to apply the various methods of cooking to an extraordinary collection of international recipes.

Many say simply buying fresh fish is intimidating. There are basic principles and simple rules you need to follow. This book will give you just the tools you need to feel confident in your ability to judge quality and to handle and prepare the many varieties of fish in a methodical way. The recipes in this book range from curries to continental cuisine to dishes that speak of Hawaiian regional cuisine, but all are easy to prepare using readily available ingredients and simple techniques, and the dishes are tasty and appealing to the eye.

Hawai'i is known as one of the most ethnically diverse communities in the modern world, drawing people from all over Asia, the Pacific, Europe, and the Americas. The tempting tastes and flavors that all these people brought to the Islands, combined with the inspiration of Hawai'i's own culinary traditions, find their way into my recipes. For their tempting tastes and flavors, I use techniques, ingredients, and seasonings from the cuisines of many ethnic cultures along with my own exotic style of cooking influenced by the cooking traditions of Sri Lanka and Europe, where I had my formal training.

Within these pages are recipes to prepare fish in many exciting ways from starters to soups, from salads to sandwiches, and entrees from hot to cold. There are recipes for curing and smoking and unique recipes such as fish head curry. Because of the curiosity many have for curries, especially fish curries, a selection of recipes for fish curries in different styles will tempt you to try them all. As the taste and attractiveness of any fish dish will be enhanced by the use of appropriate sauces, dips and relishes, and accompanying starches, recipes are included for these as well. It is my hope that readers will be drawn into the fascinating and rewarding world of fish cookery through this book and with these recipes.

How to Use This Book

THE FIRST STEP IN COOKING ANY dish is to understand your ingredients. Read the introductory sections of this book completely in order to understand fish and to cook it well. Various sections will help you understand the structure of fish, how to select and buy the freshest fish; how to store fish; how to handle fish, how to select a recipe and prepare the fish accordingly. The What Fish Is This? section will help you get to know both familiar and unfamiliar fishes and will guide you in making the best choices for your dishes. Before you start cooking a particular fish dish, read the recipe thoroughly. All measures are given in both American (Imperial) and metric, and it is important to use one set of measures or the other without mixing the two. Both weight and volume measurements are used in recipes.

Although volume is commonly used to measure liquids, it is also used in recipes for dry ingredients that are too small to be weighed accurately—for example, cups and spoons and fractions thereof. Although not as accurate as weight, these volume measurements take less time. Measurements, temperatures, and timing are given as a guide, but use your best judgment. You may find that your oven cooks more quickly than some others, or that your family prefers more or less spice. All of the ingredients listed are readily available in most large city supermarkets and ethnic markets. Unfamiliar herbs, spices, ingredients, and terms appear in **bold** text in the recipes and are clearly defined in the glossary.

Simple preparation techniques and methods are used in the recipes, but before you get started on the recipes, read the Cooking Methods section, where cooking methods are explained thoroughly. Reference recipes (basics) are in bold with the relevant section. For example, the recipe for **Bouillabaisse** (see Soups and Stews) calls for 6 cups (1.5 L) of fish stock. The recipe directs the reader to the **Fish Stock** recipe (see Stocks) to prepare the basic stock.

Throughout this book, feel free to substitute where necessary. When fresh tomatoes are called for in sauces and braised dishes, you may substitute canned tomatoes. Olive oil and butter are used throughout the book; however, you may substitute the fat of your choice. Black pepper used for seasoning should be understood as ground black pepper and is best freshly ground whenever possible. When whole peppercorns are used it will be specified in recipes. Salt in a recipe is mentioned once even though a recipe uses salt more than once. Specific amounts for salt are not given; seasoning with salt should be done to your taste or to the taste of those you cook for. The onions called for in recipes are those known as brown onions or round onions; if green onion or red onion is used it will be specified.

Many recipes call for glass or enamel dishes or **nonreactive** dishes to marinate fish in. This is a term used to describe dishes, pans and cooking equipment made of materials that do not react to acids and brines and so do not form compounds that could discolor the cookware or the food or form toxic substances. Glass, stainless steel, and ceramic are nonreactive as long as their surfaces are undamaged. And, of course, use the section on fish categories and varieties creatively to find substitutions whenever and wherever you have difficulty obtaining a particular fish. Cooking is more than following a recipe—it is an adventure. Explore the world that is fish cookery, enjoy, and delight your family and guests.

A Word about Sustainability

OVER THE YEARS, INCREASED HUMAN CONSUMPTION of and high demand for fish has led to overfishing in many areas. World fish stocks have started to decline markedly, and certain species are even threatened with extinction. Governmental agencies in countries around the world, together with fishermen and the fishing industry, work to create sustainable seafood initiatives that aim to make seafood a reliable renewable resource. Laws and regulations continue to be enacted to ensure that fisheries are managed sustainably so that the fish are allowed to breed and populate at rates sufficient to guarantee their future. Local restaurants, chefs, seafood markets, wholesalers, and retailers have also joined together and formed alliances to create sustainable seafood initiatives. Chefs in countries around the world have started to promote environmentally friendly and sustainable fish in their restaurants. They have replaced overfished species with fresh, local underused species, and there has been great success in introducing customers to these local kinds of seafood. These initiatives not only help to promote the population growth of overfished species, but also help to support local fishing industries, which have been undermined by imported fish.

Customers can do their part to help in these efforts. If you love fish, learn how to judge the quality of fish in the market, how to identify the species of fish and its country of origin, and how the fish are harvested, handled, and processed. It is important to eat fresh, local, and sustainable fish not just for a healthy lifestyle, but also for a healthier environment. Resources from our oceans are invaluable and must be safeguarded. We can all agree to do our part by buying and cooking responsibly.

From the Ocean

UNDERSTANDING FISH

The first step in preparing delicious fish is to understand your main ingredient—the fish. Once you are familiar with the inherent attributes of the different fishes, you will become very comfortable with choosing a method of preparation and will know how long to cook each fish for optimum texture and flavor. Knowledge is power, and knowing your ingredients is the key to a perfect meal.

About Fish

STRUCTURE AND MUSCLE COMPOSITION

Fish are aquatic vertebrates, with backbones, internal skeletons of cartilage and bones, fins for swimming, and gills for breathing The flesh of fish consists of water, protein, fat, and small amounts of minerals and vitamins. Unlike beef and chicken, fish has very little connective tissue and so cooks very quickly, even at a low temperature. Because fish has very little connective tissue, it flakes easily when cooked.

Skeletal structure

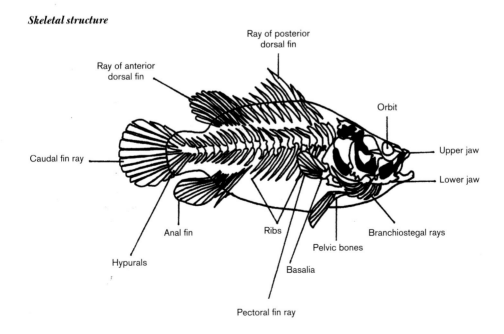

FISH CATEGORIES AND VARIETIES

The two categories of fish products are finfish and shellfish. Finfish have fins and internal skeletons of bone and cartilage. Shellfish have external shells but no internal bone structure. Finfish, or fish as we refer to it hereafter, includes both freshwater and saltwater varieties. In addition, with today's advanced aquaculture techniques, fish can be raised in ponds or ocean pens.

Based on their shape and skeletal structure, fish are divided into two groups— round fish and flat fish. Round fish have a backbone on the upper edge of their round or oval bodies and eyes on both sides of their heads; they swim in a vertical position. Salmon, red snapper, and tuna are examples of round fish.

Whole round fish

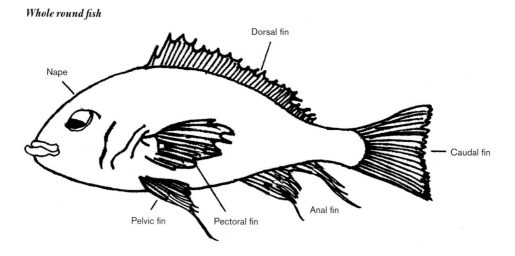

Flat fish have a backbone running horizontally through the center of the fish. They have compressed bodies with eyes on top of their heads; they swim in a horizontal position. Sole, halibut, and flounder are examples of flat fish. Some flat fish, such as sole, have dark skin on the upper side to hide them from predators, and some can even change color according to their surroundings. Flat fish have lean white flesh and a mild delicate flavor. The flesh when cooked flakes easily. One of the most prized of all flat fish is Dover sole. Flat fish may be cooked using the cooking methods for lean fish detailed below. Beyond the basic shape, flat or round, fish may be further loosely divided into lean or fatty, depending on their fat content. The fat content of fish varies significantly between species. Fish that are low in fat, such as snapper, flounder, sole, and cod, are called lean fish. Fatty fish are those high in fat, such as salmon, trout, tuna, butterfish, and mackerel. Some fish fall in between lean and fatty, such as wahoo, jacks, and swordfish.

Whole flat fish

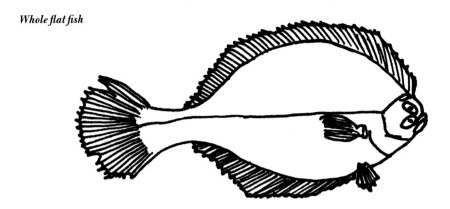

Lean fish has almost no fat and therefore can become easily dry when overcooked. Since lean fish has a tendency towards dryness, it is often served with a sauce, which enhances moisture and adds richness. Lean types of fish are best when poached—a moist heat cooking method. This method helps preserve moistness. Lean fish when broiled or baked—a dry heat cooking method—should be basted with butter or a fat of your choice. The added fat gives taste to the fish and also helps to preserve moistness.

Lean fish may also be fried or sautéed—dry heat cooking methods using fat. The oil or butter used to sauté or fry provides the fat the lean fish lacks and gives a luscious taste to the fish. Generally, fried or sautéed methods call for dredging the fish in flour or crumbs before cooking, leaving the fish crusty outside and juicy inside.

All the cooking methods can be used successfully for fatty fish, such as salmon. The fish's natural fat content will help to keep the fish moist and will help prevent unpalatable dryness. Just as with lean fish, fatty fish may be poached. Fatty fish are also well suited to broiling and baking. These cooking methods help to eliminate the oiliness of the fish. Fish with a high fat content may also be successfully fried or sautéed. Large fish may be browned in fat and finished in the oven. Fat fish fillets may be sautéed, and smaller fat fish like trout may be pan-fried. Care should be taken to avoid excessive fat by draining or mopping off visible oil with paper towels before serving.

FISH AND NUTRITION

Fish is an important part of a healthy, nutritious diet. It is low in fat and low in calories, but high in protein. Fish contains some saturated fat, although generally less than red meat. Fish provides vitamins A, B, and D and minerals such as calcium. Calcium is found more in smaller fish with edible bones, such as anchovies, sardines, and herrings. Their bones are softer and can be eaten when cooked or canned. Fish is also high in fatty acids called omega-3. Omega-3 fatty acids are unsaturated and may help to lower blood cholesterol levels and provide other potential health benefits.

Salmon, mackerel, tuna, and herring are a good source of omega-3 fatty acids. Since nutrition has become a major concern, it is good to know that fish can be prepared in simple ways and with simple sauces to reduce calories. The most commonly used cooking methods, like broiling, grilling, steaming, and poaching, need little or no fat. Because of these same dietary concerns, many people choose lean rather than fatty fish.

Fish Sense

Good fish cookery begins at the shoreline or at the fish market. The next best thing to catching your own fish is to buy your fish from a reliable fish market. For starters, the fish market should be impeccably sanitary and clean looking. The air should be fragrant with the sweet smell of sea breezes and devoid of any whiffs of strong fishy odor. Fish should be neatly displayed on crushed ice. Fresh fish will shine and glisten; it is not dull skinned and drab looking. A good fish market will have a fast turnover of its items for sale, and by the end of the day there will be little for sale. Patronize a reputable fishmonger.

TO BUY OR NOT TO BUY

Fish is one of the most perishable foods. Smell, look, and feel are important when buying fish. The fishy smells that turn many people away from fish are actually signs of decomposition of the product. It helps to have a checklist for freshness before you purchase fish:

Odor

> Fresh fish should have a sweet, fresh, ocean-breeze smell; any strong fishy odor or ammonia smells are sure signs of aged fish. This is the primary check for freshness.

Eyes

> The fish's eyes should be full, bulging, clear, and shiny. Cloudy and sunken eyes mean the fish is drying out and losing its freshness.

Gills

> Fish gills should be bright red or pink rather than muddy gray or brown, a sign of poor quality.

Texture

The texture of the fish should be firm and elastic. It should bounce back when pressed with your finger. It should not feel soft, nor should your finger leave an indentation easily. These are signs of poor quality and age.

Scales, fins, and color

The fins and fish scales should be shiny and tight on the skin; dry fins and scales may be signs of mishandling. The characteristic skin color should not be blemished with bloody patches along the ventral area. Cut fish like steaks and fillets should be moist and glistening, and the edges should not be brown or discolored and dry.

Your senses of smell, sight, and touch must be your guide to buying fish: when in doubt throw it out! Beware when you see fish at a reduced price; sometimes, if the price is too low, you can be sure it is not worth buying.

THE FISHMONGER

Growing up in a coastal town close to the Indian Ocean, we knew our fisherman and fisherwoman by name. It pays to get to know your fishmonger and build a relationship with him or her. When you are in the fish market, the fishmonger can help you. At the fish market, you will see a variety of fish in many different forms on display. Some fish may be familiar, but other lesser-known fish show up quite often at the market. Your fishmonger can help you with the names and qualities of these fish and where they come from. With the fishmonger's help, you can bring home the most economical and the freshest catch available for the day. Once you know the fishmonger well, he or she will suggest to you the best buy for the day and will be happy to prepare your pick any way you want, be it cleaned, scaled, skinned, or filleted. When you buy fish steaks, you can ask that the fishmonger cut them from a bigger chunk of fish. To be sure of having the freshest fish, you should avoid buying the ready-cut pieces. If you purchase a whole fish, the fishmonger will be glad to dress it, steak it, or fillet it for you if you so desire.

The fishmonger will occasionally share a recipe or two with his regular customers. The fishmonger may even give you a complimentary parcel of freshly trimmed fish bones for your fish stock or even a fish head, which is delicious curried, as done in Singapore. If you patronize the supermarket, get to know the manager in the fish department; he or she can be as helpful as the friendly fishmonger. Whether you shop at the local fish market or the supermarket, have a cooler with a few packs of ice in it, so you can keep your fish cool until you get home.

FISH MARKET FORMS

Fish is generally available in a variety of market forms: whole fish, drawn fish, dressed or pan-dressed fish, fillets, butterfly fillets, and steaks.

Whole fish

Fish is intact as caught.

Drawn fish

Most fresh fish is sold drawn, that is, scaled with the viscera (internal organs) and gills removed. Buying a drawn fish has its advantages. Because of minimal handling it would have lost fewer of its juices.

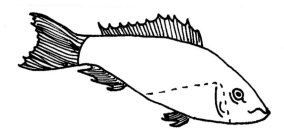

Dressed fish

These are fish with scales, viscera, head, tail, and fins removed. Dressed fish are also referred to as pan-dressed fish. Although the fish head is usually removed, sometime the head is left on for presentation. Small fish such as trout and scad may be also pan-dressed with the head on.

Fillets

These are the boneless sides of the fish and can be sold with or without the skin. Sometimes there could be small bones remaining in a fillet. Round fish produce two fillets, one from each side of the fish. Flat fish such as sole produce two or four fillets. Two whole fillets may be cut from the top and the bottom of the fish or two may be cut from the top of the fish and two from the bottom of the fish.

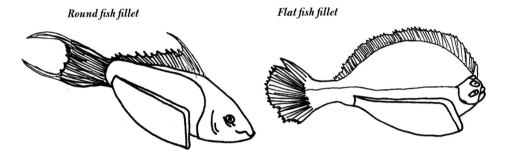

Round fish fillet   **Flat fish fillet**

Butterfly fillets

These are pan-dressed fish, boned and opened up like a book, both sides of the fish still joined by the back skin. Sometimes the head and tail are kept on for presentation.

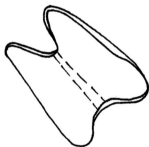

Steaks

These are cross-cut slices of the whole fish, usually ½ to 2 inches (1.2 to 5 cm) thick, each containing a section of the backbone and skin. The steaks may contain some bones.

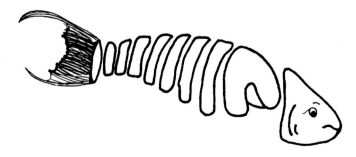

SASHIMI

Sashimi, a traditional Japanese delicacy, consists of very fresh raw fish or other seafood thinly sliced, with the dimensions depending on the type of fish or seafood used. A wide variety of fish such as tuna, marlin, and red snapper can be used for sashimi. However, tuna remains the most popular choice, with bigeye and yellowfin tuna both excellent choices for sashimi. The grade of fish matters. Sashimi grade, also called number 1 grade, is the preferred choice for sashimi and is available at a premium price. Number 1 grade fish has a higher fat content, a deeper red color, and moist flesh with a clean taste—all desired qualities for sashimi. Tuna for sashimi may be bought in loin sections. Sometimes the loin sections are presented sliced to show off their color and texture; this makes it easy to make a choice. One of the most prized and expensive cuts for sashimi is known as *o-toro*. "Toro" defines a section of the fish, the belly loin of fatty fish such as tuna. Because *chu-toro*, the larger section of the loin, has only a moderate amount of fat, it is the second-most prized cut for sashimi. *Akami* has no significant amount of fat. Only the freshest fish should be used in this delicacy. Tell the fishmonger that you need fish to prepare sashimi so that he or she can recommend the safest cuts on hand. Fish for sashimi should be saltwater fish, not freshwater fish.

Sashimi is considered the finest dish in Japanese cuisine; it represents Japanese cultural appreciation of refinement and subtlety. Sashimi is generally served at the beginning of a meal before strong flavors affect the palate. The presentation of sashimi is an art form that respects the quality and beauty of the ingredients used. Sashimi is served with a dipping sauce of soy sauce and **wasabi** and simple garnishes like **shiso** leaves, shredded radish, and thinly sliced pickled ginger root. Sometimes the fish tail and or the fins are used to garnish a sashimi platter to help identify the fish being eaten.

HOW MUCH TO BUY

How much fish should you buy? It depends on how it will be cooked. Generally speaking, today a 5-ounce (142 g) portion of fish fillet (trimmed and without bones) makes a good dinner entrée; if there are to be accompaniments such as potatoes and vegetables, the portion size may be even as small as 4 ounces (113 g). Luncheon portion sizes can vary from 3½ to 4 ounces (99 to 113 g), that too depending on whether the fish is served in a salad or as a hot entrée. The standard dinner entrée portion size served in restaurants is much larger. Depending on the preparation, it can vary anywhere from 6 ounces to 7 ounces (170 to 198 g) for a dinner entrée and 5 to 6 ounces (142 to 170 g) for a lunch entrée. For drawn fish, you would calculate your needs based on 1½ to 2 pounds (680 to 907 g) per portion; for dressed fish or pan-dressed fish, 10 ounces (283 g) per portion is the general rule. If you buy bone-in steaks, you need 8 ounces (226 g) per portion. Some fish lose water during the cooking process. Some fish have heavy bones and large heads. Therefore, when buying whole fish, you should consult the fishmonger unless you are an expert.

NO BONES ABOUT IT

Unless you buy fish steaks and fillets, other fish forms you purchase will have trimmings and bones that you can use. In fact, when you ask the fishmonger to pan-dress a fish for you, request that the trimmings be wrapped up separately. Among the trimmings you will have the fish head, bones, and some belly flesh. Fish trimmings and bones can be used to make a stock, and the fish head can be made into a fish-head soup, local style or curried.

FISH HEADS

Those who know say that most of the fish flavor lies in the fish head. (However it should be remembered that toxins accumulate in the heads of fish.) One of Singapore's culinary specialties is fish-head curry served in small restaurants in "Little India," in the hawker centers, inside street eateries, and in hotel restaurants including the once world-famous Raffles Hotel. The fabled fish-head curry, one of the most popular dishes across Singapore and Malaysia, is slowly catching on even in New York. It is believed that fish-head curry was made popular by an imaginative enterprising Indian in his small restaurant in Singapore.

There are different types of fish-head curry available in Singapore; they are all lip-smacking good! Each version is different in taste and style. The fiery hot fish-head curry is laced with a thick **tamarind** curry sauce with vegetables like ladies fingers (okra) and aubergines (eggplant). This repast bears adherence to Indian roots. It is even better when served on a banana leaf, Singapore style in the open air, a feast to remember. The Chinese-style curry comes in a huge bubbling clay pot brimming with vegetables, it is less spicy than the Indian version. The Thai version is made with a **lemongrass** paste in a spicy red curry sauce and is served with rice and a green mango salad. A giant fish head floating in a huge portion of delicious spicy sauce is the ideal menu item for a group of six to eight. This delicacy is loved not only by the locals but also by the numerous visitors to Singapore.

TOOLS AND METHODS FOR PREPARING FISH

Preparing Fish for Cooking

EQUIPMENT AND TOOLS

If you wish to buy a whole fish and break it down yourself make sure you have the proper tools it.

Cutting board
> The work surface for scaling, cleaning, and cutting fish should be of a material that can be sterilized after use and should be devoid of any odors. Avoid using cutting boards that are made of soft, porous material. Choose those made of hard wood or plastic. Make sure cutting boards are free of cracks and crevices and are easy to clean.

Fish scaler
> The fish scaler has an upward-curved thin blade with a serrated edge that helps to scrape and release the fish scales without breaking the skin. The other end of the scaler forms the handle. This is an essential tool for scaling fish.

Kitchen shears
> Similar to a heavy-duty pair of scissors, shears are used to cut off the fins and tails of fish and even the gills and viscera.

Fish knife
> A knife with a strong blade and sharp edge for cutting and steaking fish should be sharp and strong enough to be struck on the blunt edge with a mallet, to cut through fish heads and backbones.

Cleaver
> A heavy knife with a heavy sturdy handle may be used instead of the fish knife and should be strong enough to be struck on the blunt edge with a mallet, especially when cutting through head or the backbone of the fish.

Mallet

A large hammerlike wooden, metal, or rubber tool is used to hit on the blunt edge of the fish knife or cleaver when cutting through a fish head or the backbone of a fish.

Fillet knife

A light and flexible sharp knife 7 to 9 inches (18 to 23 cm) long should be used for filleting and slicing fish.

Tweezers

A pair of tweezers comes in handy for pulling small bones out of a fish fillet without damaging its flesh. Round fish fillets contain a row of intra-muscular bones or pin bones running halfway down the length of the fillet. In the case of a salmon fillet, these fine pin bones are usually removed with the help of tweezers. Small needle-nose pliers may be used instead.

CLEANING AND CUTTING FISH

Follow the directions for cleaning, cutting, and preparing fish ready to cook according to the recipe of your choice. When preparing fish, keep work surfaces, knives, utensils, and tools absolutely clean. Wash your hands thoroughly with hot soapy water before handling fish.

To scale the fish

Place the fish flat on a cutting board and grip it by its tail firmly with one hand. Grip the scaler in the other hand and, working from the tail to the head, scrape against the scales without damaging the flesh. When all the scales are removed, turn the fish over and remove the scales from the other side. Hold the fish by the tail under running water and rinse it to get rid of all the remaining scales. Feel the skin for any scales you may have missed. Clean the cutting board.

To trim fish fins and tail

Use shears and trim fins and tail of the fish. Fins should be cut as close as possible to the bone that connects them to the fish.

To eviscerate the fish

It is important to remove the viscera or guts. If left in the fish, the enzymes in the gastrointestinal system will cause the fish to deteriorate rapidly and lead to spoilage. It is equally important to rinse the fish thoroughly under cold running water to rid it of any gastrointestinal matter. To eviscerate, use a sharp knife and slit the belly starting with a shallow cut from the anal fin right up to the chin bone of the fish. Do not puncture the viscera. Pull it out from just under the chin and discard it. Pull out the membrane attached to the ribcage and scrape out the matter around the ribs. Rinse the fish cavity and the fish well under running cold water. The eviscerating procedure is the same for round fish and flat fish. To eviscerate small fish such as anchovies, smelts, herrings, and sardines, open up the gill flaps, firmly hold the gills with your fingers, twist, and slowly pull the gills, and the guts will follow. Discard the viscera and rinse the fish.

To remove the fish head

Make a V-shaped cut through the flesh just behind the gills on both sides of the fish. Cut the backbone at the point closest to the gills and pull off the head along with the gills. Rinse the fish under running water, making sure to wash off all traces of blood.

To remove gills

Lift the gill covers and, using shears or scissors, cut the gills at the place where they are attached to the head. Pull them out and discard them. Rinse the fish, again making sure to wash off all traces of blood.

To fillet a fish

One round fish is fabricated into two fillets, one from each side of the fish. Place the fish on the cutting board with the backbone parallel to the work surface and the fish head on the same side as your hand holding the filleting knife. Open the gill plates and place the knife behind the head. Angle the knife and cut down and away from the body. This cut should not sever the head of the fish from the body. Turn the cutting edge of the knife towards the tail of the fish and cut against the backbone under the flesh, down the length of the fish, using smooth strokes of the knife to separate the flesh from the bone. Continue cutting under the flesh along the curved rib bones towards the tail and detach the fillet from the head end. Turn the fish over and repeat to remove the second fillet. One flat fish is fabricated into four fillets, two from each side.

To skin a fillet

Place the fish with the tail pointing towards you, skin side down on your work surface. Firmly holding the skin at the tail end, slide the knife between the skin and the flesh. Angle the knife down towards the skin and, using a saw-ing motion, cut the skin away from the flesh, gripping the tail end of the skin firmly with one hand.

Dressed to "grill"

Dress a fish in the following order: scale the fish, remove the tail and fins, eviscerate the fish, and remove the head and gills. If you wish to cook a whole fish with the head on, dress the fish and remove the gills and keep the head on.

To butterfly a fish

First trim fins and tail, then scale and eviscerate the fish. If the fish head is to be kept on, remove the gills. If not, remove the fish head. To butterfly a fish with the head on, open the fish up on the stomach side and place the stomach side down on the cutting board. Press down firmly on the backbone with the palm of your hand. This is to loosen it somewhat. Turn the fish over, and beginning at the head, slide the filleting knife under the backbone. Gradually loosen and cut the backbone with the rib bones away from the flesh as you continue to cut from head to tail. Using shears, sever the bone at the tail and pull up the whole skeletal structure to detach it from the body and sever it at the head.

To cut steaks

Steaks can be cut from a round fish. First dress the fish, leaving the head on and removing the gills. Wash and place it on its side on a cutting board. Make the first cut behind the gill covers. A cleaver is best for this purpose. Using the cleaver, mark off cross-sections of steaks about ¾ inches to 1½ inches (1.9 to 3.8 cm) thick down the length of the fish. Cut each steak through the backbone, using a mallet to hammer down the back of the cleaver so it will easily go through the hard backbone.

AFTER CUTTING FISH

Sanitize

It is important to prevent bacteria from the raw fish from spreading to ready-to-eat food. Wash and sanitize all the work surfaces, equipment, and tools used. Make sure cutting boards are sanitized to prevent cross-contamination that can create a breeding ground for bacteria. As an added precaution, sanitize cutting boards by rinsing them in a solution of chlorine bleach made with 1 teaspoon of chlorine bleach to 1 quart of water. To remove the fishy smell clinging to your fingers, squeeze lemon juice over your hands and scrub with the lemon skins. Leave a minute or two, wash thoroughly with hot soapy water, and then sanitize your hands.

Cooking with Care

HANDLING AND STORING FISH

Since fish is one of the most perishable foods, it is essential to handle and store it carefully and use it quickly. Whole fish should be drawn or dressed and should be loosely wrapped, preferably in a damp cheesecloth or a damp towel to prevent it from drying out. Chilling is much faster with the viscera and gills removed (i.e., drawn or dressed). Place in the coldest area of the refrigerator. You may also keep it on ice, but it should not come in direct contact with the ice as the flesh can get freezer burn. Wrap cut fish, such as fillets and steaks, in moisture-proof packaging before placing on crushed ice in a perforated pan or a drip pan to catch the melting ice and cover the pan. Place fish away from ready-to-eat foods, such as salad ingredients and fruits. Avoid crowding in the refrigerator; allow air to circulate freely. Most important is the temperature at which the fish is stored. All fresh fish should be stored at 30°F to 32°F (-1°C to 0°C). Fresh fish should not be stored for more than a day. If you need to keep it longer, it should be frozen. However, not all home freezers are adequate for properly freezing fish. Frozen fish should be kept at a temperature of 0°F to 4°F (-18°C to -15°C) in order to stop any microbial activity. If you have to freeze fish, eviscerate, draw, or dress the fish first; wash and drain it and wrap in freezer wrap and place in freezer bags. To prevent freezer burns, make sure the packaging is airtight. Fix a sticker noting the date of freezing and type of fish. Maximum home-freezer storage time for fish should be two months for lean fish and one month for fat fish. Frozen fish should be thawed in the refrigerator, never at room temperature on the kitchen counter or sink. Thawed fish should never be refrozen because between the time the product is thawed and refrozen, bacteria may have time to form.

AVOIDING HAZARDS

While it is widely accepted there are health benefits from including more fish in the diet, there are also safety hazards associated with certain types of fish products. Fish can get spoiled or contaminated from the time of harvesting and processing to the time the fish reaches you. Get to know where your fish come from, the species, ones to avoid, and the ones to buy. Follow the basic safety tips when storing, handling, and preparing fish so you and your family can enjoy the fine taste and good nutrition of fish. If you don't prepare your fish yourself, patronize reputable restaurants.

As a consumer, have at least a basic understanding of common seafood-related illnesses. Pay attention to government and state health advisories in your area. Sources of infected seafood and suspected cases of seafood poisoning should be reported to your health department.

PREVENTING CONTAMINATION

It is important to keep a few things in mind when cooking fish. It is best to do the preparation in advance and cook the fish right before service. Marinate fish in the refrigerator; generally, you should discard the marinade after cooking the fish. If you want to use the marinade after the fish is cooked, bring it to a rolling boil so that any bacteria that could have been on the raw fish are killed. Never put cooked fish back in the container that held the raw fish. Avoid using any utensils that touched the raw fish to touch cooked fish.

SPECIAL PROBLEMS IN COOKING FISH

Overcooking is a major flaw in fish cookery. It must be repeated again that fish has very little connective tissue and is very delicate. As a result fish cooks very quickly even at low heat; thus, it's easily overcooked, thereby losing its natural juices and flavor. Overcooked fish tastes insipid and dull, its texture dry and shrunk. To preserve the taste and texture of the fish, avoid reheating. Lean fish has a mild taste; its tender, flaky flesh lends itself to a variety of seasonings and cooking methods. However, lean fish tends to dry out in the cooking process; moist-heat cooking techniques, such as poaching and steaming, will help preserve the moisture and thus enhance richness. Lean fish can also be baked in the oven with added butter or oil, or enclosed in paper, foil, or green leafy vegetables. When broiling or grilling lean fish, it is best to baste with fat or liquid to prevent it from drying out. Fat fish, in contrast, needs dry-heat methods of cooking to help eliminate excess fat.

These are only general rules of fish cookery, and both fat and lean fish may be cooked in any method you wish. However, care and attention should be taken to prevent overcooking fish.

TESTING FOR DONENESS

Reputable fisheries from around the world recommend that all fish be cooked 10 minutes for every inch of thickness, irrespective of cooking method used, except deep-frying. This guideline helps to determine doneness. Fish, which is translucent in the raw state, turns opaque and white when cooked. The flesh of raw fish is firmly attached to the bone. If the bone is present in the cooking process, the bone and the flesh separate easily, and the bone is no longer a pink color. Fish is cooked when it begins to separate into flakes. When tested with a fork, the fish breaks apart into its natural separations, called flakes. Flakes should not fall apart; if they do, the fish is overcooked. The residual heat in the fish will continue to cook the fish even after it is removed from the cooking heat source, a process known as carryover cooking.

Cooking Methods

Fish can be prepared by moist-heat cooking methods such as poaching and steaming as well as by dry-heat methods such as broiling, grilling, barbecuing, baking (roasting), sautéing, pan-frying, and deep-frying. Fish is also prepared by braising, which is a combination of moist-heat and dry-heat methods. These cooking methods are discussed below. Before using a recipe it is best to refer to the relevant cooking method and then proceed.

POACHING

Poaching is a moist-heat cooking method. There are two methods of poaching. In the submersion method, the fish is completely covered by a liquid in a straight-sided pan and simmered at very low temperature. It is important to have a well-flavored liquid to poach fish. The end result will be flavorful and delicious. Poaching liquids can be **Fish Stock** (see Stocks), a **Court Bouillon** (see Stocks), wine, water, or fruit juices; the addition of herbs, spices, and vegetables will enhance the flavor. High temperature can break up the fish and thus cause loss of flavor. Cooking temperature should be 160°F to 180°F (71°C to 82°C). Large fish like salmon, dressed with or without the head, may be wrapped in cheesecloth for poaching; this wrapping helps to preserve the shape of the fish while cooking. Smaller fish or steaks need not be wrapped for poaching, although they may be wrapped in cabbage or lettuce leaves. Lean white fish such as snapper and fat fish such as salmon and trout are all excellent for poaching. Any pan with low sloping sides and large enough to hold the fish in a single layer is good for poaching. A fish poacher with a lid, a nonreactive oval-shaped long pan with a fitted rack to lower the fish in and pull it out, is good for poaching large fish such as whole salmon. However, a roasting pan will yield the same results. If you do not have a lid for the roasting pan, you may use double thickness of aluminum foil to cover the roasting pan.

The second method, which combines both poaching and steaming methods, is called shallow poaching. This method is good for small cuts of fish such as fillets, steaks, and small dressed fish. These are placed in a straight-sided sauté pan on a bed of aromatic vegetables and herbs and partially submerged in fish stock or court bouillon. It is then brought to a simmer on the stove top and covered with buttered parchment paper or a tight-fitting lid. Cooking is completed either on the stove top or in a slow oven at 275°F (135°C).

Poached fish with wrappers removed may be served hot or cold with a sauce made from a portion of the poaching liquid sometimes reduced and enhanced with butter or egg yolk or with a **Hollandaise Sauce** or a **Béarnaise Sauce** (see Sauces, Dips, and Condiments). These egg-based sauces are traditional; today, low-fat vegetable relishes and chutneys have become very popular.

STEAMING

Steaming is another moist-heat cooking method. The fish is placed on a steamer rack, covered, and placed on a pot of aromatized boiling liquid. The steam created gently cooks the fish while preserving its natural flavors and nutrients. The liquid for steaming can be a **Court Bouillon** (see Stocks) or water aromatized with leeks, lemon or orange peel, star anise, **cinnamon** sticks, other spices, **lemongrass**, or wine.

To steam fish, first season it with salt, pepper, and lemon juice to taste. Next, place the fish on a rimmed plate that can fit on the steamer rack, cover tightly, and place on a steaming pot of aromatized water or court bouillon. A bamboo steamer may also be used for steaming. For a six-ounce portion of fish cook 4 to 6 minutes. A dressed fish with or without the head will take longer depending on its size. Another method of steaming fish is *en papillote*. Fish with seasoning and vegetable garnish enclosed in greased parchment or paper wrapper is placed in a baking pan and baked; usually the fish "parcel" is slit open at the table so guests can enjoy the escaping aroma of the fish.

Steamed fish is a popular menu item today because it is a low-fat, low-calorie preparation. Consequently, it should be served simply, with a squeeze of lemon or a relish. Of course, **Sauce Beurre Blanc** (see Sauces, Dips, and Condiments) is an ideal accompaniment for those who are not concerned with fat intake. Another Pacific Islands favorite preparation is to sprinkle freshly shredded ginger, green onion, and fresh cilantro sprigs on the steamed fish and immediately pour boiling hot peanut and sesame oil over it.

BRAISING

Braising is a combination of dry-heat and moist-heat cooking. A deep skillet or a heavy baking pan is good for braising. Dressed fish (with or without the head) and large cuts of fish are ideal for braising. The fish is first browned in a small amount of fat. Sliced or chopped vegetables such as leeks, onion, garlic, tomatoes, mushrooms, and aromatic herbs added and sautéed in the same pan. Liquid such as wine or fish stock is added to reach halfway up the fish. The fish can be cooked in the oven or stovetop on low heat. Cook uncovered or partially covered with parchment paper or with lettuce or cabbage leaves as appropriate. Baste the fish with the cooking liquid three to four times. When the fish is cooked, the cooking liquid will have reduced to a flavorful natural sauce. You may serve the sauce as is or strain it and enrich with cream and butter and serve with the fish. Rice or potatoes make good accompaniments to braised fish.

STEWING

In stewing, food is simmered in a deep skillet in a small amount of liquid, which is usually served with the food as a sauce.

BROILING

Broiling is a dry-heat cooking method using radiant heat from above, such as an overhead electric or gas element. Broiling, which is similar to grilling, is a popular method used often for fish. When broiling or grilling whole fish fillets with the skin on, it is best to score the skin by making three or four diagonal cuts at even intervals about ¼ inch (0.5 cm) deep into the fish to allow for even cooking. Broiling leaves fish with a lightly charred surface and a moist and succulent inside. To achieve this desired result, fish should be brushed with oil or fat before it is placed under the broiler or on the grill. Broiler pans or grills can be adjusted to be nearer to or farther from the heat source.

BAKING

Baking and roasting are both dry-heat methods of cooking, usually in an oven. In fish cookery the word "baking" is used rather than "roasting." In these methods the food is surrounded with hot, dry air. Very little or no liquid is added. Fatty fish are best for baking, and the best cuts are fish fillets and steaks. Common seasonings are black pepper, salt, and lemon juice. Wine and butter make good basting ingredients. Lean fish tends to dry out during the cooking process and needs basting throughout. Oven-proof glass baking dishes are good for baking as are baking pans and sheets and open casseroles.

ROASTING

"Roasting" usually applies to meats and poultry, but roast fish is elegant and attractive. A large fish roasted whole serves to six to eight guests; smaller fish roasted whole and served as individual portions are popular with many fish lovers. Drawn fish, with the skin and head on, is ideal for roasting. Make sure the fish is well scaled before roasting. The skin will encapsulate the moisture and flavor of the roasted fish and become crisp and golden brown when the fish is done. Fatty fish such as salmon, red snapper, or striped or black bass with their colorful skins are good for roasting. Fill the cavity of the fish with aromatic spices or herbs; season with lemon, lime, orange, or **tamarind** juice and sea salt and splash with wine or flavored vinegars before you place the fish in the oven for roasting. To help the skin turn crisp and prevent the fish from drying out, baste with melted butter or oil during roasting.

SAUTÉING

Sautéing is a dry-heat cooking method where food is cooked quickly in a small amount of fat; it is a popular method for cooking fish. Straight-sided or plain sauté pans or skillets are best for sautéing fish. The cooking process leaves a lightly caramelized golden color and a crusty surface on the fish that add to the flavor and look of the dish. **Clarified butter** or a combination of clarified butter and oil is the preferred fat for sautéing fish. Whole butter tends to burn before the fish is done, unless the fish is cut into small pieces. Both lean and fat fish are good to sauté. However, fat fish sometimes tends to be greasy by the end of cooking time, whereas this method provides the fat that lean fish needs to make it tasty and keep it moist. Dressed flat fish such as sole and its fillets, fillets of round lean fish such as snapper or whole round fish such as trout may be sautéed. Steaks from larger fish such as salmon or evenly portioned fillets of salmon may also be sautéed. Thin fish fillets such as fillet of sole and other delicate fish may be dusted lightly in seasoned flour before sautéing. This dusting not only prevents the fish from breaking while sautéing but also creates a golden-brown crust that enhances the flavor and the presentation of the dish.

SEARING

Searing is done to brown the surface of a food quickly at a high temperature. Searing seals the juices of the food and keeps it moist and flavorful as in the case of **Seared Tuna with Mint Chutney** (see Entrées).

PANFRYING

Panfrying food is cooked in a moderate amount of fat in a pan over moderate heat. Fish is always breaded or coated lightly with flour. Such coatings prevent the fish from coming into contact with the fat. Well-prepared panfried fish will have an attractive and crisp coating with a moist inside. Sauces such as **Rémoulade** and **Tartar Sauce** (see Sauces, Dips, and Condiments) are traditionally served with panfried fish. Today chutneys and relishes for panfried fish are very popular.

DEEP-FRYING

In deep-frying, food is submerged in hot fat. For health reasons, this cooking method is not as popular as it was some time ago. A deep fryer usually has a basket insert with a handle and a rest for propping the basket to allow the fat from the cooked food to drain off. A deep pot will also suffice for deep-frying and a slotted spoon or a skimmer for removing the fried food from the fryer. Lean fish is best suited for deep-frying. Small fish fillets, small whole fish, or thin fish slices are best for deep-frying. Fish for deep-frying should be breaded, battered, or tossed in seasoned flour. These coatings not only give a crisp attractive look but also add flavor to the fish. The secret to good deep-frying is to use an oil that does not burn at a high temperature, such as corn oil or peanut oil.

To deep fry fish, it is essential to have at least 3½ to 4 inches of fat in the fryer. The cooking temperature should be between 325°F (165°C) and 375°F (190°C). The temperature may be adjusted within these limits to allow the interior of the fish to cook without overbrowning the crust. Lower the coated fish into the fat and fry to a golden brown. Turn fish once during cooking. When done, remove from the fryer and place on absorbent paper to remove excess fat. Deep-fried fish is traditionally served with lemon and **Tartar Sauce, Rémoulade Sauce,** or **Cocktail Sauce** (see Sauces, Dips, and Condiments). **Chutneys**, **relishes**, and **dips** (see Sauces, Dips, and Condiments) are healthy choices to replace the mayonnaise-based sauces.

STIR-FRYING

A form of sautéing, stir-frying is done on very high heat in a lightly oiled pan, often a wok, sometimes a skillet. Any type of fish can be used, often cut up into bite-sized pieces or thin slices. Peanut oil is the preferred cooking fat, but other fats may be used. Common seasonings are soy, vinegar, ginger, garlic, **chili paste**, and wine; the common thickener is flavored cornstarch slurry. It is best to use as little as possible when it comes to slurries in stir-fries. Fish may be stir-fried with a choice of vegetables.

GRILLING

Grilling is a dry-heat cooking method, similar to broiling. The main difference is that the heat source in grilling comes from beneath the food. Grilling is done on an open grid; the heat may be from charcoal or an electric or gas-heated element. Grilling brings out the flavor of the fish yet keeps it tender and juicy. Charcoal grilling is most popular, and the resulting smoky charcoal flavor is a desired characteristic in grilled fish. For grilling, especially for dressed fish, you may use a grilling basket so that you can easily turn the whole fish without fear of breaking it. This is the required tool for grilling whole fish. Cooking and serving principles are similar to serving broiled fish.

BARBECUING

Barbecuing is also a dry-heat cooking method. The food is cooked over dry heat created by a wood fire or over hot coals of wood. Both give the food a smoky flavor. Both fat and lean fish are ideal for barbecuing and grilling, and dressed fish is more desirable than smaller cuts of fish. Small cuts of fish and tender-fleshed fish should be placed on perforated foil on the grill for barbecuing. Cubed fish should be threaded on skewers to barbecue. As a rule, marinate whole fish and large cuts for 30 to 40 minutes before cooking. Smaller cuts, tender-fleshed fish, and skewered fish may be brushed with a marinade while cooking. A wide spatula and long pair of tongs are the needed tools in addition to a wood-burning, gas, or charcoal grill.

CURING

Curing is a method of preserving foods. Salt curing is a process of surrounding the food with a mix of salt and flavoring agents. Salt is the common ingredient used today for home curing food, with the addition of sugar, spices, herbs, fruit juices, and wines to enhance flavor. Salt inhibits bacterial growth at the same time it dehydrates the product. The process preserves the product, adds flavor, and makes it safe to eat. Curing fish products takes less time than curing meat products. Cured fish is used for smoking. It can also be used for grilling and steaming, and in various other ways such as spreads for sandwiches in canapés and salads. Cured fish can be salty, so care should be taken when seasoning these items. Cured fish takes well to sweet, tart, and creamy flavors and to liquors such as brandy, rum, and vodka; it goes well with fruit compote, chutney, fruit relishes, and creamy horseradish to name a few.

SMOKING

The basic style of smoking is hot smoking. Heat within the range of 200°F to 250°F (93°C to 107°C) exposes food to smoke, and the food actually gets cooked in this method. Hot smoking is often used to preserve seafood products. Even though hot smoked seafood products are fully cooked when taken off the smoker, it is best that you cook these before serving as directed in my recipes. There are gas and electrical smokers available commercially for smoking foods. Pan smoking is a simple and quick method widely used in homes. To pan smoke you need one aluminum pan 4 inches (10 cm) high and another aluminum perforated pan 2 inches (5 cm) high. Place moistened wood chips in the first pan; place a wire rack in the second pan and place it over the first pan. Make sure there is room between the wood chips and the pan above. Cover with a tight-fitting lid and place on the kitchen stove on very low heat. When the wood chips start to smoke, place the food on the rack and cover tightly. Make sure you keep to the temperatures indicated above. If needed you may turn off the heat and continue to cook the food without opening the lid. Pan-smoked fish is moist and takes on the special flavors of the smoke. You may wish to try spices, herbs, and citrus peel to add flavor.

To the Plate

STARTERS

A starter is the first course of a meal. It is intended to whet the appetite. The recipes in this chapter range from cold to hot, mild to pungent, simple to fancy. They are just right for this day and age, tasty and fragrant and in small portions. The starters here include a selection of both familiar and unfamiliar fish and cooking techniques.

Spicy Seared Tuna with Mint Chutney (ʻAHI)

Gray Snapper Fries (UKU)

Fried Anchovies (NEHU)

Fried Scads with Vinegar and Mint Dip (ʻŌPELU)

Skipjack Tuna "Sambal" (AKU)

Creamed Fish on Sweet Potato Chips

Hawaiian Yellowfin Tuna "Poke" (ʻAHI)

Smoked Marlin with Avocado (KAJIKI)

Hawaiian "Lomi Lomi" Salmon

Hot and Spicy Marlin (KAJIKI)

Swordfish Kebabs (SHUTOME)

Spicy Swordfish Kebabs (SHUTOME)

Smoked Skipjack Tuna with Watercress Salad
and Horseradish Sauce (AKU)

Curried Gray Snapper Fish Balls (UKU)

Minced Striped Marlin Satay on Lemongrass Stalks (NAIRAGI)

Striped Marlin Satay with Marinated Cucumber (NAIRAGI)

Fish Cakes with Chili Crème Fraîche

Spicy Moonfish (OPAH)

Pink Snapper Ceviche (ʻŌPAKAPAKA)

Spicy Seared Bigeye Tuna (ʻAHI)

Tuna Dip (ʻAHI)

Lettuce-wrapped Steamed Red Snapper with Orange Glaze (ONAGA)

Coconut-crusted Pink Snapper with Lychee Sauce and
Arugula Salad (ʻŌPAKAPAKA)

Mahimahi Fish Fingers (DORADO)

Spicy Seared Tuna with Mint Chutney ('AHI)

Fresh tuna is luscious and rich and takes well to a spicy marinade. The chutney of fresh herbs, yogurt, and lime juice gives an enticing aroma and a tart finish—a perfect balance and color to the seared tuna.

YIELD 6 SERVINGS

6 tuna fillets, 4 to 4½ ounces (113 to 128 g) each

For marinade

1 tablespoon (15 ml) plain yogurt
1 teaspoon (5 ml) **chili paste**
1 teaspoon (5 ml) chopped onion
1 garlic clove chopped
½ teaspoon (2.5 ml) ground **cumin**
Salt to taste

To sear fish

1 tablespoon (15 ml) vegetable oil

For the dip

Mint Chutney (see Sauces, Dips, and Condiments)

DIRECTIONS

Pat fish dry with paper towel and place in a medium bowl. Combine ingredients for the marinade, add to the fish, and mix well to season. Cover and refrigerate for 1 hour. Heat oil in a skillet over high heat and sear marinated fish for 5 minutes on each side. Prepare mint chutney. Serve the tuna fillets sliced with a small bowl of chutney on the side.

Gray Snapper Fries (UKU)

*Batter-fried fish is a universal favorite. Both small fish, battered and fried whole, or chunks of boneless fish fillets are good. Small fish like smelts, fresh large-size anchovies, and sardines with the bone in are excellent for deep-frying. They should of course be scaled, **eviscerated** (see Preparing Fish for Cooking), and cleaned before use. For those who are less adventurous, there are fish fillets, such as the snapper used in this recipe, which may be cut into thin strips or chunks. Make sure you use a high quality oil for frying; my choice is a light olive oil. You may use a fry basket for easy removal and place fish on clean paper towels to drain off all the oil. Serve the fish fries hot on a platter lined with a folded napkin. **Cocktail Sauce** or **Tartar Sauce** (see Sauces, Dips, and Condiments) make delicious dips for the hot fries.*

YIELD 6–8 SERVINGS

1½ pounds (680 g) gray snapper fillets
1 tablespoon (15 ml) Worcestershire sauce
½ teaspoon (2.5 ml) cayenne pepper
2 tablespoons (30 ml) lemon juice
Salt
Black pepper
Oil for deep-frying
1½ cups (375 ml) **Simple Batter for Fish** (see Batters)

DIRECTIONS

Cut the fish into 1-inch (2.5 cm) cubes, pat dry with paper towels, and place in a bowl. Add Worcestershire sauce, cayenne, lemon juice, and salt and pepper to taste; mix to coat evenly with the seasonings. Heat oil to 350°F (175°C) for deep-frying; whisk the prepared batter, then fold fish gently into the batter. Using a fork, pick up the fish a few pieces at a time, allowing the excess batter to drain off, and drop carefully into the hot oil. Fry the fish for 4 to 5 minutes, turning the pieces over in the oil to brown evenly. Remove and drain on paper towels. Serve with cocktail or tartar sauce.

Fried Anchovies (NEHU)

Fresh anchovies are not always available, but when they are, they are a real treat. I remember as a child we often had bone-in fried anchovies. They were fresh as could be. They were about 3 to 3½-inches (7.5 to 9 cm) long and were threaded, about six of them, on a skewer made of fresh coconut-leaf ribs and then fried in fresh coconut oil. They were so good we did not need a dipping sauce. Even the smaller anchovies that are not large enough to thread on skewers are good, especially with the seasoning they get before frying. Use your choice of oil for frying. Cocktail sauce makes a tasty dip, but these crispy, small fish are just as tasty on their own.

YIELD 6 SERVINGS

1½ pounds (680 g) fresh anchovies
Salt
Pepper
⅛ teaspoon (0.63 ml) **turmeric**
¼ teaspoon (1.25 ml) cayenne pepper
1 cup (250 ml) oil for deep-frying
½ cup (62.5 g) flour
½ cup (125 ml) **Cocktail Sauce** (see Sauces, Dips, and Condiments)

DIRECTIONS

Eviscerate (see Preparing Fish for Cooking) the anchovies. Rinse them and place on paper towels to remove the moisture, season with salt, pepper, turmeric, and cayenne pepper and refrigerate for 20 minutes. For deep-frying heat oil to 350°F (175°C). Remove anchovies from the seasonings, toss in flour, and place in a strainer. Shake the strainer to remove excess flour and place half the anchovies in hot oil. Fry till golden brown and place on paper towels to absorb the oil. Similarly fry the rest of the anchovies. Serve plain or with cocktail sauce.

Fried Scads with Vinegar and Mint Dip ('ŌPELU)

*The fish in this recipe is meant to be fried bone in! Some people do not have the know-how to enjoy bone-in fried fish and are very frightened of fish bones, so be aware. If you do not want to handle bone-in fish, you may **fillet** the scad (see Preparing Fish for Cooking) or substitute snapper fillets for this recipe.*

YIELD 6 SERVINGS

12 small scad, dressed about 5 ounces (142 g) each
¼ teaspoon (1.25 ml) **turmeric**
Salt
Black pepper
1 cup (125 g) flour
Oil for deep-frying

For the dip

½ cup (125 ml) white vinegar
¼ cup (60 ml) **fish sauce**
1 tablespoon (15 ml) soy sauce
¾ cup (185 ml) water
Juice of 1 lime
1 teaspoon (5 ml) sugar
2 **chili peppers** chopped
½ cup (125 ml) roughly chopped mint leaves

DIRECTIONS

Wash fish and dry with paper towels. Add turmeric with salt and pepper to taste, and mix to coat the fish, refrigerate for 30 minutes. Heat the oil to 350°F (175°C) for deep-frying. Remove the fish from the seasonings. Season the flour with salt and pepper to taste and toss the fish in the flour to coat evenly. Deep-fry until the fish is golden brown and crisp. For the dip, mix the remaining ingredients in a small bowl and serve with the hot fried fish.

Skipjack Tuna "Sambal" (AKU)

Sambal is a mixture fried with a lot of chilies and seasonings. This hot and spicy preparation is a favorite in south Asian cooking. Sambals may also be made with meat and can accompany rice and other starches. For this dish, heap the tuna sambal in small portions on potato chips, and endive or lettuce leaves, or toasted bread. It is also good just served with fresh pineapple and mango slices.

YIELD 6 SERVINGS

1½ pounds (680 g) tuna fillets

For the marinade

1 teaspoon (5 ml) chopped garlic
1 teaspoon (5 ml) chopped ginger
1 teaspoon (5 ml) ground **coriander**
1 tablespoon (15 ml) **tamarind** juice
1 tablespoon (15 ml) **fish sauce**
1 teaspoon (5 ml) black pepper
Salt

For grilling

1 tablespoon (15 ml) vegetable oil

For seasoning the sambal

1 tablespoon (15 ml) finely sliced shallots
1 tablespoon (15 ml) finely sliced **serrano chilies**
3 **Kaffir lime** leaves finely shredded
1 tablespoon (15 ml) finely chopped tender **lemongrass** stalks
1 tablespoon (15 ml) lime juice
½ cup (125 ml) chopped tomatoes

DIRECTIONS

Heat the grill. Skin, trim and slice the tuna 1 inch (2.5 cm) thick. Place the sliced tuna in a bowl, add the ingredients for the marinade, and rub into the tuna with salt to taste. Grill for 2 minutes on each side, brushing with oil while grilling. Place in a fresh bowl when done. Flake the tuna when cool enough to handle, add the seasoning ingredients and tomatoes, and toss to combine the flavors thoroughly. Taste and season with salt if needed.

Creamed Fish on Sweet Potato Chips

Creamed fish may be made with most types of leftover cooked fish, as long as the fish is not heavily seasoned. Sometimes leftover fish can be somewhat dry, so it is best to poach it before use. Sweet potato chips, toast points, crackers, or sliced cucumbers are all good vehicles for the creamed fish.

YIELD 6 SERVINGS

8 ounces (227 g) cooked fish
Salt

To cream the fish
½ cup (125 ml) sour cream
1 tablespoon (15 ml) snipped dill
⅛ teaspoon (0.63 ml) cayenne
   pepper
1 tablespoon (15 ml) finely chopped
   onion
1 tablespoon (15 ml) chili sauce
½ teaspoon (2.5 ml) black pepper
1 tablespoon (15 ml) lemon juice

Holder for creamed fish
24 crisp sweet potato chips

DIRECTIONS

Remove any bones or skin from the fish. Using a fork, break it up into flakes. Put it into a bowl, add the rest of the ingredients, mix thoroughly, and heap on the chips.

Hawaiian Yellowfin Tuna "Poke" ('AHI)

*Crunchy **ogo** cloaking the shiny, firm chunks of fish, spiked with the heat of the **chili peppers**, laced with the soothing sesame oil—the first mouthful creates a taste and texture sensation. This is an exotic and enticing dish.*

YIELD 6 SERVINGS

1 pound (454 g) tuna fillets
½ cup (125 ml) coarsely chopped
   ogo
2 tablespoons (30 ml) chopped
   onion
2 tablespoons (30 ml) thinly sliced
   green onion
4 fresh hot **chili peppers**, finely
   minced
2 teaspoon (10 ml) light soy sauce
1 teaspoon (5 ml) sesame oil
1 tablespoon (15 ml) iced water
Sea salt, to taste

DIRECTIONS

Cut fish into ½-inch (0.1 cm) cubes. Place in a bowl, add the remaining ingredients, and toss to combine all the flavors. Cover and refrigerate for at least one hour before serving.

Smoked Marlin with Avocado (KAJIKI)

Home-smoked fish is always better than store bought (see Cured and Smoked). Smoked fish can be salty, so be careful when seasoning the mixture.

YIELD 6 SERVINGS

8 ounces (227 g) **Smoked Marlin Fillet** (see Cured and Smoked)
¾ (185 ml) cup sour cream
1 tablespoon (15 ml) horseradish
1 tablespoon (15 ml) dill
Lemon juice
Salt
Black pepper
2 avocados, peeled and sliced

DIRECTIONS

Grill the smoked fish about 5 to 6 minutes on each side and then flake. In a bowl whisk sour cream and horseradish; fold in the dill, lemon juice, and salt and pepper to taste. Fold in the flaked fish. Heap the mixture on the avocado slices and serve with crackers or toasted bread.

Hawaiian "Lomi Lomi" Salmon

*"Lomi lomi" salmon, a Hawaiian favorite, is traditionally served with **poi**. Lomi lomi salmon is so good it may also be served as a dip for taro or potato chips, as a relish, or as a filling or topping for hors d'oeuvres. When using salted salmon, it is important to wash it thoroughly to remove excess salt. Usually "lomi lomi" salmon is served in small portions. To make your own **Salted Salmon** (see Smoked and Cured).*

YIELD 6 SERVINGS

8 ounces (227 g) salted salmon
Cold water
2 tablespoons (30 ml) chopped onion
2 medium tomatoes, peeled, seeded, and chopped
1 tablespoon (15 ml) chopped green onion
2 to 3 ice cubes

DIRECTIONS

Soak the salted salmon in cold water and refrigerate overnight. Remove and discard the salmon skin; remove any bones present and wash the salmon in cold running water to get rid of as much of the salt as possible. Chop the salmon into small dice, and place in a glass or ceramic bowl; add onion, tomatoes, green onion, and ice cubes; mix well and refrigerate for an hour before serving.

Hot and Spicy Marlin (KAJIKI)

This dish can be prepared quickly and can be made with your choice of fish. Cubed, firm-fleshed fish will hold its shape in the finished dish.

YIELD 4 SERVINGS

1 pound (454 g) marlin fillets
1 teaspoon (5 ml) **chili paste**
1 large pinch **turmeric**
Salt
4 tablespoons (60 ml) olive oil
1 onion, thinly sliced
½ teaspoon (2.5 ml) dark soy sauce
2 tablespoons (30 ml) lime or lemon juice
½ cup (125 ml) orange juice
2 cups (500 ml) shredded iceberg lettuce
2 tomatoes, sliced

DIRECTIONS

Cut fish into 1-inch (2.5 cm) cubes; add chili paste, turmeric, and salt to taste and mix well to coat fish. Heat 2 tablespoons (30 ml) of oil in a sauté pan; sauté fish on high heat for 6 minutes, or until fish is cooked. Remove to a plate and place aside. Add remaining olive oil to the pan and sauté the onions on low heat until soft; stir in the soy sauce and the lime (or lemon) and orange juices and deglaze the sauté pan (that is, swirl the liquid to dissolve the brownings in the bottom of the sauté pan). Fold in the cooked fish to combine with the onions. Cover and cook on low heat for 2 to 3 minutes. Arrange shredded lettuce and tomatoes on a platter and spoon the fish on top.

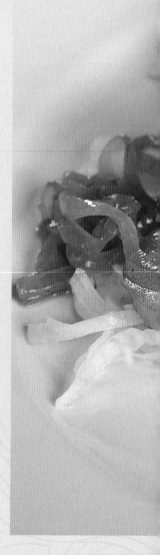

Swordfish Kebabs (SHUTOME)

These kebabs are a popular starter for an outdoor party as well. In this case you can serve the kebabs straight from the out-door grill. Soak the wooden skewers in water at least an hour to prevent burning them on the grill. Perfect accompaniments are naan bread, **Cucumber Raita** *(see Sauces, Dips, and Condiments), and chutney of your choice.*

6 SERVINGS

12 wooden skewers
1 cup water for soaking skewers
1 pound (454 g) swordfish fillets
Salt
Pepper
1 tablespoon (15 ml) flour
12 cherry tomatoes
12 chunks pineapple
12 basil leaves
12 chunks red onion
2 tablespoon (30 ml) olive oil

DIRECTIONS

Soak the skewers in water. Heat the grill. Remove skin and any bones from the fish and cut into bite-size pieces and season with salt and pepper; dust lightly with flour and thread on skewers alternating with cherry tomatoes, pineapple, basil leaves, and red onion. Brush with olive oil and grill, turning over the skewers once or twice to ensure the fish is cooked through.

Spicy Swordfish Kebabs (SHUTOME)

Any firm-textured fish can be substituted for swordfish, if desired. It is a good idea to marinate the fish overnight in the refrigerator. Wooden skewers should be soaked in cold water for an hour or so to prevent burning them on the grill. Naan bread, **Cucumber Raita** *(see Sauces, Dips, and Condiments), and chutney of your choice are perfect accompaniments to these spicy kebabs.*

YIELD 6 SERVINGS

12 to 18 wooden skewers
1 cup water for soaking skewers
1½ pounds (680 g) swordfish fillets
1 teaspoon (5 ml) finely chopped ginger
1 tablespoon (15 ml) finely chopped onion
1 tablespoon (15 ml) black pepper
1 teaspoon (5 ml) ground **cumin**
¼ teaspoon (1.25 ml) paprika
1 teaspoon (5 ml) salt
2 tablespoons (30 ml) tomato ketchup
1 tablespoon (15 ml) lemon juice
½ cup (125 ml) plain yogurt
2 tablespoons (30 ml) olive oil
6 sprigs fresh cilantro

DIRECTIONS

Soak the skewers in water. Trim and remove skin and any bones from the fish, and cut into 1-inch (2.5 cm) cubes. Place in a bowl; add ginger, onion, and the spices. Add salt, ketchup, lemon juice, and yogurt and mix to coat fish. Store in a covered dish and refrigerate for at least 2 hours. Heat the grill. Thread fish cubes on skewers and brush with olive oil. Grill for 6 to 8 minutes turning the kebabs two or three times to ensure even cooking. Place skewers on a platter and garnish with cilantro.

Smoked Skipjack Tuna with Watercress Salad and Horseradish Sauce (AKU)

The smoky fish flavored by the piquant sour cream dressing makes a delicious mouthful; the occasional bite of the peppery watercress and tart green apples spiked with hot green peppercorns is the ultimate taste sensation.

YIELD 6 SERVINGS

10 ounces (280 g) **Pan-smoked Skipjack Tuna** (see Cured and Smoked) sliced
1 cup (250 ml) watercress sprigs
6 thinly sliced red radishes
1 green apple, peeled, cored, and thinly sliced
1 tablespoon (15 ml) green peppercorns
1 cup (250 ml) sour cream
¼ cup (60 ml) creamed horseradish
1 tablespoon (15 ml) chopped dill
1 tablespoon (15 ml) lemon juice
Salt

DIRECTIONS

Preheat the grill. Grill the smoked fish slices 2 to 3 minutes on high heat. Arrange the watercress and the red radishes and apple slices on a platter; flake and place the fish on the slices. In a bowl whisk together the green peppercorns, sour cream, horseradish, and dill with lemon juice and salt to taste and drizzle on the fish.

Curried Gray Snapper Fish Balls (UKU)

In small portions these delectable fish balls make a tempting beginning to a meal. They can also be served with rice as a main dish. Naan bread, chapati, or toasted bread go well with the fish. Any fast-cooking fish can be substituted in this recipe.

YIELD 6 SERVINGS

1½ pounds (680 g) snapper fillets, skin removed, coarsely minced
2 green chilies, seeded and chopped
2 teaspoons (10 ml) finely chopped ginger
½ cup (125 ml) chopped mint
2 egg whites
Salt

For the sauce
1 tablespoon (15 ml) oil
¼ cup (60 ml) finely chopped onion
1 tablespoon (15 ml) **curry powder**
⅛ teaspoon (0.63 ml) **turmeric**
½ teaspoon (2.5 ml) cayenne pepper
1½ cups (375 ml) coconut milk
1 cup (250 ml) water
Juice of 1 lemon
Salt

DIRECTIONS

Mix the minced fish with the green chilies, ginger, mint, egg whites, and salt to taste. Form into balls 1-inch (2.5 cm) in diameter and place aside. Heat oil in a sauté pan; add onion and cook to a light gold color. Add spices, then stir in coconut milk and water. Stirring continuously, bring to a slow simmer and season with lemon juice and salt to taste. Drop the fish balls into the simmering curry sauce, cover the sauté pan, and simmer for 5 to 6 minutes or until the fish balls are cooked.

Minced Striped Marlin Satay on Lemongrass Stalks (NAIRAGI)

*Spears of **lemongrass** may be used instead of wooden or metal skewers for this delicious hot and spicy satay. The lime juice in the minced fish mixture brings out the best in the satay, and the additional squeeze of lime gives it that ultimate finishing touch. You may substitute shredded, dried coconut for the freshly grated coconut called for in the recipe. In this case rehydrate the coconut by sprinkling with several tablespoons of cold water before use.*

YIELD 6 SERVINGS

1 pound (454 g) marlin fillets, skin removed
1 cup (250 ml) fresh grated coconut
2 tablespoons (30 ml) dried shrimp, soaked, excess water squeezed out

Seasonings

1 tablespoon (15 ml) chopped ginger
1 tablespoon (15 ml) chopped shallots
2 red **serrano chilies**, chopped fine
1 tablespoon (15ml) ground **coriander**
2 tablespoons (30 ml) **tamarind** juice
2 tablespoons (30 ml) brown sugar
1 tablespoon (15 ml) peanut butter
2 tablespoons (30 ml) lime juice
Salt

To mould and grill

12 **lemongrass** stalks, each 8 inches (20 cm) long
2 tablespoons (30 ml) peanut oil

Garnish

6 lime wedges

DIRECTIONS

Combine the fish, coconut, and dry shrimp, and grind in a food processor to a smooth paste. Remove to a bowl. Mix in the seasonings with lime juice and salt to taste. Heat the grill. Mold a tablespoonful of the minced fish mix around the lemongrass stalks, brush with peanut oil, and grill on medium heat. Place on a platter and garnish with lime wedges.

Striped Marlin Satay with Marinated Cucumber (NAIRAGI)

Exotic spices lured Marco Polo and many spice merchants to the Spice Islands for centuries. Today these same spices lure tourists to exotic foods like satay, which are highlights of Malay, Indonesian, and Singaporean cuisines. Added nuances to the already exotic cuisines are provided by fragrant roots and grasses, coconut milk, peanuts, and a complex mixture of seasonings. The sauce is laden with shreds of coconut and crunchy bits of peanuts. Wooden skewers should be soaked in water at least for an hour to prevent them from burning on the grill. Serve the satay with **Marinated Cucumber** *(see Sauces, Dips, and Condiments).*

YIELD 6 SERVINGS

24 wooden skewers
2 cups (500 ml) water for soaking skewers
1½ pounds (680 g) marlin fillets, skin removed

Spicy marinade

1 shallot peeled and sliced
2 green chilies, seeded
1 teaspoon (5 ml) chopped ginger
1 tablespoon (15 ml) soy sauce
1 tablespoon (15 ml) brown sugar
½ teaspoon (2.5 ml) ground **coriander**
½ teaspoon (2.5 ml) ground **cumin**
¼ cup (60 ml) hot water
2 tablespoons (30 ml) crunchy peanut
   butter
Lime juice
Salt

For grilling

3 tablespoons (45 ml) peanut oil

Satay sauce

1 teaspoon (5 ml) ground **coriander**
1 teaspoon (5 ml) ground **cumin**
¼ teaspoon (2.5 ml) **turmeric**
1 tablespoon (15 ml) minced, tender
   lemongrass stalks
1 tablespoon (15 ml) finely chopped
   onion
1 teaspoon (5 ml) finely chopped ginger
1 teaspoon (5 ml) finely chopped garlic
1 tablespoon (15 ml) crunchy peanut
   butter
1 tablespoon (15 ml) fresh grated coconut
1½ cups (375 ml) coconut milk

DIRECTIONS

Soak skewers in water. Cut fish in 1-inch (2.5 cm) cubes, thread on skewers, and place in a glass dish. Using a food processor, process the ingredients for the marinade with lime juice and salt to taste. Pour on the skewered fish and turn over to coat evenly. Marinate for 30 minutes. Heat the grill. Brush the fish skewers with peanut oil and grill on medium heat for 4 to 5 minutes on a side, turning once or twice to ensure even cooking. For the satay sauce, process all the ingredients except the coconut milk to a smooth paste. Heat the coconut milk in a pan, then whisk in the processed ingredients with salt to taste and simmer on low heat stirring constantly, for 6 to 8 minutes. Serve the satay sauce in a sauceboat to pour on the satay.

Fish Cakes with Chili Crème Fraîche

These fish cakes are made with cooked fish. They are well seasoned, moist inside and crusty on the outside.

YIELD 4 SERVINGS

1 pound (454 g) cooked fish
1 tablespoon (15 ml) finely chopped onion
1 teaspoon (5 ml) minced ginger
1 tablespoon (15 ml) Worcestershire sauce
2 tablespoons (30 ml) mayonnaise
2 eggs, yolks and whites separated
Salt
Black pepper
1 cup (250 ml) fresh bread crumbs or **panko**
1 tablespoon (15 ml) vegetable oil
½ cup (125 ml) **Chili Crème Fraîche** (see Sauces, Dips, and Condiments)

DIRECTIONS

Flake the fish and place in a bowl with the onion, ginger, Worcestershire sauce, mayonnaise, egg yolks, and salt and pepper to taste. Mix to combine all the ingredients; using your fingers, form into 8 round flat cakes. Whip the egg whites to a soft peak; dip the fish cakes in the egg whites and dredge in bread crumbs or panko to coat evenly. Heat oil in nonstick pan and fry the fish cakes on medium heat for 2 minutes on each side or until golden brown. Serve with chili crème fraîche.

Spicy Moonfish (OPAH)

This is an exotic dish and is impressive served in small portions on attractive appetizer plates. Garnish with sliced mango or pineapple and a few mint leaves to counteract the heat in the dish.

YIELD 6 SERVINGS

1 pound (454 g) moonfish fillets

Spice paste

6 fresh red chilies
6 shallots
1 tablespoon (15 ml) roasted peanuts
1 teaspoon (5 ml) **shrimp paste**
½ cup (125 ml) water

For the wok

2 tablespoons (30 ml) peanut oil
1 cup (250 ml) coconut milk
¼ cup (60 ml) **tamarind** juice
1 stalk **lemongrass**, bruised
Salt

DIRECTIONS

Cut the fish into 1-inch (2.5 cm) cubes and refrigerate. Using a blender, grind the ingredients for the spice paste, adding enough water to get a smooth consistency. Heat a wok and add the oil; then add the ground spice paste and cook on low heat for 3 to 4 minutes, stirring constantly. Add the coconut milk, tamarind juice, and lemongrass and season with salt to taste. Add fish and simmer for 5 to 6 minutes or until the fish is cooked through. Pick out and discard lemongrass.

Pink Snapper Ceviche ('ŌPAKAPAKA)

Freshness is essential when putting together ceviche. Be sure that your fish is as fresh as possible. The fish must marinate overnight, so be sure to start this dish the evening before you intend to serve it. Use a glass container for marinating the fish. The acid in the citrus juice used will "cook" the fish.

YIELD 6 SERVINGS

1 pound (454 g) snapper fillets
¾ cup (175 ml) freshly squeezed lime juice
1 red onion, finely chopped
2 medium tomatoes, coarsely chopped
2 **serrano chili** peppers chopped fine
1 tablespoon (15 ml) olive oil
Sea salt
Black pepper
½ cup (125 ml) thick coconut milk

DIRECTIONS

Remove skin and any bones from the fish and slice thinly. Place fish in a glass dish and pour the lime juice over it; cover and refrigerate overnight. Drain and dry the fish on paper towels. Place onions, tomatoes, peppers, and olive oil in a glass dish, add the fish with salt and pepper to taste. Toss to combine the ingredients, then mix in the coconut milk. Refrigerate for 30 minutes. Serve chilled.

Spicy Seared Bigeye Tuna ('AHI)

*The spicing here is very Sri Lankan. I use a spoonful of my favorite chutney beside the fish. The must-have garnish is the fried **poppadom**. This interesting flavor combination has won admiration from guests at special events.*

YIELD 6 SERVINGS

½ recipe **Sauce Beurre Blanc** (see Sauces, Dips, and Condiments)
1½ pounds (680 g) center-cut tuna fillets
2 tablespoons (30 ml) olive oil
1 tablespoon (15 ml) coarsely ground **coriander**
1 tablespoon (15 ml) coarsely ground **cumin**
1 teaspoon (5 ml) crushed red pepper
1 tablespoon (15 ml) white sesame seeds, toasted crisp
1 teaspoon (5 ml) sea salt
6 **poppadom**
6 mint sprigs

DIRECTIONS

Prepare the sauce beurre blanc and keep it hot. Heat an iron skillet on the stove. Remove the skin from the tuna and cut into 3 to 4 rectangular log shapes; brush with some of the olive oil. Mix the spices, sesame seeds, and sea salt and place on a plate. Roll the fish "logs" in the spices to coat all sides thoroughly. Brush the hot skillet with the remaining olive oil. When the skillet is sizzling hot, sear each piece of fish about 30 seconds, rolling the fish logs in the skillet to sear the outside. Place the seared fish on a cutting board and slice thin; arrange on 6 plates, spoon beurre blanc around the fish, and garnish with poppadom and mint sprigs.

Tuna Dip ('AHI)

This dip may be served with toasted bread or crackers or used as a filling for tart shells that could be served as an hors d'oeuvre. I like to serve it with sweet potato chips. This is also one way of putting "usable" trimmings of any fresh tuna to good use.

YIELD 6 TO 8 SERVINGS

8 ounces (227 g) tuna fillets
4 ounces (113 g) softened cream cheese
¼ cup (60 ml) plain yogurt
½ teaspoon (2.5 ml) crushed red pepper
1 tablespoon (15 ml) finely chopped onion
1 tablespoon (15 ml) lemon zest
1 tablespoon (15 ml) lemon juice
¼ cup (60 ml) sliced mint leaves
Salt
Black pepper

DIRECTIONS

Place fish on a sanitized cutting board and chop to a coarse texture; place in a bowl and refrigerate. In a separate bowl, beat the cream cheese and add the yogurt, crushed red pepper, onion, lemon zest and juice and beat to a smooth consistency. Mix in the mint, chopped fish, and salt and pepper to taste. Spoon into a serving bowl, cover and refrigerate for an hour before serving.

Lettuce-wrapped Steamed Red Snapper with Orange Glaze (ONAGA)

Any snapper will do well for this recipe. The simply seasoned steamed fish is best served by itself, so the taste of the fresh fish stands out. It makes an outstanding starter course for an elegant dinner.

YIELD 4 SERVINGS

Juice of 1 orange
½ cup (125 ml) balsamic vinegar
4 large leaves of butter lettuce
4 red snapper fillets, 4 ounces (113 g) each
1 tablespoon (15 ml) finely chopped ginger
2 tablespoons (30 ml) rice wine vinegar
A few drops sesame oil
Salt
Black pepper
4 orange slices

DIRECTIONS

Place orange juice and balsamic vinegar in a pan on medium heat; reduce to 3 tablespoons (45 ml) or to a glaze and put aside. Dip lettuce leaves in boiling water for 1 second and instantly cool the leaves by dipping in ice water. Season the fish with the ginger, vinegar, sesame oil, and salt and pepper to taste. Remove lettuce leaves from the ice water, dry out with paper towels, and spread open on a cutting board. Place a portion of fish on each leaf. Fold the 2 ends of each leaf to enclose the fish, and then fold in the 2 sides of each leaf to secure the fish in the parcels. Place fish in a steamer basket and steam over simmering water for 4 minutes. Drizzle some of the orange glaze on each plate, top with fish parcels, drizzle with the remaining glaze, and place an orange slice on each fish parcel.

Coconut-crusted Pink Snapper with Lychee Sauce and Arugula Salad ('ŌPAKAPAKA)

This rich-tasting fish makes a good starter course for a special dinner. I use olive oil to fry the fish, but you can use the oil of your choice.

YIELD 6 SERVINGS

1 10-ounce (283 g) can of seedless lychees in syrup
1 tablespoon (15 ml) white vinegar
1 tablespoon (15 ml) sherry
1 tablespoon (15 ml) sugar
1 teaspoon (5 ml) soy sauce
1 teaspoon (5 ml) Worcestershire sauce
½ cup (62.5 g) plus 1 tablespoon (15 ml) flour
1 egg
1 cup (250 ml) water
6 snapper fillets, 4 ounces (113 g) each
Salt
Black pepper
¾ cup (180 ml) shredded dry coconut
Vegetable oil for deep-frying

Arugula salad

1 cup (250 ml) trimmed arugula leaves
2 tablespoons (30 ml) macadamia nut bits
1 tablespoon (15 ml) fried bacon bits
1 tablespoon (15 ml) lemon juice
2 teaspoons (10 ml) olive oil
Salt
Black pepper

DIRECTIONS

To make the lychee sauce, blend together the lychee with syrup, vinegar, sherry, sugar, soy sauce, and Worcestershire sauce until the sauce is smooth; put aside. For deep-frying, heat oil to 350°F (175°C). Place ½ cup (62.5 g) flour, egg, and water in a bowl and whisk to form a thin batter. Season the fish with salt and pepper to taste and dust with 1 tablespoon (15 ml) flour. Shake off excess flour and dip fish in the batter and then in the coconut. Deep-fry the fish to a golden color. Place on crumpled paper or paper towels to drain off excess oil. Spoon a pool of lychee sauce on each appetizer plate and place a piece of fish on each. Toss the ingredients for the arugula salad with salt and pepper to taste and spoon a small portion of arugula salad beside each portion of fish.

Mahimahi Fish Fingers (DORADO)

This tasty finger food is ideal for a cocktail party. It is easy to prepare and delicious too. See how fast it disappears.

YIELD 6 SERVINGS

1 pound (440 g) mahimahi fillets
1 cup (250 ml) melted butter at room temperature

For the cheese mix

½ cup (125 ml) grated Parmesan cheese
½ cup (125 ml) fresh bread crumbs
1 tablespoon (15 ml) chopped green onion
1 tablespoon (15 ml) chopped parsley
1 tablespoon (15 ml) seeded and chopped green chilies
½ teaspoon (2.5 ml) crushed red pepper
Salt
Freshly ground black pepper

For dipping sauce

½ cup (125 ml) chili sauce
1 teaspoon (5 ml) prepared horseradish
1 tablespoon (15 ml) lemon juice

DIRECTIONS

Remove skin from the fillets; trim and cut fish into pieces 2 inches (5 cm) long and ½ inch (1.3 cm) thick; place in a bowl and pour on the melted butter to coat the fish. Heat oven to 350°F (176°C). For the cheese mix, combine cheese and all the dry ingredients in a bowl. Take the butter-coated fish and dip each piece one by one in the combined cheese mixture to coat; place in a baking pan and bake for 25 minutes. Mix the ingredients for the dipping sauce in a small bowl and serve with fish fingers.

SOUPS AND STEWS

The word "soup" originally meant "a cup of nourishment."
Today, soups are valued for their simplicity as well as their
nourishment. In small portions, they tease the palate; in large
ones, they become satisfying meals in themselves. The soups and
stews in this section range from light to hearty; many recipes
feature exotic ingredients and unusual cuts of fish like bone-
in sea bass. Here you will find a selection of soups and stews,
hot and cold, using legumes and grains, fruits and vegetables,
herbs and spices all with the flavor of fish as the central focus.
A good stock is the foundation of good soups and stews; for Fish
Stock see Stocks.

Short-tail Red Snapper Soup with Leeks (ʻEHU)

Avocado Kamehameha with Sashimi (ONAGA)

Pink Snapper Soup with Fennel (ʻŌPAKAPAKA)

Fish Mulligatawny

Short-tail Red Snapper Soup with Tamarind (ʻEHU)

Pacific Island Jackfish Soup (ULUA)

Hawaiian Sea Bass Gumbo (HĀPUʻUPUʻU)

Tomato Goatfish Soup (KŪMŪ)

Mahimahi Chowder (DORADO)

Mahimahi Corn Chowder (DORADO)

Dal and Swordfish Soup (SHUTOME)

Hot and Sour Short-tail Red Snapper Soup (ʻEHU)

Curried Short-tail Red Snapper Soup (ʻEHU)

Fisherman's Hawaiian Sea Bass Stew (HĀPUʻUPUʻU)

Jackfish and Green Papaya Soup (ULUA)

Bouillabaisse with Hawaiian Sea Bass, Gray Snapper, and Moonfish
(HĀPUʻUPUʻU, UKU, AND OPAH)

Spicy Hawaiian Sea Bass Stew (HĀPUʻUPUʻU)

Moonfish Stew with Rhubarb (OPAH)

Baked Short-tail Red Snapper and Vegetable Stew (ʻEHU)

Creamy Mustard Wahoo Stew (ONO)

Short-tail Red Snapper Soup with Leeks ('EHU)

This is a simple and light soup that is also easy to prepare. The recipe calls for fish stock; you may use commercially prepared fish stock if you do not have homemade stock. The leeks must be thoroughly washed to get rid of the sandy soil that gets between the leaves. The final rinse should be under running water. The snapper, tender leeks, and peeled tomatoes cook rapidly so care should be taken not to overcook.

YIELD 4 SERVINGS

2 ounces (57 g) chopped bacon

¼ cup (60 ml) chopped onion

1 tablespoon (15 ml) flour

3 cups (750 ml) **Fish Stock** (see Stocks)

2 cups (500 ml) milk

1 small bay leaf

2 heavy pinches dry thyme

1 pound (454 g) red snapper fillets cut into 1-inch (2.5 cm) dice

½ pound (227 g) leeks, light green and white parts only, thinly sliced

2 tomatoes peeled, seeded, and diced, about 1½ cups (375 ml)

Pinch of cayenne pepper

Big pinch of **nutmeg**

Salt

Black pepper

DIRECTIONS

Place a 2 quart (2 L) pot on moderate heat, add bacon and cook till bacon is crisp. Add onion and cook till soft. Stir in the flour and keep stirring for 2 minutes until the roux is an ivory color. Pour in the fish stock and milk and whisk to incorporate with the contents in the pot. Add bay leaf and thyme and simmer uncovered for 15 minutes. Add fish, leeks, and tomatoes; season with cayenne, nutmeg, salt and pepper to taste. Cover and let simmer for 5 minutes. Remove from heat; keep covered and let stand for 5 more minutes before serving.

Avocado Kamehameha with Sashimi (ONAGA)

*This beautiful soup was originally served at Honolulu's famous restaurant The Willows. At The Willows it was served in regular soup bowls without the **sashimi** garnish, but it looks exotic when served in chilled martini glasses with a crown of glistening sashimi. It makes a lovely first course for an elegant dinner. Some avocados are starchier than others and can make the soup too thick; in this case add more chicken broth to thin out the soup to the consistency you like. The chicken broth should be very light so the subtle flavor of the avocado can shine through.*

YIELD 6 SERVINGS

4 ounces (113 g) red snapper fillets, thinly sliced for **sashimi**
½ teaspoon (2.5 ml) olive oil
1 teaspoon (5 ml) lemon juice
A sprinkling of sea salt
1 large avocado, peeled, pit removed
1 teaspoon (5 ml) chopped onion
⅛ teaspoon (0.63 ml) cayenne pepper
1½ cups (375 ml) very light chicken broth
2 tablespoons (30 ml) sherry
1½ cups (375 ml) half-and-half
Salt
Pepper

DIRECTIONS

Spread fish on a plate and drizzle with the olive oil and lemon juice; sprinkle with sea salt and refrigerate. Blend the rest of the ingredients in a blender until smooth. Season the soup with salt and pepper to taste and refrigerate for 2 to 3 hours. Ladle into chilled martini glasses and place a portion of sashimi on each soup.

Pink Snapper Soup with Fennel ('ŌPAKAPAKA)

*To some it is a messy business to cut up a whole snapper. In this case ask your fish-monger to cut it up for you, or use cut up snapper bones. Snapper stock gives a fine, delicate flavor to the soup. It is always best to strain the stock through a cheesecloth to get rid of any scales before using. Once the snapper fillet is added, care should be taken not to overcook the fish. Snapper cooks very fast. Serve with garlic bread and a green salad with sliced **fennel**, an ideal accompaniment.*

YIELD 8 SERVINGS

4 pounds (2 kg) whole pink snapper, gutted and cleaned
¼ cup (60 ml) olive oil
1 bulb of **fennel**, sliced
2 onions, sliced
2 trimmed leeks, white and light green parts thinly sliced
8 cloves unpeeled garlic, crushed
2 pounds (907 g) tomatoes, diced
1 teaspoon (5 ml) fennel seed
1 bay leaf
½ cup (125 ml) dry white wine
6 cups (1.5 L) cold water
Sea salt
Black pepper
A pinch of **saffron** threads soaked in 1 tablespoon (15 ml) of hot water
1 teaspoon (5 ml) lemon zest

DIRECTIONS

Fillet the fish, cut into 2-inch (5 cm) pieces, and refrigerate. Cut up the bones and head; clean and wash. Heat olive oil in a 1-gallon (4 L) pot on moderate heat and brown the vegetables and garlic. Add fish bones and fish head and cook on high heat 4 to 5 minutes. Add the tomatoes, fennel seed, bay leaf, wine, and cold water. Simmer uncovered and undisturbed for 40 minutes. Pass the soup stock through a sieve lined with a cheesecloth. Pour about 4 cups (1 L) of the soup stock into a pan and season with salt and pepper to taste. Add the cut-up fish fillet, saffron, and lemon zest and simmer 3 to 4 minutes.

Fish Mulligatawny

This soup is a tasty rich broth flavored with vegetables and aromatized with choice spices. There are many versions of this velvety and luscious soup. It is believed that the local Indian cooks created this for the British rajas around two centuries ago. The British love this soup, and it still appears on the royal menus when foreign guests are entertained. The soup may also be made with vegetables, chicken, rabbit, or beef. It is important to start with a very good fish stock.

YIELD 4–6 SERVINGS

6 cups (1½ L) **Fish Stock** (see Stocks)

2 cups (500 ml) clam juice

1 medium potato, peeled and cut into small dice

1 medium size onion, peeled and cut into small dice

2 tomatoes cut into small dice

2 stalks lemongrass

1 tablespoon (15 ml) minced garlic

1 tablespoon (15 ml) minced ginger

6 **cardamom** pods, crushed

2-inch (5 cm) piece of **cinnamon** stick

1 teaspoon (5 ml) roasted **cumin** seed

2 teaspoons (10 ml) roasted **coriander** seed

¼ teaspoon (2.5 ml) **turmeric**

1 teaspoon (5 ml) crushed peppercorns

2 tablespoons (30 ml) **tamarind** juice

Juice of 1 lime

Salt

To enrich the soup

1 tablespoon (15 ml) butter

2 shallots, thinly sliced

¼ cup (60 ml) coconut milk

2 teaspoons (10 ml) **fennel** seeds, roasted to a dark color and coarsely crushed

DIRECTIONS

Place fish stock and clam juice in a 1-gallon (1 L) pot; add potatoes, onions, tomatoes, lemongrass, garlic, ginger, and the spices and bring to a boil. Turn heat to low and simmer for 30 minutes. Use a wooden spoon to crush the vegetables as you stir the stock. Season the soup stock with the tamarind, lime juice, and salt to taste and continue to cook for 10 minutes. Pass the soup stock through a strainer pressing on the vegetables to extract the pulp and place the liquid aside. (You may also use a food mill for this purpose.) To enrich the soup, heat the butter in the pot, add shallots and sauté on low heat until shallots turn a dark caramel brown. Pour in the strained soup stock; add the coconut milk and simmer uncovered for 5 to 6 minutes. Remove soup from heat and sprinkle with crushed roasted fennel seeds. Cover and let stand for 5 minutes before serving.

Short-tail Red Snapper Soup with Tamarind ('EHU)

*This is a spicy soup aromatized with herbs and spiked with fresh chilies. Serve with **poppadom**.*

YIELD 4 SERVINGS

1 tablespoon (15 ml) olive oil
4 red snapper fillets, 4 ounces (113 g) each
3 cups (0.7 L) water
2 tablespoons (30 ml) **tamarind** juice or to taste
1 tablespoon (15 ml) grated ginger
Salt
1 red **serrano chili**, chopped fine
1 green serrano chili, chopped fine
2 shallots thinly sliced
1 large tomato, peeled, seeded, and diced
1 tablespoon (15 ml) chopped cilantro
1 tablespoon (15 ml) sliced green onion

DIRECTIONS

Heat the oil in a 2-quart (2 L) saucepan on high heat and sear the fish for about 3 minutes. Add water, tamarind, ginger, and salt to taste. Cover the pan and simmer on low heat for 5 minutes. Add chilies, shallots, tomato, cilantro, and green onion and simmer 5 more minutes.

Pacific Island Jackfish Soup (ULUA)

Spinach combines well with fish and coconut milk and gives a velvety texture in your mouth at the first spoonful. It is rich, silky, and comforting as well. This tasty soup is easy to make; you may use any fish you like in the soup. Cream is an elegant substitute for coconut milk.

YIELD 2 TO 3 SERVINGS

1 tablespoon (15 ml) vegetable oil
1 medium onion, chopped
2 tablespoons flour (30 ml)
3 cups (750 ml) **Fish Stock** (see Stocks)
1 cup (250 ml) thick coconut milk
½ pound (227 g) Jackfish fillets, thinly sliced
Pinch of **nutmeg**
Salt
Black pepper
1 bunch fresh spinach leaves, trimmed and washed

DIRECTIONS

Heat the oil in a 2-quart (2 L) saucepan; add onion and sauté to a golden brown. Stir in flour and cook the roux 2 to 3 minutes until blond in color. Gradually stir in the stock; cover and simmer on low heat for 10 minutes. Add coconut milk and fish and cook 3 to 4 minutes. Season the soup with nutmeg and salt and pepper to taste. Add spinach and simmer uncovered for 2 more minutes.

Hawaiian Sea Bass Gumbo (HĀPUʻUPUʻU)

Gumbo is good with any fish. Because sea bass does not fall apart when cooked, it is the best. Sea bass with the bone is delicious in this country-style recipe; however, you may use fish without bones if you prefer. Creole gumbos are not considered complete without rice and okra. Sliced frozen okra is as good as fresh. Many are put off by okra's mucilaginous quality, which is its main characteristic. To keep okra from turning slimy, cook it in acidulated water. In this recipe, I add a tablespoon of lime or lemon juice as a seasoning to keep the okra from turning too slimy.

YIELD 4 SERVINGS

1½ pounds (680 g) bone-in sea bass
4 strips bacon, cut into small dice
1 medium onion, chopped
2 stems celery, sliced
1 tablespoon flour (15ml)
2 cups (500 ml) stewed tomatoes
1 tablespoon (15 ml) tomato paste
1 tablespoon (15 ml) minced garlic
1 bay leaf
½ teaspoon (2.5 ml) dry thyme
4 cups (1 L) salt-free light chicken broth
Salt
Black pepper
1 cup (250 ml) cooked rice
5 ounces (142 g) frozen sliced okra
1 tablespoon (15 ml) lime or lemon juice

DIRECTIONS

Cut the fish into 2-inch x 2-inch (5 x 5 cm) pieces. Cover and refrigerate. Heat a 1-gallon (4 L) soup pot; add bacon and cook till bacon is crisp. Add onion and celery and cook until onion is wilted. Stir in the flour and cook on low heat for about 5 minutes to a light brown roux. Stir in the stewed tomatoes, tomato paste, garlic, bay leaf, and thyme, whisk in the chicken broth, and season with salt and pepper to taste. Simmer for 15 minutes. Add the rice, okra, lemon or lime juice, and the refrigerated fish. Simmer covered for 20 minutes.

Tomato Goatfish Soup (KŪMŪ)

This recipe looks long, but once you get the ingredients together it takes no time to finish it. It may also be done in two steps; make the stock first and cook the fish just before you serve. Goatfish is delicate and makes an appealing first course for an elegant dinner. You may also use snapper or other similar fish.

YIELD 4 SERVINGS

1 tablespoon (15 ml) olive oil
¼ cup (60 ml) sliced onion
¼ cup (60 ml) sliced leeks, white part only
2 celery stems, sliced
2 parsley stems
1 tablespoon flour (15 ml)
4 large tomatoes, sliced
4 cloves crushed garlic
1 bay leaf
½ teaspoon (2.5 ml) **cumin** seed
8 black peppercorns
4 cups (1 L) **Fish Stock** (see Stocks)
Salt
½ cup (125 ml) sherry
1 tablespoon (15 ml) lemon juice
2 goatfish about 1 pound (450 g) each, filleted
1 tablespoon (15 ml) snipped dill
4 lemon slices

DIRECTIONS

Heat olive oil in a medium sauté pan and sauté vegetables on medium heat until the onions turn a light golden color. Stir in flour and cook for 2 minutes. Add tomatoes, garlic, bay leaf, and spices and stir in the stock. Simmer uncovered for 25 minutes. Pass the soup stock through a fine strainer into another clean pan and season with salt to taste. Add sherry, lemon juice, and fish and cover and simmer 7 minutes. Ladle the soup into bowls, sprinkle with dill, and float a slice of lemon on each portion.

Mahimahi Chowder (DORADO)

Chowders are thick, hearty American soups of French origin with milk or tomatoes and shellfish, finfish, or vegetables (often including potatoes) to which other ingredients are added to give flavor. Using cream in place of milk makes the chowder silky textured and luscious. You may replace mahimahi with swordfish.

YIELD 6 SERVINGS

2 ounces (57 g) bacon, chopped
1 onion cut into small dice
2 celery stems, cut into small dice
3 tablespoons flour (45 ml)
4 cups (1 L) **Fish Stock** (see Stocks)
1 bay leaf
1 large potato, peeled and cut into medium dice
2 cups (500 ml) hot milk
¾ cup (185 ml) heavy cream
½ teaspoon (2.5 ml) dry thyme
1 tablespoon (15 ml) Worcestershire sauce
¼ teaspoon (1.25 ml) cayenne pepper
Salt
Black pepper
1½ pounds (680 g) mahimahi fillets cut into medium dice
1 tablespoon (15 ml) chopped parsley

DIRECTIONS

Heat a 1-gallon (1 L) heavy-bottom saucepan over medium heat. Add the bacon and cook, stirring, until the bacon is crisp. Add onions and celery and sauté until the onions are soft. Turn the heat to low, stir in the flour, and cook for 4 to 5 minutes. When the flour cooks to an ivory color roux, whisk in the stock. Cook 10 minutes; then add the bay leaf and potatoes and bring to a simmer. Cook about 20 minutes on low heat, stirring occasionally. When the liquid is thickened and smooth stir in the milk, cream, thyme, Worcestershire sauce, and cayenne pepper and season with salt and pepper to taste. Simmer for 15 minutes. Fold in the fish and simmer for about 8 minutes more. Keep the soup covered for 5 more minutes. Spoon the hot chowder into bowls and garnish with a sprinkling of parsley.

Mahimahi Corn Chowder (DORADO)

*This chowder is similar to the recipe for **Mahimahi Chowder** (this section) above. Simply reducing the quantity of fish and adding some corn makes a delicious fish and corn chowder.*

YIELD 6 SERVINGS

2 ounces (57 g) bacon cut into small bits
1 medium onion, cut into small dice
2 celery stems, cut into small dice
2 tablespoons flour (30 ml)
3 cups (750 ml) **Fish Stock** (see Stocks)
8 oz (227 g) frozen or fresh corn kernels
2 cups (500 ml) hot milk
1 cup (250 ml) cream
½ teaspoon (2.5 ml) dry thyme
Salt
Freshly ground black pepper
1 pound (454 g) mahimahi fillets, cut into small dice
1 tablespoon (15 ml) chopped parsley

DIRECTIONS

Heat a 1-gallon (4 L) heavy-bottom saucepan over medium heat. Add the bacon and cook, stirring, until the bacon is crisp. Add onions and celery and sauté until the onions are soft. Turn the heat to low, stir in the flour, and cook for 4 to 5 minutes. When the flour cooks to an ivory color roux, stir in the stock and whisk to avoid having lumps. Bring to a simmer, stirring occasionally, cook 15 minutes on low heat. Add the corn and stir in the milk, cream, and thyme. Season the soup with salt and pepper to taste. Add fish and simmer for 10 minutes. Serve in bowls with a sprinkling of parsley.

Dal and Swordfish Soup (SHUTOME)

*There are many varieties of lentils, also known as dal, available in the markets. You may use any kind in this soup. Spices are commonly used with lentils to enhance taste. I use **cumin**, which is a vital ingredient in Indian and Sri Lankan cooking, to spice up this soup. You can use fish and vegetables of your choice. Serve this soup as a light meal or a snack.*

YIELD 4 SERVINGS

2 ounces (57 g) red lentils

5 cups (1.2 L) water

½ cup (125 ml) chopped onions

1 teaspoon (5 ml) ground **cumin**

1 bay leaf

1 tablespoon (15 ml) olive oil

8 ounces (227 g) swordfish fillets, cut into 1-inch (2.5 cm) cubes

1 cup (250 ml) diced tomatoes

1 cup (250 ml) corn kernels

1 cup (250 ml) diced zucchini

Salt

Black pepper

1 tablespoon (15 ml) chopped mint

DIRECTIONS

Wash lentils and place in a 1-gallon (4 L) size pan with water, onions, cumin, and bay leaf; simmer on medium heat for about 30 minutes or until the lentils are soft. Discard the bay leaf; puree the lentil soup and set aside. Heat oil in a saucepan and sauté the fish for 4 to 5 minutes; add the lentil soup along with the tomatoes, corn, and zucchini. Season with salt and pepper to taste and simmer on medium heat for about 20 minutes or until the vegetables are cooked. Sprinkle with chopped mint and serve hot.

Hot and Sour Short-Tail Red Snapper Soup ('EHU)

This is a simple, satisfying meal for a cold night. For some, it is unusual to see whole green chilies floating in a soup! Many of us, however, enjoy this sight, and we love biting into the chilies too. If you don't like them whole in the soup, you may use just one green chili finely sliced.

YIELD 4 SERVINGS

1 snapper 3½ to 4 pounds (1.6 to 1.8 kg), dressed
3 pints (1.5 L) water
2 tablespoons (30 ml) long-grain brown or white rice
1 cup (250 ml) peeled, diced sweet potato
4 cloves of garlic, crushed
2 tablespoons **besan** flour (30 ml)
8 long beans cut in 2-inch (5 cm) pieces
⅛ teaspoon (0.63 ml) **turmeric**
4 whole green chilies
2 tablespoons (30 ml) **tamarind** juice
Salt
Black pepper
1 bunch spinach leaves, washed and trimmed

DIRECTIONS

Fillet the fish, cut into 2-inch (5 cm) pieces, and refrigerate. Wash the fish head and bones; place them in a 1-gallon (1 L) pot with water and cook 35 to 40 minutes. Strain the stock into a clean, smaller pot. Add the rice, sweet potato, and garlic; cover and simmer for 20 minutes. Whisk in besan flour; add the long beans, turmeric, green chilies, and tamarind with salt and pepper to taste. Simmer for 10 minutes. Add the fish and spinach leaves; cover and cook 5 minutes. Serve hot.

Curried Short-Tail Red Snapper Soup

This creamy curried fish soup is enhanced with exotic spices. **Turmeric** *gives the soup an appealing light yellow color;* **fenugreek** *seeds add an exotic aroma. Once the coconut milk is added, it is necessary to stir the soup continuously to avoid curdling. The end result is a light, velvety smooth soup, specked with green* **curry leaves**, *spices, and bits of tomatoes. If curry leaves are unavailable, use a bay leaf instead. In this case remove and discard the bay leaf before serving the soup. Because snapper cooks quickly and has a delicate taste, it is the best fish to use in this recipe.*

YIELD 4 SERVINGS

1 tablespoon (15 ml) oil
2 tablespoons (30 ml) sliced shallots
1 teaspoon (5 ml) minced ginger
1 green chili, seeded and thinly sliced
2 tomatoes, peeled, seeded, and chopped
10 **curry leaves**
⅛ teaspoon **turmeric**
2-inch (5 cm) piece of **cinnamon** stick
¼ teaspoon (1.25 ml) **fenugreek** seeds
1 teaspoon (5 ml) ground **cumin**
1 teaspoon (5 ml) ground **coriander**
2 cups (500 ml) water
2 cups (500 ml) coconut milk
Salt
1 tablespoon (15 ml) lime juice
1 pound (454 g) red snapper fillets, cut into 2-inch (5 cm) pieces

DIRECTIONS

Heat oil in a 2-quart (2 L) size saucepan; sauté shallots for 2 minutes or until the shallots turn a gold color. Add ginger, green chilies, tomatoes, and curry leaves and cook for 5 minutes until tomatoes are soft and saucy. Add the rest of the spices and stir in the water and the coconut milk; simmer for 6 minutes, stirring continuously. Season the soup with salt and lime juice to taste. Add the fish and simmer for 10 more minutes. Remove and discard the cinnamon stick. Spoon the soup into serving bowls and serve hot.

Fisherman's Hawaiian Sea Bass Stew (HĀPUʻUPUʻU)

Fishermen always serve the best of their catch in their hearty soups. You may substitute any other firm-fleshed fish and vegetables of your choice.

YIELD 4 SERVINGS

2 pounds (907 g) sea bass fillets
2 tablespoons (30 ml) olive oil
1 medium onion, chopped fine
6 whole peeled garlic cloves
1 teaspoon (5 ml) crushed red pepper
3 pints (1.5 L) **Fish Stock** (see Stocks)
Salt
Black pepper
2 cups (500 ml) peeled and cubed winter melon
1 cup (250 ml) sweet corn kernels
1 cup (250 ml) trimmed and cut up long beans
2 medium tomatoes cut into wedges

DIRECTIONS

Cut the fish into 2-inch (5 cm) pieces and refrigerate. Heat the oil in a 1-gallon (4 L) heavy-bottomed soup pot; add the onion and cook to a light gold color. Add the garlic, crushed red pepper, and fish stock and simmer for 10 minutes. Season with salt and pepper to taste; add all the vegetables and simmer for 15 minutes or until the vegetables are cooked soft. Add the fish and simmer for 15 minutes.

Jackfish and Green Papaya Soup (ULUA)

Green papaya is used as a vegetable in Asian cooking. If green papaya is unavailable, substitute winter melon or summer squash. This hot and tangy soup has Balinese flavors. The papaya is soothing as it melts in the mouth. Rice is the best accompaniment to this satisfying and homely soup.

YIELD 4 SERVINGS

2 small green papayas
1 tablespoon (15 ml) oil
½ cup (125 ml) sliced shallots
1 teaspoon (5 ml) chopped ginger
1 stalk **lemongrass**, crushed
2 hot green chilies sliced fine
1 tablespoon (15 ml) ground **coriander**
⅛ teaspoon (0.63 ml) **turmeric**
1 teaspoon (5 ml) **shrimp paste**
1 teaspoon (5 ml) **chili paste** to taste
5 cups (1.2 L) light chicken stock
2 **Kaffir lime** leaves, finely sliced
1 pound (454 g) jackfish fillets, cut into 1-inch (2.5 cm) slices
Lime juice
Salt

DIRECTIONS

Peel the papayas, wash, cut in half lengthwise, and remove the seeds. Slice the papayas lengthwise into 4 or 6 slices, and slice again crosswise into pieces about ¼ inch (0.64 cm) thick; put aside. Heat the oil in a 2-quart (2 L) pot and fry the shallots until golden. Add the ginger, lemongrass, green chilies, coriander, turmeric, shrimp paste, and chili paste; stir to combine. Add the chicken stock and bring to a slow simmer. Continue to simmer uncovered for about 10 minutes. Add the papaya, Kaffir lime leaves, and fish; cover and simmer about 30 minutes until the papaya is soft. Season the soup with lime juice and salt to taste.

Bouillabaisse with Hawaiian Sea Bass, Gray Snapper, and Moonfish (HĀPUʻUPUʻU, UKU, AND OPAH)

Don't be put off by the length of this recipe! It is not complicated at all. Most of the recipe may be made a day or two ahead, and finished close to serving time. The dish originated in the Mediterranean. Fishermen there knew how to use the best of their catch, and they also loved to use fish like sea bass with the bone in. They also used any variety of fish they had on hand. You may use any fish and without the bones if you desire; this is an opportunity to use underutilized fish species as well. If you don't have any fresh fish stock a commercial stock is fine. Hot, crusty, garlic-buttered French bread and a dry white wine are the best accompaniments to this dish.

YIELD 10 TO 12 SERVINGS

¼ cup (60 ml) olive oil

1 celery stem, thinly sliced

1 small onion, coarsely chopped

1 leek, white part, thinly sliced

1 tablespoon (15 ml) chopped garlic

1 bay leaf

2 cups (500 ml) peeled, seeded, and diced tomatoes

1 cup (250 ml) clam juice

1 cup (250 ml) white wine

3 pints (1.5 L) **fish stock** (see Stocks)

1 **fennel** bulb, thinly sliced

Salt

Black pepper

2 pounds (907 g) sea bass fillets, cut into 2-inch (5 cm) pieces

1 pound (454 g) gray snapper fillets, cut into 2-inch (5 cm) pieces

½ pound (227 g) moonfish fillets, cut into 2-inch (5 cm) pieces

⅛ teaspoon (0.63 ml) **saffron** threads

1 tablespoon (15 ml) chopped parsley

½ cup (125 ml) **Rouille** (see Sauces, Dips, and Condiments)

DIRECTIONS

Heat the oil in a 6-quarts (6 L), heavy-bottom soup pot; add the celery, onion, leeks, and garlic and cook on medium heat until onions turn transparent. Add the bay leaf, tomatoes, clam juice, wine and fish stock and simmer for 20 minutes. Add the fennel with salt and pepper to taste. Add the fish and the saffron. Cover the soup and simmer for 15 minutes. Add parsley and spoon the fish soup into a tureen. Serve the rouille alongside in a sauceboat.

Spicy Hawaiian Sea Bass Stew

(HĀPUʻUPUʻU)

When using sea bass, make sure its tough scales are removed and the fish is thoroughly washed to make sure no scales remain. Cut the fish into large chunks; it is finger-licking good this way!

YIELD 6 SERVINGS

2 pounds (907 g) sea bass fillets
1 tablespoon (15 ml) olive oil
1 teaspoon (5 ml) crushed **cumin** seed
1 teaspoon (5 ml) crushed **coriander** seed
½ teaspoon (2.5 ml) crushed red pepper
¼ teaspoon (1.25 ml) cracked black pepper
3 pints (1.5 L) hot water
Pinch of **saffron** threads
4 red potatoes, unpeeled, cut into quarters
2 carrots, peeled and cut into large dice
1 medium red onion, peeled and cut into large dice
1 leek, trimmed and washed, white part cut into large dice
2 large ripe tomatoes, cut into large dice
6 cloves of garlic, sliced
Salt
¼ cup (60 ml) grated Parmesan cheese (optional)

DIRECTIONS

Cut the fish into 2-inch (5 cm) pieces. Cover and refrigerate. Heat the oil in a 4-quart (4 L) soup pot and add the cumin, coriander, and red and black pepper. Cook spices, stirring, for 1 minute. Add water and saffron, all the vegetables, and garlic with salt to taste. Cover pot and cook on medium heat 20 minutes or until the potatoes are cooked. Add the fish, reduce heat to low, cover and simmer 10 minutes. Serve in bowls with a sprinkling of Parmesan cheese on each serving.

Moonfish Stew with Rhubarb (OPAH)

Moonfish has a sweet flavor that partners well with the sour rhubarb. Serve with rice and wilted greens such as beet greens or kale.

YIELD 2 SERVINGS

1 pound (454 g) moonfish fillets

1 tablespoon (15 ml) olive oil

2 medium red onions, thinly sliced

1 tablespoon (15 ml) minced ginger

½ cup (125 ml) white wine

1½ cups (375 ml) water

Juice of 1 orange

1 tablespoon (15 ml) lemon juice

Zest of 1 lemon

1 teaspoon (5 ml) crushed red pepper

1 stem rhubarb, peeled and cut into 1-inch (2.5 cm) lengths

Salt

Pepper

½ teaspoon (2.5 ml) sugar

½ cup (125 ml) chopped mint leaves

DIRECTIONS

Cut the fish into 1-inch (2.5 cm) cubes. Heat olive oil in a sauté pan and sauté onions on medium heat for 2 to 3 minutes. Add ginger, wine, water, orange, lemon juice and zest, red pepper, and rhubarb with salt and pepper to taste; sprinkle with sugar and bring to a slow simmer. Add the cubed fish, cover pan, and simmer on low heat 6 to 8 minutes, or until the fish is done. Fold in mint and serve with rice.

Baked Short-Tail Red Snapper and Vegetable Stew ('EHU)

This baked fish dish with lots of vegetables is a meal by itself. It is between a soup and a stew with a mix of wonderful flavors and textures. You may use any whole snapper to prepare in this method. Use an attractive baking pan that will fit the fish, and serve out of the pan at the table.

YIELD 4 SERVINGS

1 pound (454 g) unpeeled Yukon gold potatoes, thinly sliced
3 pounds (1.4 kg) whole dressed red snapper
Juice of 1 lemon
1 tablespoon (15 ml) Worcestershire sauce
Salt
Black pepper
4 ounces (113 g) melted butter
¼ cup (60 ml) broken up fresh dill sprigs
1 pound (454 g) tomatoes, sliced
8 garlic cloves, thinly sliced
2 red bell peppers, seeded and thinly sliced
4 ounces (110 g) mushrooms, sliced
1 small zucchini, thinly sliced
½ pound (227 g) leeks, thinly sliced (white parts only)
2 medium onions, thinly sliced
½ cup (125 ml) white wine
½ cup (125 ml) vegetable broth

DIRECTIONS

Heat the oven to 375°F (190°C). Place the sliced potatoes in the bottom of a baking pan. Season the fish with lemon, Worcestershire sauce, and salt and pepper to taste. Place the fish on the potatoes, spoon half the melted butter on, and lay the dill and tomato slices on top. Strew the garlic over the tomatoes and place the bell peppers, mushrooms, zucchini, and leeks on top. Heat the remaining butter in a sauté pan and sauté onions until golden; season with salt and pepper to taste and spoon over the vegetables. Pour the wine and broth over, cover tightly with foil, and bake for 45 minutes or until the fish flakes when tested.

Creamy Mustard Wahoo Stew (ONO)

Any snapper or wahoo may be used in this fast-cooking stew. It is a meal in itself or can be served with potatoes and vegetables. It can also be served with rice.

YIELD 4 SERVINGS

4 wahoo steaks about 8 ounces (227 g) each
Salt
Black pepper
⅛ teaspoon **turmeric**
2 medium tomatoes, thinly sliced
2 medium onions, thinly sliced
2 cloves crushed garlic
1 russet potato, peeled and thinly sliced
¼ pound (113 g) string beans cut into 2-inch (5 cm) pieces
1 tablespoon (15 ml) sliced green onion
1½ cups (375 ml) water
½ cup (125 ml) dry white wine
2 tablespoons (30 ml) lime juice

To enrich the stew

1 tablespoon (15 ml) Dijon country mustard
2 tablespoons (15 ml) cream or coconut milk

DIRECTIONS

Season the fish with salt and pepper, rub in the turmeric, and refrigerate. Place the rest of the ingredients in a straight-sided sauté pan; bring to a boil, cover, and simmer on medium heat for 10 minutes. Lay the fish over the cooked vegetables, cover the sauté pan, and simmer on low heat for 7 minutes more. To enrich the stew, whisk mustard and cream together in a bowl and stir into the stew. Taste and season with more salt if needed.

SALADS AND SANDWICHES

Salads play a major role in today's healthy diets. Salads partnered with fish make nutritious yet small meals that are much in vogue today. This chapter presents a selection of such dishes that are simply produced. For added nutrition, taste, and flavor, these dishes are combined with vegetables, greens, legumes, and pasta. Spices and herbs are added for extra flavor and fragrance.

*General directions for **broiling**, **grilling**, **poaching**, and **sautéing** can be found in Cooking Methods.*

Grilled Yellowfin Tuna with Spinach, Goat Cheese, and Mango Chutney ('AHI)

Wahoo Rice Salad (ONO)

Sautéed Swordfish and Roasted Corn Salad (SHUTOME)

Sautéed Swordfish with Tomato Salad (SHUTOME)

Broiled Gray Snapper with Pickled Onion, Goat Cheese,
    and Spinach Salad (UKU)

Broiled Wahoo and Avocado Salad (ONO)

Spicy Bigeye Tuna Salad ('AHI)

Salmon with Minty Orange Vinaigrette

Poached Trout with Potatoes in Herb Mayonnaise

Fish with Slaw

Skipjack Tuna Salad with Bacon and Sherry Vinaigrette (AKU)

Grilled Bigeye Tuna with Greens and Blue Cheese Dressing ('AHI)

Grilled Mahimahi with Tomato and Seaweed Vinaigrette (DORADO)

Marlin with Spinach and Papaya (A'U)

Sautéed Short-tail Red Snapper with Potato and Arugula Salad (EHU)

Skipjack Tuna and Pineapple (AKU)

Niçoise-style Bigeye Tuna Salad ('AHI)

Chermoula Grilled Pink Snapper with Spinach Raita ('ŌPAKAPAKA)

Blackened Yellowfin Tuna Caesar ('AHI)

Grilled Bigeye Tuna with Watercress, Orange, and Beet Salad ('AHI)

Warm Spinach Salad with Fried Smelts

Grilled Mahimahi Sandwich with Cilantro and Basil Pesto (DORADO)

Bigeye Tuna with Basil and Tomato Bruschetta ('AHI)

Grilled Skipjack Tuna and Goat Cheese Bruschetta (AKU)

Crostini Sandwich with Yellowfin Tuna ('AHI)

Curried Fish Crostini

Grilled Yellowfin Tuna with Spinach, Goat Cheese, and Mango Chutney ('AHI)

This is a lovely dish to behold, and the combination of goat cheese and mango chutney is heavenly. Any fish suitable for grilling may be substituted for tuna.

YIELD 6 SERVINGS

6 tuna fillets, 4 ounces (113 g) each
⅛ teaspoon (0.63 ml) cayenne pepper
1 tablespoon (15 ml) balsamic vinegar
Salt
2 tablespoons (30 ml) olive oil
1 bunch spinach leaves, washed, trimmed, spun,
    and chilled
½ medium red onion, thinly sliced
Juice of ½ a lemon
Black pepper
4 ounces (113 g) goat cheese
2 tablespoons (30 ml) mango chutney

DIRECTIONS

Preheat the grill. Season the fish with cayenne pepper, balsamic vinegar, and salt to taste; brush with olive oil (save the balance of the olive oil for the dressing). On medium heat, grill the tuna to medium rare, 2 to 3 minutes on each side. Place spinach and onion in a bowl; add the remaining olive oil, the lemon juice, and salt and pepper to taste. Toss to coat the spinach and spoon onto plates. Place one piece of grilled fish on each portion of spinach, crumble goat cheese on top of the fish, and then spoon mango chutney on top of the cheese.

Wahoo Rice Salad (ONO)

*I use **basmati** rice, but any white or brown rice is equally good. Any cooked fish may be used in this elegant and substantial luncheon salad. The dressing is an exotic curry dressing that is savory and makes the salad colorful as well. For garnish use sliced fruit or small bunches of grapes and mint sprigs.*

YIELD 4 SERVINGS

2 cups (500 ml) cooked rice
2 cups (500 ml) cooked, flaked wahoo
1 cup (250 ml) diced fresh pineapple (or substitute canned pineapple)
½ cup (125 ml) seedless red grapes, halved
2 tablespoons (30 ml) chopped almonds

Dressing

1 tablespoon (15 ml) olive oil
2 tablespoons (30 ml) chopped green onion
2 tablespoons (30 ml) **curry powder**
1 teaspoon (5 ml) dry mustard
½ cup (125 ml) sour cream
½ cup (125 ml) mayonnaise
1 tablespoon (15 ml) mango chutney
Juice of 1 lemon
Black pepper
Salt
4 mint sprigs

DIRECTIONS

Place rice, fish, pineapple, grapes, and almonds in a bowl. For the dressing, heat the oil and sauté the green onion until soft. Add the curry powder and mustard and cook for 1 minute on low heat. Remove from heat and fold in the rest of the ingredients, adding pepper and salt to taste. Add to the salad mix and gently fold to combine with the dressing. Taste and adjust seasoning, mold onto a dish and garnish with mint.

Sautéed Swordfish and Roasted Corn Salad (SHUTOME)

This is a great salad to serve at an outdoor dinner. Any firm-fleshed fish will be delicious prepared in this manner.

YIELD 4 SERVINGS

2 ears of corn, soaked in cold water for 1 hour
1 pound (454 g) swordfish fillets, cut into large dice
Salt
Black pepper
2 tablespoons (30 ml) olive oil
2 beefsteak tomatoes, cut in wedges
1 medium red onion, chopped
½ cup (125 ml) chopped cilantro
½ cup (125 ml) chopped basil leaves
1 teaspoon (5 ml) finely chopped garlic
2 teaspoons (10 ml) honey
Juice of 1 orange

DIRECTIONS

Place the soaked corn in the husk on a hot grill and cook for about 30 minutes, rolling on the grill occasionally. When the husk is browned the corn should be cooked. Remove the husk and scrape the corn kernels into a salad bowl. Season fish with salt and pepper; heat a tablespoon of olive oil in a skillet and cook the fish on high heat for about 4 to 5 minutes; add to the corn. Add the remaining tablespoon of olive oil to the salad along with the rest of the ingredients with salt to taste and toss to combine.

Sautéed Swordfish with Tomato Salad

(SHUTOME)

YIELD 4 SERVINGS

1 small red onion, finely chopped

1 teaspoon (5 ml) finely chopped garlic

1 tablespoon (15 ml) white wine vinegar

Juice of 1 lemon

2 ounces (60 ml) olive oil

Salt

Black pepper

2 red vine-ripened tomatoes, sliced (or a mix of red and yellow tomatoes)

8 red tear-drop tomatoes, halved

8 yellow tear drop tomatoes halved

¼ cup (60 ml) chopped parsley

¼ cup (60 ml) shredded basil leaves

¼ cup (60 ml) peanut oil

4 swordfish fillets, 4 ounces (113 g) each

2 tablespoons (30 ml) cornstarch

2 eggs, beaten

DIRECTIONS

Combine onions, garlic, vinegar, and lemon juice in a bowl; add olive oil with salt and pepper to taste and whisk. Fold in the tomatoes and the herbs. Refrigerate. Heat peanut oil in a skillet. Season fish with salt and pepper to taste. Dust with cornstarch, dip in egg, and sauté in the hot skillet on medium heat for 3 to 4 minutes on each side. Spoon the tomato salad onto plates and place a portion of fish on each.

Broiled Gray Snapper with Pickled Onion, Goat Cheese, and Spinach Salad (UKU)

The pickled onions in this dish can be done in a few minutes, and they make it special. Pickled onions and goat cheese go well together, and with the spinach make a great combination—a treat for lunch served on a platter.

YIELD 4 SERVINGS

4 snapper fillets, 4 ounces (113 g) each

Marinade

Juice of 1 orange

1 teaspoon (5 ml) balsamic vinegar

1 teaspoon (5 ml) chopped garlic

1 teaspoon (5 ml) cracked black pepper

1 tablespoon (15 ml) olive oil

Salt to taste

Pickled red onion

1 tablespoon (15 ml) olive oil

2 small red onions, peeled and sliced into ¼-inch (.64 cm) rings

1 tablespoon (15 ml) white wine vinegar

1 tablespoon (15 ml) white wine

1 tablespoon (15 ml) balsamic vinegar

1 tablespoon (15 ml) brown sugar

A large pinch of ground **cloves**

A pinch of ground **cinnamon**

Spinach and goat cheese salad

1 bunch spinach leaves, washed, trimmed, spun, and chilled

3 tablespoons (45 ml) olive oil

2 tablespoons (30 ml) lemon juice

Black pepper

4 ounces (113 g) goat cheese

DIRECTIONS

Place fish in a nonreactive dish; pour the marinade over the fish, mix, and refrigerate for 30 minutes. Heat the broiler. For the pickled onions, heat olive oil in a sauté pan, then add and sauté the onions on medium heat for 2 minutes. Spoon the sautéed onions into a glass bowl and place aside. Add the rest of the pickling ingredients to the sauté pan with salt to taste and bring to a simmer; immediately remove from heat and pour over the onions. **Broil** (see Cooking Methods) the fish and place aside. To assemble the salad, place the spinach in a bowl; add the olive oil, lemon juice, and black pepper with salt to taste. Toss the spinach salad and place on a platter or individual plates. Break up the goat cheese, strew it on the spinach salad, and place broiled fish on the salad. Place a spoonful of pickled onion on each portion of fish.

Broiled Wahoo and Avocado Salad (ONO)

This salad is a good starter to a meal, or it can be a light luncheon salad on its own.

YIELD 4 SERVINGS

1 pound (454 g) wahoo fillets, broiled (see Cooking Methods)

2 tablespoons (30 ml) chopped celery

2 tablespoons (30 ml) chopped onion

1 peeled, seeded avocado, cut into ¼-inch (0.64 cm) dice

1 cup (250 ml) diced tomatoes

Dressing

½ cup (125 ml) yogurt

¼ cup (60 ml) mayonnaise

1 tablespoon (15 ml) lemon juice

½ teaspoon (2.5 ml) Tabasco sauce

Salt

Black pepper

2 cups (500 ml) baby spinach, washed, spun, and chilled

DIRECTIONS

Cut the broiled fish into medium dice and place in a salad bowl with the celery, onion, avocado, and tomato. For the dressing, whisk together yogurt, mayonnaise, lemon juice, Tabasco, and salt and pepper to taste. Add to the salad and fold gently to combine all the ingredients. Arrange spinach on salad plates and spoon a portion of the fish and avocado salad onto the spinach.

Spicy Bigeye Tuna Salad ('AHI)

This fish salad garnished with sliced fruit and served in small portions makes an elegant appetizer.

....

YIELD 4 SERVINGS

....

1 tablespoon (15 ml) light soy sauce
2 tablespoons (30 ml) olive oil
1 pound (454 g) tuna fillets

Dressing

¼ cup (60 ml) finely chopped red onion
½ teaspoon (2.5 ml) **chili paste**
2 tablespoons (30 ml) lime juice
2 tablespoons (30 ml) **fish sauce**
2 teaspoons (10 ml) sugar
¼ cup (60 ml) hot water
1 cup (250 ml) broken-up butter lettuce
¼ cup (60 ml) mint leaves
1 cup (250 ml) sliced fruit (pineapple, mango, or plums, kiwi, or your choice of fruits)

DIRECTIONS

Mix together soy sauce and 1 tablespoon (15 ml) olive oil, brush on the fish, and place aside. Heat a skillet with the rest of the olive oil and sear the fish on high heat about 3 minutes on each side, to medium-rare doneness. For the dressing, place onions, chili paste, lime juice, fish sauce, sugar, and hot water in a bowl and whisk to combine. Slice the fish, add to the dressing, and toss to mix with the seasoning. Arrange lettuce, mint leaves, and fruit on a platter and spoon the fish along with the dressing.

Salmon with Minty Orange Vinaigrette

The hot broiled whole salmon fillet is served with the cold minty orange salad.

YIELD 4 SERVINGS

1 pound (454 g) salmon fillet
Salt
1 tablespoon (15 ml) olive oil

Minty orange salad

2 oranges, peeled and segmented
1 small red onion, sliced and loosened into rings
½ cup (125 ml) shredded mint leaves
1 teaspoon (5 ml) cracked black pepper
1 teaspoon (5 ml) **cumin** seed, roasted
Juice of 1 orange
Juice of ½ lemon
1 teaspoon (5 ml) capers
2 tablespoons (30 ml) olive oil
Salt

DIRECTIONS

Heat the broiler. Season the salmon with salt to taste and rub with the olive oil; place on broiler rack and broil 6 minutes on each side. Place on a platter. Toss the rest of the ingredients with salt to taste, spoon around the salmon, and serve.

Poached Trout with Potatoes in Herb Mayonnaise

A good substitute for trout is red snapper. In this case use a 2 to 2½ pound (907 grams to 1.1 kg) dressed snapper. If you think that making a court bouillon is a lot of work, take a shortcut: substitute water and wine and add lots of herbs such as dill, parsley, and bay leaves.

YIELD 4 SERVINGS

4 dressed trout, 8 to 10 ounces (227 to 284 g) each
6 cups (1.5 litres) **Court Bouillon** (see Stocks)
1 teaspoon (5 ml) sea salt
1 pound (454 g) Yukon gold potatoes, boiled

Herb mayonnaise

3 egg yolks
2 teaspoons (10 ml) Dijon mustard
1 tablespoon (15 ml) white wine vinegar
1 teaspoon (5 ml) minced garlic

2 tablespoons (30 ml) hot water
½ cup (125 ml) parsley sprigs
1 cup (250 ml) watercress leaves
½ cup (125 ml) arugula leaves
1 tablespoon (15 ml) chopped green onion
½ cup (125 ml) olive oil
Salt
Pepper

Garnish

½ cup (125 ml) watercress sprigs
1 lemon, sliced thin

DIRECTIONS

Place the trout in a pan, add the cold court bouillon, sprinkle with sea salt, and bring slowly to a simmer; cover pan and simmer for 5 minutes. Turn off the heat and let the trout cool in the poaching liquid. Peel and dice the potatoes. For the herb mayonnaise, place egg yolks, mustard, vinegar, garlic, and hot water in a food processor and blend for 30 seconds. Add parsley, watercress, arugula, and green onion and blend for 30 seconds. With the machine running, add the olive oil in a stream; blend a few seconds and season with salt and pepper. Add the herb mayonnaise to the warm potatoes and toss to combine. Remove trout from the poaching liquid, place on a platter, and using two forks peel away the skin, leaving the heads on. Arrange lettuce on plates, top with a trout, and spoon potato salad on the side. Garnish the trout with watercress and lemon slices.

Fish with Slaw

YIELD 4 SERVINGS

1 pound (454 g) fish fillets, **poached** (see Cooking Methods),
 or use leftover cooked fish
4 ounces (113 g) head cabbage
4 ounces (113 g) red cabbage
4 ounces (113 g) Chinese cabbage
4 ounces (113 g) romaine lettuce
½ small red onion, thinly sliced
1 tablespoon Dijon mustard
½ cup (125 ml) mayonnaise
2 tablespoons (30 ml) chopped dill pickle
2 tablespoons (30 ml) lemon juice
Black pepper
Salt

DIRECTIONS

Flake the fish and refrigerate. Shred the cabbages and lettuce and place in a bowl with the onion. Add the rest of the ingredients and toss lightly with pepper and salt to taste. Fold in the cooked flaked fish. Serve cold.

Skipjack Tuna Salad with Bacon and Sherry Vinaigrette (AKU)

This is a fast-cooking dish, with a pan-made sauce that is terrific on the fish accented with the crispy bacon. It is suitable to prepare for large numbers.

YIELD 4 SERVINGS

8 strips of bacon
1 tablespoon (15 ml) olive oil
4 tuna fillets, 4 ounces (113 g) each
8 mushrooms, thinly sliced
1 small red onion, thinly sliced
Salt
Black pepper
8 ounces (227 g) spinach, trimmed, washed, and chilled
2 shallots, minced
1 teaspoon (5 ml) Dijon mustard
2 teaspoons (10 ml) sherry vinegar
1 tablespoon (15 ml) red wine

DIRECTIONS

Cut the bacon into ½-inch (1.28 cm) pieces, place in a skillet, and cook on high heat, stirring constantly. Remove the bacon when crisp; place aside and discard half the bacon fat in the skillet. Add olive oil to the skillet, turn heat to high, and sear the fish about 2 minutes on each side, remove from skillet and set aside. Add mushrooms and onion to the skillet, season with salt and pepper to taste, and sauté for 1 minute. Place spinach on a platter; arrange the mushrooms, onion, and fish on the spinach. Place the skillet on high heat; add shallots, mustard, sherry vinegar, and wine with salt and pepper to taste, deglaze the skillet and drizzle the sauce on the salad. Strew the crispy bacon over the salad.

Grilled Bigeye Tuna with Greens and Blue Cheese Dressing ('AHI)

Tuna is good in this recipe. The salad is rich, laced with an equally rich, cheese-laden dressing.

YIELD 4 SERVINGS

4 tuna fillets, 4 ounces (113 g) each

3 cups (375 ml) mixed greens, trimmed, washed, and chilled (spinach, watercress, arugula, etc.)

2 large tomatoes, cut into 1-inch (2.5 cm) cubes

1 small avocado, peeled, seed removed, and cut into 1-inch (2.5 cm) cubes

4 strips crisp cooked bacon, crumbled

Dressing

1 ounce (28 g) crumbled blue cheese

½ cup (120 ml) sour cream

¼ cup (60 ml) plain yogurt

1 tablespoon (15 ml) white vinegar

1 teaspoon (5 ml) Worcestershire sauce

⅛ teaspoon (0.63 ml) cayenne pepper

Salt

DIRECTIONS

Grill the fish (see Cooking Methods); cover and keep warm. Place the greens, tomato, avocado, and bacon in a bowl. For the dressing, whisk together the rest of the ingredients in a bowl with salt to taste and add to the greens. Toss to combine, spoon onto a chilled platter, and place the warm grilled fish on the salad.

Grilled Mahimahi with Tomato and Seaweed Vinaigrette (DORADO)

The strong seasonings and flavorings of the seaweed salad are a good match for grilled fish. The seaweed used in the salad gives a crunchy bite and together with the juicy tomatoes makes the plain grilled fish so appetizing.

YIELD 4 SERVINGS

4 mahimahi fillets, 4 ounces (113 g) each
2 teaspoons (10 ml) finely chopped ginger
2 teaspoons (10 ml) finely chopped garlic
2 tablespoons (30 ml) lime juice
Salt
4 tablespoons (60 ml) olive oil
2 medium tomatoes, peeled, seeded, and diced
½ cup (125 ml) **ogo**, coarsely chopped
1 red jalapeño pepper, seeded and chopped
¼ cup (60 ml) chopped mint leaves
1 tablespoon (15 ml) sliced green onion
½ teaspoon (2.5 ml) crushed red pepper
2 tablespoons (30 ml) **mirin**
1 tablespoon (15 ml) rice wine vinegar

DIRECTIONS

Heat the grill and season the fish with ginger, garlic, 1 tablespoon (15 ml) lime juice, and salt to taste. Place the fish on the hot grill, brush with olive oil, and cook 3 to 4 minutes on each side. Toss the tomatoes and seaweed with the rest of the ingredients, and the remaining olive oil and lime juice; season with salt to taste. Serve with hot grilled fish.

Marlin with Spinach and Papaya (A'U)

This is a surprisingly quick and easy dish to prepare. The tartar sauce that crowns the dish ties together the flavors of all the ingredients.

YIELD 4 SERVINGS

4 marlin fillets, 4 ounces (113 g) each
1 tablespoon (15 ml) olive oil
1 teaspoon (5 ml) chopped garlic
1 teaspoon (5 ml) chopped ginger
Lemon juice
Salt
Black pepper
1 bunch spinach leaves, washed and trimmed
1 small ripe papaya, peeled and sliced
2 tablespoons (30 ml) chopped walnuts
1 medium onion, thinly sliced
2 tablespoons (30 ml) rice wine vinegar
1 tablespoon balsamic vinegar
¼ cup (60 ml) **Tartar Sauce** (see Sauces, Dips, and Condiments)

DIRECTIONS

Heat the oven to 350°F (175°C). Pat fish dry with paper towels. Mix together the oil, garlic, ginger, lemon juice, and salt and pepper to taste. Coat the fish thoroughly with this mixture. Heat an oven-safe skillet to smoking hot and sear the fish for 2 minutes on each side; place the skillet with the fish in the oven to let the fish cook through, about 4 minutes. Toss spinach, papaya, walnuts, onion, rice wine vinegar, and balsamic vinegar with salt and pepper to taste and spoon onto a platter. Place the fish on the salad; spoon a dollop of tartar sauce over fish.

Sautéed Short-Tail Red Snapper with Potato and Arugula Salad (EHU)

Arugula in the potato salad adds a special touch of flavor to this fish dish. Arugula has a strong, spicy, peppery flavor, so I use it in combination with other greens and lots of lemon. Lemon counteracts the peppery flavor somewhat, but does not take away the character of this delicious green leaf. I leave the arugula leaves whole, but you may slice them if you like to make them less pungent.

YIELD 4 SERVINGS

6 red potatoes, boiled and cut into large dice
1 cup (250 ml) arugula leaves, broken up into bite-size pieces
2 tablespoons (30 ml) snipped fresh dill
2 tablespoons (30 ml) chopped green onion
¼ cup (60 ml) mayonnaise
¼ cup (60 ml) sour cream
2 tablespoons (30 ml) lemon juice
Salt
Black pepper
4 short-tail red snapper fillets, skin on, about 5 ounces (142 g) each
1 tablespoon (15 ml) flour
2 tablespoons (30 ml) olive oil
8 lemon slices
2 teaspoons (10 ml) capers

DIRECTIONS

Place potatoes, arugula, dill, and green onion in a bowl. Whisk mayonnaise, sour cream, and lemon juice with salt and pepper to taste; pour onto the potato mixture and toss to combine; place in the refrigerate. Season the fish with salt and pepper and dust the skin side lightly with flour. Heat olive oil in a sauté pan and place the fish skin side down in the pan; cook on high heat for 3 to 4 minutes, until the skin is crusty and golden. Turn the fish over and cook 2 to 3 minutes. Remove fish from the pan and place on plates, skin side up. To the sauté pan add lemon slices and capers and cook for ½ a minute or until the lemon slices wilt. Spoon 2 lemon slices and a few capers on each portion of fish and spoon a portion of potato and arugula salad beside the fish.

Skipjack Tuna and Pineapple Salad (AKU)

*The fish is seared on high heat to seal its juices in. These fish slices partnered with juicy pineapple studded with bits of macadamia nuts are luscious in the mouth. The addition of finely sliced **curry leaves** is a great combination. You may do without the curry leaves and use fresh mint as a substitute.*

YIELD 4 SERVINGS

4 tuna fillets, 4 ounces (113 g) each
1 tablespoon (15 ml) olive oil
½ teaspoon (2.5 ml) cracked black pepper
½ teaspoon (2.5 ml) crushed red pepper
1 teaspoon (5 ml) ground **cumin**
1 teaspoon (5 ml) ground **coriander**
1 teaspoon (5 ml) white sesame seeds, toasted
1 teaspoon (5 ml) sea salt
1 cup (125 ml) diced fresh pineapple
¼ cup (60 ml) macadamia nut bits
¼ cup (60 ml) diced red bell pepper
¼ cup (60 ml) chopped cilantro
1 teaspoon (5 ml) minced ginger
2 tablespoons (30 ml) finely sliced **curry leaves**
Juice of 1 lime
Juice of 1 orange

DIRECTIONS

Brush both sides of the fish with olive oil. Toss together spices, sesame seeds, and salt; coat both sides of the fish with the mixture and place aside for 30 minutes. Heat an ungreased skillet to the smoking point and sear fish for 2 to 3 minutes on each side, to a rare doneness. For the pineapple salad, mix together the rest of the ingredients with salt to taste, and spoon onto plates. Place a portion of fish on the pineapple salad.

Niçoise-style Bigeye Tuna Salad ('AHI)

This is a version of the classic salad from Nice, France. Hot garlic bread is my favorite to serve with the salad.

YIELD 6 SERVINGS

1 pound (454 g) trimmed tuna fillet
4 tablespoons (60 ml) olive oil
Salt
Black pepper
4 tablespoons (60 ml) lemon juice
1 tablespoon (15 ml) Dijon mustard
1 teaspoon (5 ml) finely chopped garlic
1 cup (250 ml) torn lettuce leaves
2 vine-ripened tomatoes, cut into wedges
2 red potatoes, cooked and cut into wedges
4 ounces (113 g) baby green beans, trimmed and blanched
8 anchovy fillets, bones removed
1 tablespoon (15 ml) capers
¼ cup (60 ml) black olives
½ small red onion, thinly sliced
2 hard-cooked eggs, sliced

DIRECTIONS

Heat the grill. Place the fish in a dish, brush with olive oil (reserve the balance), and season with salt and pepper to taste. Grill the fish 2 to 3 minutes on a side until just seared outside but still rare in the center; slice when the fish is cool. For the dressing, whisk together the reserved olive oil, lemon juice, mustard, and garlic with salt and pepper to taste. Arrange lettuce, tomatoes, potatoes, and beans on a platter. Place the fish on the center of the salad. Strew with the anchovies, capers, black olives, and onion, and drizzle on the dressing. Place the egg slices around the edge of the platter.

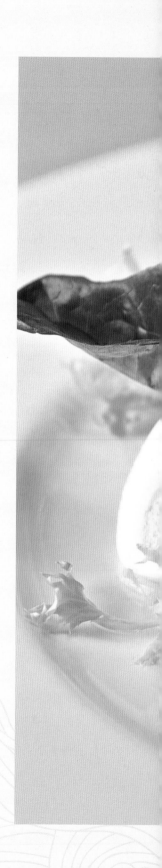

Chermoula Grilled Pink Snapper with Spinach Raita ('ŌPAKAPAKA)

The spice mix used to marinate the fish is hot, and when grilled, the fish is crusty on the outside and moist and juicy inside. The cooked spinach raita is a tasty salad, simple and easy to make, and is an exotic partner to fish. It tones down the heat of the fish. Naan bread is a good accompaniment.

YIELD 4 SERVINGS

1 pink snapper, about 4 pounds (1.8 kg), dressed
1 cup (250 ml) **Chermoula** (see Sauces, Dips, and Condiments)
1 recipe **Spinach Raita** (see Sauces, Dips, and Condiments)
Juice of 1 lemon
Juice of 1 orange
½ cup (125 ml) melted butter

DIRECTIONS

Score the fish, making two ½-inch (1.28 cm) deep diagonal cuts about 4 inches (10 cm) long and 2 inches (2.5 cm) apart on both sides of the fish; rub in the chermoula and refrigerate for 1 hour. Preheat the broiler. Make spinach raita and refrigerate. Mix lemon and orange juice with melted butter in a bowl and place aside. Place the fish on a broiler rack on a pan and broil on medium heat about 20 minutes on each side, basting often with the juice-butter mix. Serve with cold spinach raita.

Blackened Yellow Fin Tuna Caesar ('AHI)

The Caesar salad is a cooling bed, excellent for spicy blackened fish. It is a perfect luncheon dish. For a change I sometimes use romaine lettuce hearts in the Caesar salad.

YIELD 4 SERVINGS

1 small head romaine lettuce

3 anchovy fillets, bones removed

1 teaspoon (5 ml) finely chopped garlic

2 tablespoons (30 ml) lemon juice

2 teaspoons (10 ml) Worcestershire sauce

Salt

Black pepper

¼ cup (60 ml) olive oil

4 tuna fillets, 4 ounces (113 g) each

1 ounce (28 g) grated Parmesan cheese

DIRECTIONS

Wash, spin, and break up the lettuce into bite-size pieces; cover and refrigerate. For the dressing mash anchovies and garlic together in a salad bowl; add lemon juice, Worcestershire sauce, salt and pepper to taste and whisk in the olive oil. Prepare blackened fish according to directions for **Blackened Bigeye Tuna** (see Entrées). Toss lettuce with the dressing; add cheese, toss again, and spoon a serving on each plate. Place a portion of blackened fish on each portion of salad.

Grilled Bigeye Tuna with Watercress, Orange, and Beet Salad (ʻAHI)

*The **coriander** I use in this recipe goes well with the beets and orange. I grind whole coriander seeds rather coarse so they are gritty. If you don't have coriander seeds on hand, use regular ground coriander.*

YIELD 4 SERVINGS

4 tablespoons (60 ml) olive oil
1 tablespoon (15 ml) red wine vinegar
2 teaspoons (10 ml) coarse-ground **coriander**
Salt
Black pepper
1 pound (454 g) trimmed tuna fillet
1 bunch watercress, trimmed, washed, and chilled
1 orange peeled and segmented
2 tablespoons (30 ml) lemon juice
2 medium-size beets roasted, peeled, and sliced
2 hard-cooked eggs, sliced

DIRECTIONS

Reserve 2 tablespoons (30 ml) of the olive oil. Whisk together the remaining 2 tablespoons (30 ml) olive oil, vinegar, coriander, and salt and pepper to taste; pour over the fish; refrigerate to marinate for 30 minutes. Grill (see Cooking Methods) the fish to rare, about 3 minutes on a side. Break watercress into sprigs and place in a bowl with the orange segments. Toss the watercress salad, adding the reserved olive oil and lemon juice with salt and pepper to taste. Spoon onto 4 plates and arrange the beets and eggs round the salad. Dust the beets and eggs with a little salt and pepper. Slice the fish and place a portion on each salad.

Warm Spinach Salad with Fried Smelts

These spice-crusted fried smelts are addictive! They can be a meal by themselves, but served with a warm spinach salad they are a substantial repast. Coleslaw also makes a good partner to fried smelts with cocktail sauce. I use olive oil for frying smelts; you may use your choice of oil. It is important to clean the smelts thoroughly before use.

YIELD 6 SERVINGS

2 cups (500 ml) fresh baby spinach, washed and spun

1½ to 2 pounds (680 to 907 g) smelts, eviscerated (see Preparing Fish for Cooking)

¾ cup (185 ml) all-purpose flour

2 teaspoons (10 ml) ground **coriander**

1 teaspoon (5 ml) cayenne pepper

Salt

Black pepper

Olive oil for frying fish

3 strips of bacon, diced

½ red onion, thinly sliced

2 cloves garlic, thinly sliced

2 tablespoons (30 ml) red wine vinegar

1 teaspoon (5 ml) Dijon mustard

2 teaspoons (10 ml) sugar

2 tablespoons (30 ml) olive oil

6 lemon wedges

DIRECTIONS

Chill the spinach in the refrigerator. Clean the smelts; wash and place on paper towels to remove any moisture. Heat the oil to 375°F (190°C). In a bowl, combine the flour with the coriander, cayenne pepper, and salt and pepper to taste. Add the smelts to the seasoned flour and toss to coat evenly. Add ⅓ of the smelts to the oil. Fry for 1 to 2 minutes and drain on paper towels. Fry all the smelts in this manner. For the salad, heat a skillet over medium heat and cook the bacon until crisp. Remove the bacon and discard the bacon fat; add the onion and garlic to the skillet and cook until the onions are wilted; set aside. To the skillet add vinegar and using a wire whisk scrape the brownings in the skillet (a process known as deglazing). Add the mustard and sugar and whisk in the olive oil with salt and pepper to taste. Place the spinach leaves and wilted onions in a bowl, pour the hot bacon dressing over, add the cooked bacon, and toss to combine. Spoon the salad onto individual plates, place a portion of fried smelts on each salad and garnish with lemon wedges.

Grilled Mahimahi Sandwich with Cilantro and Basil Pesto (DORADO)

This dish is ideal for an elegant lunch and is easy to make, too. Once again you may substitute your choice of fish and bread.

YIELD 4 SERVINGS

1 cup (250 ml) fresh cilantro leaves
1 cup (250 ml) fresh basil leaves
¼ cup (60 ml) olive oil
¼ cup (60 ml) walnuts
2 cloves of garlic
Salt
Black pepper
4 mahimahi fillets, about 4 ounces (113 g) each
2 tablespoons (30 ml) butter
8 thick bread slices
2 ounces (57 g) grated Parmesan cheese
2 large tomatoes, sliced ¼ inch (0.64 cm) thick into 8 slices

DIRECTIONS

Heat the grill. For the pesto, place the cilantro, basil, olive oil, walnuts, and garlic in a food processor, add salt and black pepper to taste, and blend to a slightly coarse texture. Season the fish with salt and pepper, brush with a spoonful of pesto, and cook on the hot grill for 3 minutes on a side. Butter the bread slices on both sides and toast lightly on the grill; spread with pesto and sprinkle with the cheese; top 4 slices of toasted bread with two slices of tomatoes each and a portion of grilled fish. Spoon pesto on the fish and partially cover each with a slice of toasted bread.

Bigeye Tuna with Basil and Tomato Bruschetta ('AHI)

This delicious bruschetta can be used as a light luncheon dish. It is easy to make. Made in small portions, these make elegant appetizers. Any fish on hand may be substituted.

YIELD 4 SERVINGS

8 ounces (227 g) tuna fillet
Salt
Black pepper
3 tablespoons (45 ml) olive oil
4 mashed anchovy fillets (bones removed)
1 tablespoon (15 ml) finely chopped onion
1 teaspoon (5 ml) finely minced garlic
1 teaspoon (5 ml) Worcestershire sauce
8 slices French bread, ½ inch (1.28 cm) thick
8 basil leaves
4 thick slices tomatoes
1½ ounces (43 g) grated Parmesan cheese

DIRECTIONS

Heat the broiler. Season fish with salt and pepper and brush with olive oil; reserve the rest of the olive oil. Broil fish about 4 minutes on a side to cook through. Break the fish into flakes and place in a bowl. Add the mashed anchovy, black pepper, onion, half of the minced garlic, and the Worcestershire sauce; gradually drizzle in 1 tablespoon (15 ml) olive oil; use a wooden spoon to roughly mash the fish. Brush the remaining olive oil and garlic on both sides of each of the bread slices. Broil the bread about half a minute on each side. Spoon the fish mixture on 4 bread slices; place under the broiler for 2 minutes and remove to each of the 4 plates. Place the basil leaves on the 4 remaining slices of bread and top each with a tomato slice. Sprinkle with Parmesan cheese and broil for a few seconds. Serve together with the fish-topped bruschetta on the plates.

Grilled Skipjack Tuna and Goat Cheese Bruschetta (AKU)

You may change the fish and the cheese to fit your taste and still make it tasty and enticing.

YIELD 4 SERVINGS

4 tuna fillets, 4 ounces (113 g) each
Salt
Black pepper
2 tablespoons (30 ml) olive oil
8 slices Italian bread, ½ inch (1.28 cm) thick
2 whole garlic cloves, crushed
4 ounces (113 g) goat cheese
1 teaspoon (5 ml) minced chives
4 plum tomatoes, cut into small dice
8 arugula leaves

DIRECTIONS

Heat grill. Season the fish with salt and pepper and brush with olive oil. Save the remaining oil. Grill fish on high heat about 2 minutes on each side. Brush bread with olive oil and grill on both sides. While the bread is still hot, rub the crushed garlic on both sides of each slice. Mix the goat cheese with the chives, season with salt and pepper to taste, and spread on the grilled bread. Place a piece of grilled fish on the goat cheese. Season tomatoes with salt and pepper, toss with one tablespoon (15 ml) olive oil, and spoon on the fish; top each with 2 arugula leaves; lean a slice of grilled bread on each.

Crostini Sandwich with Yellow Fin Tuna ('AHI)

This open sandwich is filling and makes a good lunch. It is important to toast the bread to a crispy crunch.

....

YIELD 4 SERVINGS

....

¼ cup (60 ml) olive oil

¼ teaspoon (1.25 ml) crushed red pepper

¼ cup (60 ml) shredded basil leaves

4 tuna fillets, 4 ounces (113 g) each

Salt

Black pepper

8 slices French bread, ½ inch (1.28 cm) thick

1 medium red onion, thinly sliced

2 medium tomatoes, thinly sliced

1 ounce (28 g) shaved Parmesan cheese

DIRECTIONS

Heat the grill. Mix together the olive oil, crushed red pepper, and basil; set aside to season for 30 minutes. Season the tuna with salt and pepper and a little of the seasoned olive oil; cook on a very hot grill 2 to 3 minutes on each side. Brush the bread slices lightly with the seasoned olive oil and toast them on the grill, about a minute on each side. To the remaining seasoned olive oil add the sliced onion and tomatoes; toss to coat. Place the onions and tomatoes on 4 toasted bread slices, sprinkle with cheese, and place on plates. Place tuna on the remaining toast and place on each plate.

Curried Fish Crostini

These delicious crostini can be assembled with cooked fish for a lovely lunch. You may serve a green salad to make it a filling one. In small portions these make elegant starters or appetizers.

YIELD 4 SERVINGS

1 baguette

1 tablespoon (15 ml) butter, melted

2 cups (500 ml) flaked, cooked fish

1 red delicious apple, peeled, cored, and cut into small dice

½ cup (125 ml) coarsely chopped celery

2 tablespoons (30 ml) roasted, chopped cashew nuts

Dressing

2 teaspoons (10 ml) butter

2 tablespoons (30 ml) chopped green onion

1 tablespoon (15 ml) **curry powder**

1 teaspoon (5 ml) dry mustard

1 teaspoon (5 ml) Worcestershire sauce

½ cup (125 ml) sour cream

½ cup (125 ml) mayonnaise

1 tablespoon (15 ml) mango chutney

Juice of 1 lemon

Black pepper

Salt

DIRECTIONS

Heat the grill. Slice the baguette diagonally into 8 slices, each ½ inch (1.28 cm) thick. Brush each slice with melted butter and set aside. Place the fish, apple, celery, and cashew nuts in a bowl. For the dressing, melt the butter in a skillet, add the green onion, and sauté until soft. Add the curry powder and cook for 1 minute on low heat. Remove from heat and fold in the rest of the ingredients, adding pepper and salt to taste. Add to the fish mix and gently fold to combine with the dressing. Taste and adjust seasoning. Toast the bread on the grill for 1 to 2 minutes or until crisp and the edges of the bread turn golden brown. Place a slice of grilled bread on each plate, heap the fish salad on top, and partially lean another slice of grilled bread on each serving.

ENTRÉES

The entrée is the star of the meal. This chapter has a selection of recipes, simple and uncomplicated, with fish as the center of the plate. There are a few entrées for those who love a challenge. These intriguing and exciting fish dishes are tasty and appealing to the eye too. Vegetables and a wide variety of herbs and spices are used to import tempting tastes and seductive flavors. Recipes for sauces are also given in the "On the Side" chapter of this book; you can use them when you would like a change.

Simply Poached Salmon

Poached Long-tail Red Snapper Fillets (ONAGA)

Simply Steamed Hawaiian Sea Bass (HĀPUʻUPUʻU)

Pink Snapper Steamed in Banana Leaves (ʻŌPAKAPAKA)

Hawaiian-style Steamed Threadfin (MOI)

Steamed Moonfish Bundles (OPAH)

Steamed Threadfin (MOI)

Stewed Hawaiian Sea Bass with Rhubarb (HĀPUʻUPUʻU)

Gray Snapper en Papillote (UKU)

Simply Braised Short-tail Red Snapper (ʻEHU)

Braised Gray Snapper in Pomegranate Sauce (UKU)

Braised Short-tail Red Snapper with Okra (ʻEHU)

Braised Goatfish (KŪMŪ)

Broiled Long-tail Red Snapper Fillets with Wilted Spinach and Tomato Relish (ONAGA)

Broiled Salmon Steak with Pineapple and Ginger Salsa

Simply Broiled Swordfish (SHUTOME)

Broiled Yellowfin Tuna with Black Olive and Arugula Pesto (ʻAHI)

Wasabi-crusted Mahimahi (DORADO)

Broiled Salmon with Red Apple Relish and Port Wine Glaze

Broiled Pesto-crusted Gray Snapper Fillets (UKU)

Simply Baked Salmon

Baked Rainbow Trout

Spicy Cheese-crusted Mahimahi (DORADO)

Baked Long-tail Red Snapper in a Salt Crust (ONAGA)

Baked Gray Mullet with Roasted Red Bell Pepper Vinaigrette (ʻAMAʻAMA)

Stuffed Baked Long-tail Red Snapper (ONAGA)

Gray Snapper Tagine (UKU)

Baked Goatfish in Tomato Sauce (KŪMŪ)

Simply Roasted Red Snapper (ONAGA)

Honey-glazed Roast Gray Snapper with Peaches (UKU)

Roasted Miso Salmon

Roasted Long-tail Red Snapper (ONAGA)

Pan-cooked Pink Snapper Fillets with Greens (ʻŌPAKAPAKA)

Swordfish with Penne Pasta and Spinach (SHUTOME)

Simply Sautéed Pink Snapper Fillets (ʻŌPAKAPAKA)

Broiled Swordfish in Tomato Sauce (SHUTOME)

Lemon-glazed Pink Snapper (ʻŌPAKAPAKA)

Blackened Bigeye Tuna (ʻAHI)

Bigeye Tuna Steaks with Pearl Onions and Cashews (ʻAHI)

Fruity Seared Yellowfin Tuna with Basil Sauce (ʻAHI)

Furikake-crusted Salmon

Stir-fried Moonfish with Eggplant, Tomato, and Basil (OPAH)

Hawaiian Sea Bass in Black Bean Sauce (HĀPUʻUPUʻU)

Long-tail Red Snapper Curried in Yogurt Sauce (ONAGA)

Chili-fried Cod (PACIFIC COD)

Goanese-style Hawaiian Sea Bass Curry (HĀPUʻUPUʻU)

Hawaiian Sea Bass and Pineapple Curry (HĀPUʻUPUʻU)

Curried Scads with Okra (AKULE)

Marlin and Spinach Curry (KAJIKI)

Wahoo with Onion and Mustard Sauce (ONO)

Devilled Swordfish (SHUTOME)

Curried Wahoo Steaks (ONO)

Hot Hawaiian Sea Bass Curry (HĀPUʻUPUʻU)

Curried Short-tail Red Snapper (ʻEHU)

Fried Short-tail Red Snapper in Thai Curry Sauce (ʻEHU)

Singapore-style Wahoo Fish Head Curry (ONO)

Simply Poached Salmon

Poached salmon is cooked by the submersion method; using a flavorful fish stock gives delicious results. For that special touch, I skin the salmon after cooking and lightly sprinkle sea salt just before service. However, if you like to see the skin on, do not remove it. As accompaniments serve mashed potatoes, cooked greens of your choice, and **Hollandaise Sauce** *(see Sauces, Dips, and Condiments).*

YIELD 12 TO 15 SERVINGS

6 to 7 pounds (2.7 to 3.2 kg) **drawn** salmon (see Understanding Fish)
5 quarts (4.7 L) cold **Fish Stock** (see Stocks)
Sea salt or salt
15 sprigs dill
15 lemon wedges

DIRECTIONS

Wash the salmon inside and out under running cold water. Wrap it in a double thickness of dampened cheesecloth. Leave at least 6 inches (15.25 cm) of cheesecloth at each end to serve as handles to lift the salmon out of the poaching liquid. Twist the two ends of the cheesecloth and tie with string. Place the salmon in a roasting pan with a lid and tie the ends of the cheesecloth to the handles of the roasting pan. Pour the cold fish stock over the salmon, making sure the liquid rises at least 1 inch (2.5 cm) over the salmon. Cover the roasting pan with the lid, place on the stove over medium heat, and gradually bring to a slow simmer. Simmer 40 to 45 minutes. When the salmon is done, untie the cheesecloth from the handles and lift the salmon out of the roasting pan using the cheesecloth ends as handles. Place on a cutting board and carefully open the cheesecloth. With a sharp knife remove the skin and the gray-colored flesh down the middle of the cooked salmon. Sprinkle sea salt on the salmon to taste. Using a serving platter large enough to hold the salmon, hold the ends of the cheesecloth and turn the salmon over, onto the platter. Gently remove the cheesecloth and discard. Remove the skin and the gray flesh down the center of this side of the salmon as you did on the other side and sprinkle with sea salt to taste. Garnish the salmon platter with fresh dill sprigs and lemon wedges. Use a serving spoon and fork, lift the top fillet off the center bone. When the top fillet is served, lift the center bone, and with the serving spoon and fork serve the second fillet.

Poached Long-Tail Red Snapper Fillets (ONAGA)

These shallow-poached snapper fillets are delicious, especially with a sauce made using the reduced poaching liquid enriched with a little butter. Steamed vegetables, rice, potatoes, or pasta are all good accompaniments. Salmon, sole, and bass fillets may also be prepared in this manner.

YIELD 2 SERVINGS·

2 red snapper fillets, 5 ounces (142 g) each
Salt
Black pepper
1 tablespoon (15 ml) butter
1 shallot, thinly sliced
2 tablespoons (30 ml) thinly sliced leeks, white parts only
2 ounces (57 g) sliced mushrooms
1 sprig of thyme
¼ cup (60 ml) white wine
½ cup (120 ml) **Fish Stock** (see Stocks)

To enrich the sauce

1 tablespoon (15 ml) cold butter
Lemon juice
1 tablespoon (15 ml) chopped parsley

DIRECTIONS

Season the fish fillets with salt and black pepper to taste and set aside. On low heat melt butter in a sauté pan and add shallots, leeks, mushrooms, and a sprig of thyme. Lay the fish on the vegetables, pour the wine and fish stock into the pan, and bring to a simmer. Cover the fish with a piece of parchment (cut to fit the size of the pan) and simmer on medium heat 5 to 6 minutes. Remove the fish gently to a dish and reserve in a warm place. Place the sauté pan with the vegetables back on medium heat, reduce the liquid to about 4 tablespoons (60 ml), and whisk in the butter. Season sauce with a squeeze of lemon juice, pour over the fish and sprinkle with chopped parsley.

Simply Steamed Hawaiian Sea Bass (HĀPUʻUPUʻU)

The fish is simply steamed over a small amount of aromatized boiling water. These additional flavors will infuse the fish and make its aroma appetizing. Place the fish on a rimmed platter so the cooking liquids will not spill out. Cover tightly, to make sure the steam does not escape when steaming. Serve with **Sauce Beurre Blanc** *(see Sauces, Dips, and Condiments) and steamed rice.*

YIELD 4 SERVINGS

4 portions sea bass fillet, 6 ounces (170 g) each

Seasonings

1 tablespoon (15 ml) minced garlic
1 tablespoon (15 ml) white wine
1 teaspoon (5 ml) grated lemon zest
1 tablespoon (15 ml) lemon juice
Sea salt
Black pepper

Aromatized water

1 cup (250 ml) water
Peel of 1 lemon
1 **cinnamon** stick
4 **cloves**
1 bay leaf

DIRECTIONS

Pat the fish with paper towels to remove excess moisture. Place on a platter with a rim; add seasonings with salt and pepper to taste, and place on a steamer rack. Place ingredients for aromatized water in a steamer pot and bring to a fast boil. Place the steamer rack with the fish over the boiling aromatized water, cover steamer tightly, and steam 4 to 6 minutes.

Pink Snapper Steamed in Banana Leaves ('ŌPAKAPAKA)

The wrapping of banana leaves imparts an earthy flavor to the fish and preserves its natural juices. You may use foil, but it is not as exotic as banana leaves. The banana leaves should not be eaten. Any soft-fleshed white fish like snapper, halibut, or pomfret fillets may be used for this recipe. Serve with **Yellow Rice** *(see Accompanying Staples) and chutney.*

....

YIELD 4 SERVINGS

....

4 banana leaves cut into 12-inch (30.5 cm) squares
1 tablespoon (15 ml) vegetable oil
4 portions snapper fillets, 6 ounces (170 g) each
Salt

Herbs and seasonings paste

½ cup (125 ml) mint leaves
½ cup (125ml) cilantro leaves
½ cup (125 ml) fresh grated coconut
2 **serrano chilies**, sliced
1 tablespoon (30 ml) sliced shallots
1 tablespoon sliced ginger
½ teaspoon (2.5 ml) ground **cumin**
½ teaspoon ground **coriander**
2 tablespoons (30 ml) lime juice
2 teaspoons (10 ml) sugar

DIRECTIONS

Wash, dry, and warm the banana leaves over low heat on a stove until they are pliable. Brush insides of the leaves with the oil. Season the fish with salt to taste. In a blender, blend all the ingredients for the herb and seasoning paste, adding salt to taste. When the paste is smooth, divide it into 4 portions. Coat both sides of each fillet with a portion of the paste and place one fillet on each leaf; fold top and bottom edges of the leaves over the fish, and fold sides over to form 4 neat parcels. Place the fish parcels in a bamboo steamer, cover, and steam over boiling water 8 to10 minutes. Remove and serve on plates, allowing guests to open their own fish bundles.

Hawaiian-style Steamed Threadfin (MOI)

In the Hawaiian Islands, threadfin is a popular fish served in restaurants. It is best when it is steamed or deep-fried. One whole threadfin, about 12 to 14 ounces (340 to 397 g), makes a good portion. Goatfish is a substitute for this style of cooking.

YIELD 2 SERVINGS

2 dressed threadfin with heads on
2 teaspoons (10 ml) salt
1 teaspoon (5 ml) sugar
2 teaspoons (10 ml) soy sauce
¼ cup (60 ml) ginger julienne
½ cup (125 ml) green onion julienne
½ cup (125 ml) thinly sliced shitake mushrooms

For the sauce

½ cup (125 ml) chicken stock
¼ teaspoon (1.25 ml) sugar
¼ teaspoon (1.25 ml) salt
½ teaspoon (2.5 ml) sesame oil
1 teaspoon (5 ml) oyster sauce
1 fresh red chili, thinly sliced
1 tablespoon (15 ml) chopped cilantro

DIRECTIONS

Wash the fish and pat dry with paper towels. Score both sides of each fish making a diagonal cut ½-inch (1 cm) deep and 2 inches long (95 cm) on each side. Rub fish with the salt, sugar, and soy and refrigerate 15 minutes. Scatter some of the ginger on a rimmed platter and place the seasoned fish over the ginger. Sprinkle the rest of the ginger, green onions, and mushrooms on fish. Place the plate on the steamer rack, insert into steamer, cover, and steam for about 15 minutes. For the sauce, strain the liquid from the steamed fish into a pan; add the chicken stock, sugar, salt, sesame oil, and oyster sauce and simmer for 1 minute; adjust seasoning if needed. Add the red chili and cilantro to the sauce, pour it over the fish, and serve with rice.

Steamed Moonfish Bundles (OPAH)

These fish bundles are wrapped in ti leaves and steamed in the style of Hawaii lau lau. When steamed, ti leaves give a tempting aroma and make a lovely presentation. However, the ti leaves are not to be eaten! If ti leaves are not available, you may use cabbage leaves, lettuce leaves, or even kitchen foil. Serve with steamed rice and soy sauce to drizzle over the fish.

YIELD 4 SERVINGS

4 moonfish fillets, 5 ounces (142 g) each
Sea salt
1 teaspoon (5 ml) crushed red pepper
1 tablespoon lemon juice
8 ti leaves

Vegetables and seasoning

4 lemon slices
4 tomato slices
4 onion slices
A handful of **ogo**, trimmed and cut into 1-inch (2.5 cm) pieces
4 tablespoons (60 ml) sliced green onions
4 teaspoons (20 ml) olive oil

DIRECTIONS

Season fish with sea salt, red pepper, and lemon juice and refrigerate. Wash and wipe the ti leaves. Turn the leaves to have the underside of the leaves facing up. Make a cut on the midrib without cutting through the midrib and the leaf. Bend the leaf at the point of the cut and peel off the mid-rib still not breaking and damaging the leaf. Place 2 ti leaves in a cross pattern on the work surface, cut side down. Place one fish fillet on the center of the leaves where they cross each other. Place a slice of lemon, a slice of tomato, and a slice of onion on each portion of fish. Top with a tablespoon of seaweed and green onion and drizzle with a teaspoon of olive oil. Pick up the two stem ends and the two tail ends of the leaves and hold close to the fish tightly with one hand to form a bundle. Using your free hand, tear one stem end of a leaf in two, twist the two torn leaf strips in opposite directions, and tie a knot to tightly secure the bundle. Similarly complete the other fish bundles. Place in a bamboo steamer and steam over boiling water for 6 to 8 minutes. Remove and serve on plates, allowing guests to open their own fish bundles.

Steamed Threadfin (MOI)

Steamed Threadfin (MOI)

A favorite in the Pacific Islands, the main seasoning in this delicious dish is soy sauce. More flavors are added by pouring hot oil over the steamed fish. You can steam a variety of fish in this manner.

YIELD 4 TO 5 SERVINGS

3 pounds (1.4 kg) dressed threadfin with heads on
2 tablespoons (30 ml) dark soy sauce
2 tablespoons (30 ml) lemon juice
1 small onion, thinly sliced

To aromatize the fish

4 green onions, thinly sliced
2 tablespoons (30 ml) roughly chopped cilantro
1 tablespoon (15 ml) sliced **chili pepper**
1 tablespoon (15 ml) ginger julienne
¼ cup (60 ml) peanut oil
2 teaspoons (10 ml) sesame oil

DIRECTIONS

Wash the fish and pat dry with paper towels. Rub the soy sauce and lemon juice on the fish and stuff onion slices in the belly cavity of each fish. Place on a rimmed platter and then on a steamer rack. Put the rack in the steamer, cover tightly, and steam over boiling water for about 25 to 30 minutes. Remove the platter with the fish from the steamer; to aromatize the fish, strew the green onion, cilantro, chili pepper, and ginger on the fish. In a small frying pan, heat peanut oil until smoking and pour over the vegetables on the fish; drizzle with sesame oil on fish. Serve with rice.

Stewed Hawaiian Sea Bass with Rhubarb (HĀPUʻUPUʻU)

Rhubarb is a vegetable with pink to red long stems. They have a tart flavor and are often used in baked goods. Rhubarb is also used in pies, often mixed with strawberries; hence, it is known as the pie plant.

However, its large green leaves are toxic and should not be eaten. Sea bass has a mild sweet taste and goes well with the tart flavor of the rhubarb stem.

YIELD 4 SERVINGS

1½ pounds (680 g) sea bass fillet
3 tablespoons (45 ml) butter
2 medium red onions, thinly sliced
1 tablespoon (15 ml) chopped ginger
½ cup (125 ml) white wine
1 cup (250 ml) water
Juice of 1 orange
1 tablespoon (15 ml) lemon juice
1 teaspoon (5 ml) crushed red pepper
Salt
Pepper
1 stem rhubarb, peeled and cut into 1-inch (2.5 cm) lengths
½ a green apple, peeled and sliced
½ teaspoon (2.5 ml) sugar
½ cup (125 ml) mint leaves

DIRECTIONS

Cut fish into 1-inch (2.5 cm) cubes. Heat butter in a skillet and sauté onion about 2 to 3 minutes. Add ginger, wine, water, orange and lemon juice, crushed red pepper, and salt and pepper to taste. Bring to a slow simmer and add fish. Cover skillet and simmer on low heat for 6 minutes. Add rhubarb, apple, and sugar and simmer for 8 minutes or until fish flakes when tested with a fork. Fold in the mint leaves and serve with rice.

Gray Snapper en Papillote (UKU)

*Serve these Mediterranean-style fish parcels on dinner plates and allow guests to slit open their own; the well-seasoned fish with a mix of crunchy vegetables and herbs will give out a tempting aroma to savor. Natural juices created in the cooking process can be spooned on to the **Saffron Rice** (see Accompanying Staples) that goes well as an accompaniment. A cooked green vegetable can be added to enhance the meal. I chose gray snapper for this recipe, but all snappers are suitable for this style of cooking.*

YIELD 6 SERVINGS

6 gray snapper fillets, 6 ounces
(170 g) each
2 teaspoons (10 ml) chopped garlic
½ teaspoon (1.25 ml) paprika
Salt
Black pepper
6 pieces parchment paper,
15 inches (38 cm) square
4 ounces (113 g) butter
2 egg yolks, beaten lightly
2 medium onions, thinly sliced
2 red bell peppers, seeds removed,
thinly sliced

4 garlic cloves, thinly sliced
4 tablespoons (60 ml) sliced leeks,
white parts only
2 tablespoons (30 ml) chopped
tomatoes
2 tablespoons (30 ml) chopped
parsley
2 tablespoons (30 ml) lemon juice
2 tablespoons (30 ml) white wine
1 tablespoon (15 ml) balsamic
vinegar

DIRECTIONS

Heat the oven to 400°F (204°C). Pat the fish dry with paper towels and season with garlic, paprika, and salt and pepper to taste. Place the parchment squares on a work surface and brush with butter. Reserve the balance of the butter for the fish. Brush the edges of the parchment squares with egg. Place a piece of fish on each square about 2 inches (5 cm) from the edge of the side closest to you. Mix the vegetables and the rest of the ingredients together and spoon equally over fish and top each with some of the reserved butter. Fold the top edges of the parchment squares toward you to cover the fish. Crimp the edges all around the squares securely to enclose the parcels. Place fish parcels on a sheet pan and bake at 400°F (204°C) for 10 to 12 minutes. When the parchment parcels turn a golden brown, the fish is done. Place on hot dinner plates and serve, letting your guests open their own fish parcels.

Simply Braised Short-Tail Red Snapper ('EHU)

Use a deep skillet or a heavy baking pan for braising. Rice or potatoes make a good accompaniment to braised fish. In place of short-tail red snapper, you may use any fish that is less than three pounds; anything over this can be tough when cooked. Fish such as mullet or any other snapper are also good for braising.

YIELD 4 SERVINGS

2 tablespoons (30 ml) olive oil
2 pounds (900 g) dressed red snapper
1 onion, thinly sliced
2 leeks, white parts only, halved lengthwise and sliced into 2-inch (5 cm) pieces
1 red bell pepper, seeded and cut into strips
1 tablespoon (15 ml) chopped garlic
2 cups (500 ml) peeled, seeded, and chopped plum tomatoes or canned tomatoes
1 cup (250 ml) white wine
1 tablespoon (15 ml) white vinegar
1 bay leaf
2 sprigs fresh thyme
½ cup (125 ml) fish stock or water
1 teaspoon (5 ml) black pepper
Salt
1 cup (250 ml) quartered mushrooms

DIRECTIONS

Heat oil in a deep, wide medium-size skillet; add fish and sear on high heat for 3 to 4 minutes on each side. Remove fish to a plate and set aside. Add the onions and leeks to the skillet and sauté until onions are a light golden color. Add the bell pepper, garlic, tomatoes, wine, vinegar, bay leaf, thyme, fish stock, black pepper, and salt to taste; bring to a simmer. Place fish in the skillet, add mushrooms, cover, and simmer on low heat for 35 minutes.

Braised Gray Snapper in Pomegranate Sauce (UKU)

The pink-fleshed gray snapper is excellent for braising. The aromatics and seasonings, especially the sweet and tart pomegranate juice, enrich the braising liquid, giving a rich sauce by the end of cooking time. To accompany this elegant snapper dish I serve sautéed greens like beet tops or kale and roasted red potatoes.

YIELD 5 TO 6 SERVINGS

5 pounds (2.3 kg) dressed gray snapper
Salt
1 tablespoon (15 ml) flour
4 tablespoons (60 ml) butter

To braise

1 medium onion, finely chopped
1 tablespoon (15 ml) finely chopped ginger
1 teaspoon (5 ml) crushed red pepper
2-inch (5 cm) piece of **cinnamon** stick
1 bay leaf
1 sprig of thyme
1 cup (250 ml) fish stock
1 cup (250 ml) pomegranate juice
1 cup (250 ml) dry white wine
Juice of 1 lemon

DIRECTIONS

Heat the oven to 375°F (190°C). Score the fish on both sides making two diagonal cuts 1 inch (2.5 cm) deep, 2 inches (5 cm) long, and 5 inches (12.5 cm) apart. Rub the fish with salt and dust with flour. Heat butter in a large oven-proof skillet; sear the fish about 4 to 5 minutes on each side on high heat. Place the fish aside. Add the onion to the skillet and sauté on high heat for 3 minutes. Add the rest of the ingredients and bring to a simmer; season with salt to taste. Place the fish back in the skillet, bring to a simmer once again, cover the skillet, place in the oven and cook for 40 minutes. Place fish on a platter and strain sauce over.

Braised Short-tail Red Snapper with Okra ('EHU)

A native of Africa, okra is one of those vegetables that people either like or hate. Many are put off by its mucilaginous quality, which is its main attraction. Pick small okra that are not discolored. The large okra with seeds protruding from under their skin are coarse and fibrous. Certainly there are other vegetables you can use in place of okra; try long beans cut up into 2-inch (5 cm) pieces along with a large handful of spinach leaves. Rice does well with this dish.

YIELD 2 TO 3 SERVINGS

2 pounds (900 g) red snapper, dressed

To cook the fish

3 tablespoons (45 ml) olive oil
2 small onions, sliced lengthwise into ⅛-inch (3.2 mm) thick slices
2 tablespoons (30 ml) sliced garlic
2 **serrano chilies**, seeded and sliced
1 teaspoon (5 ml) ground **coriander**
1 teaspoon (5 ml) ground **cumin**
1 teaspoon (5 ml) crushed red pepper
⅛ teaspoon (0.63 ml) **turmeric**
2 large tomatoes, peeled and chopped, or 1 cup (250 ml) canned tomatoes
1 cup (250 ml) white wine
½ cup (125 ml) water
Salt
Black pepper

Vegetables

½ pound (250 g) fresh okra, stems and tails trimmed
Juice of half a lemon

DIRECTIONS

Score fish on both sides making diagonal cuts 1 inch (2.5 cm) deep and 2 inches (4 cm) long. Heat olive oil in a skillet. On high heat sear fish on both sides. Add onions, garlic, chilies, and spices to skillet, and cook for 2 to 3 minutes. Add tomatoes, wine, and water with salt and pepper to taste. Shake the skillet, cover and simmer on medium heat for 15 minutes. Turn fish over; add okra and lemon juice; cover skillet and simmer for 10 more minutes. Check with a fork for doneness and remove from heat.

Braised Goatfish (KŪMŪ)

The whole braised fish makes a homely meal for two, when you can use your fingers to bone the fish. When made with goat-fish fillets, this may be served as a first course with a matching wine.

YIELD 2 SERVINGS

2 whole dressed goatfish, about 1 pound (500 g) each
1 cup (250 ml) **Nage** (see Stocks)
½ cup (125 ml) **Sauce Beurre Blanc** (see Sauces, Dips, and Condiments)
½ cup (125 ml) sliced shitake mushrooms
2 tablespoons (30 ml) sliced leeks, white part only
4 chive leaves

DIRECTIONS

Clean, wash, and dry fish with paper towels and refrigerate. Make the nage and strain. Make beurre blanc and place aside. Place fish in a pan; pour in the nage; add mushrooms and leeks and bring to a slow simmer. Cover pan and simmer on low heat for 15 minutes, turning the fish over once during the cooking time. Place fish on 2 hot deep plates and spoon vegetables around fish. Reduce nage to ¼ cup and stir in beurre blanc; spoon some over and around the fish; garnish with chives.

Broiled Long-tail Red Snapper Fillets with Wilted Spinach and Tomato Relish (ONAGA)

*Any soft-fleshed fish like snapper can be used in this recipe. It is simply delicious when served with **Roasted Garlic Mashed Potatoes** (see Accompanying Staples). It is an easy-to-prepare crowd pleaser.*

YIELD 4 SERVINGS

4 red snapper fillets, 6 ounces (170 g) each
2 tablespoons (30 ml) red wine
1 teaspoon (5 ml) chopped ginger
1 teaspoon (5 ml) chopped garlic
1 teaspoon (5 ml) ground **cumin**
Salt
Black pepper
2 tablespoons (30 ml) olive oil

Tomato relish

1 large, firm, ripe tomato cut into small dice
1 tablespoon (15 ml) chopped onion
1 tablespoon (15 ml) chopped green onion
1 tablespoon (15 ml) chopped mint
¼ teaspoon (1.25 ml) cracked black pepper
2 tablespoons (30 ml) lemon juice

Wilted spinach

1 bunch spinach leaves, washed and trimmed
A large pinch of **turmeric**
A pinch of grated **nutmeg**
¼ cup (60 ml) sour cream, whisked smooth

DIRECTIONS

Heat the broiler. Pat the fish dry with paper towels. Place in a dish and add wine, ginger, garlic, cumin, and salt and black pepper to taste. Mix to coat the fish. Refrigerate and leave to marinate for 30 minutes. Remove fish from marinade, place on a broiler pan, brush with olive oil, and broil for about 4 to 5 minutes on each side. For relish, toss together tomatoes, onion, green onion, mint, cracked black pepper, and lemon juice in a container and season with salt to taste; place aside. Heat the rest of the olive oil in a sauté pan; add spinach leaves, turmeric, and nutmeg, and season with a pinch of salt. Using tongs, move spinach around in the pan for 2 minutes to wilt. Stir in sour cream and instantly spoon onto plates; place a portion of fish on each plate and spoon tomato relish on top of the fish.

Broiled Salmon Steak with Pineapple and Ginger Salsa

The recipe is quite simple, and can be put together at short notice. Salmon cooks fast, so take care not to overcook it. Salmon should be slightly underdone rather than overdone. The flavor of the sweet and slightly sour fresh salsa complements broiled salmon perfectly.

YIELD 4 SERVINGS

4 salmon steaks, 6 ounces (170 g) each

Marinade

2 tablespoons (30 ml) olive oil
2 tablespoons (30 ml) white wine
2 tablespoons (30 ml) lemon juice
¼ cup (60 ml) chopped dill
½ teaspoon (2.5 ml) crushed black pepper
Salt

For pineapple salsa

1 cup (250 ml) diced fresh pineapple
1 tablespoon (15 ml) chopped ginger
2 tablespoons (30 ml) small diced red onion
¼ sliced green onion
¼ cup (60 ml) chopped mint
1 red jalapeño pepper, seeded and finely chopped
1 tablespoon (15 ml) honey
Juice of 2 limes

DIRECTIONS

Heat the broiler. Pat salmon dry with paper towels. Combine the ingredients for the marinade; add salmon to the marinade and refrigerate for 15 minutes. Place the salmon on a broiler rack over broiler pan and broil for about 4 minutes on each side, until lightly brown. When salmon is done toss ingredients for salsa with salt to taste. Serve hot salmon with salsa.

Simply Broiled Swordfish (SHUTOME)

Swordfish is somewhat fatty and is ideal for broiling since its own fat keeps it moist during the cooking process. It is best to marinate the fish before cooking to preserve its moisture. Rice or pasta and a simple salad with a piquant dressing are good accompaniments to simply broiled fish.

YIELD 4 SERVINGS

4 swordfish loin steaks, about 5 ounces (142 g) each
1 tablespoon finely chopped ginger
Juice of 1 orange
1 teaspoon **chili sauce**
Salt
Black pepper
1 tablespoon (15 ml) olive oil
1 orange cut into wedges
1 tablespoon (15 ml) **Garlic Butter** (see Sauces, Dips, and Condiments)

DIRECTIONS

Season fish with ginger, orange juice, chili sauce, and salt and pepper to taste; place in the refrigerator for 20 minutes to marinate. Heat the broiler. Brush the fish on both sides with olive oil. Place on a broiler rack and broil for 5 minutes under medium heat, brush with oil and using a spatula turn over fish. Brush the top side again with oil and cook 2 to 3 minutes more. Garnish each portion with a wedge of orange and a pat of garlic butter.

Broiled Yellowfin Tuna with Black Olive and Arugula Pesto ('AHI)

This Niçoise-style fish with arugula pesto and juicy fresh tomato salad is rich and satisfying. Most of all it is easy to put together. With the addition of crusty garlic bread and some red wine, it is great for a special luncheon.

YIELD 6 SERVINGS

6 tuna steaks, 5 ounces (142 g) each

Marinade

1 tablespoon (15 ml) lemon juice
1 tablespoon (15 ml) lemon zest
1 tablespoon (15 ml) olive oil
1 teaspoon (5 ml) crushed red
    pepper
Black pepper
Sea salt

For pesto

1 cup (250 ml) arugula leaves
1 cup (250 ml) basil leaves
¼ cup (60 ml) pitted Niçoise olives
2 garlic cloves, crushed
3 anchovy fillets
2 ounces (60 ml) olive oil
Juice of 1 lemon
Salt

For tomato salad

2 medium vine-ripened tomatoes,
    sliced
2 green onions, thinly sliced
1 red onion, thinly sliced
½ pound (227 g) green beans,
    broken into 1-inch (2.5 cm) pieces
    and steamed
¼ cup (60 ml) pitted Niçoise olives
3 tablespoons (45 ml) olive oil
1 tablespoon (15 ml) lemon juice
1 tablespoon (15 ml) red wine
    vinegar
1 teaspoon (5 ml) chopped garlic
2 hard-cooked eggs, peeled and
    sliced

DIRECTIONS

Pat fish dry with paper towels; spoon ingredients for marinade over, adding black pepper and salt to taste, and refrigerate for 30 minutes. Heat the broiler. To make pesto, blend ingredients for pesto to a smooth paste, with salt to taste. For salad, toss tomatoes, green and red onion, green beans, and olives with olive oil, lemon juice, red wine vinegar, and garlic; spoon onto a platter; arrange sliced egg on the outer edge. Broil fish for 4 minutes on each side and place on the salad. Spoon the pesto on top of the fish.

Wasabi-crusted Mahimahi (DORADO)

This mahimahi dish is easy to make for a fast dinner. Serve with **Garlic Mashed Potatoes** *(see Accompanying Staples)*

YIELD 4 SERVINGS

4 mahimahi fillets, 5 ounces (142 g) each
2 tablespoons (30 ml) lemon juice
Salt
Black pepper
1 tablespoon (15 ml) olive oil

For crust

½ cup (125 ml) fresh white bread crumbs
1 tablespoon (15 ml) toasted sesame seeds
1 teaspoon (5 ml) lemon zest
2 teaspoons (10 ml) **wasabi** paste
3 tablespoons (45 ml) mayonnaise

Vegetables

4 baby bok choy

DIRECTIONS

Heat the broiler. Season fish with lemon juice and salt and pepper to taste. Place fish on a rack on a broiler pan, brush with olive oil, and broil for 3 minutes. Turn over, brush with olive oil again, and broil for 3 minutes more. Mix together ingredients for crust; spoon onto fish and press down firmly so mix adheres to the fish. Broil about 6 inches (15 cm) away from heat for 2 to 3 minutes or until crust is a light golden color. Steam bok choy and serve with fish.

Broiled Salmon with Red Apple Relish and Port Wine Glaze

Vegetables, fruits, and herbs all enhance this salmon dish. It is a simple dish, yet one that you can serve to guests.

YIELD 4 SERVINGS

4 salmon fillets, about 5 ounces (142 g) each
2 tablespoons (30 ml) melted butter
1 teaspoon (5 ml) chopped fresh thyme leaves
Salt
Black pepper

Port wine glaze

½ cup (125 ml) red port wine
½ cup (125 ml) balsamic vinegar

Red apple relish

1 red apple, cored and cut into small dice
3 red radish cut into small dice
1 tablespoon (15 ml) diced red onion
1 tablespoon (15 ml) snipped chives
1 tablespoon (15 ml) chopped dill
2 tablespoons (30 ml) lemon juice

DIRECTIONS

Heat the broiler. Brush salmon with melted butter and thyme; season with salt and pepper to taste. Place salmon on a broiler rack on a broiler pan and broil 4 minutes; turn over and broil 4 minutes more. While salmon is cooking, place port wine and balsamic vinegar in a small pan and reduce to 3 tablespoons (45 ml). For red apple relish, toss ingredients in a bowl and season with salt to taste. Place broiled salmon on hot plates, drizzle glaze around salmon, and spoon relish on salmon. Serve with mashed potatoes.

Broiled Pesto-crusted Gray Snapper Fillets (UKU)

The luscious pesto that coats fish and pasta is redolent of savory herbs; all it needs is tomatoes in one form or another. A simple tomato and green salad to accompany will make this a great meal.

YIELD 4 SERVINGS

4 gray snapper fillets, about 5 ounces (142 g) each
2 tablespoons (30 ml) white wine
1 teaspoon (5 ml) lemon zest
Black pepper
Salt

Pesto

2 cups (500 ml) loosely packed fresh basil leaves
4 cloves garlic
2 tablespoons (30 ml) walnuts
¼ cup (60 ml) water
½ cup (125 ml) grated Parmesan cheese
1 teaspoon (5 ml) black pepper
1 tablespoon (15 ml) lemon juice
¼ cup (60 ml) olive oil

Pasta

4 portions cooked pasta
¼ cup (60 ml) light chicken broth or cream

DIRECTIONS

Heat the broiler. Marinate the fish in the wine, lemon zest, and black pepper and salt to taste. For the pesto, use a processor to blend the basil, garlic, walnuts, and water to a smooth paste; add the cheese, black pepper, and lemon juice; slowly add olive oil and blend till the oil is well incorporated. Place fish fillets on a rack over a broiler pan and place under the broiler for 4 minutes. Lower the broiler rack, turn fish over, spread some pesto evenly on top surfaces of the fish fillets, and broil away from heat 4 minutes more. On high heat, toss the cooked pasta with the extra pesto, chicken broth or cream, and salt and pepper to taste; cook till pasta is hot and well coated with pesto. Serve with the broiled fish.

Simply Baked Salmon

*This salmon is seasoned, wrapped in foil, and baked to a melt-in-your-mouth goodness. Make sure the foil fully encloses the salmon so that steam does not escape when baking. Salmon is traditionally served with **Hollandaise Sauce** (see Sauces, Dips, and Condiments); **Sauce Beurre Blanc** (see Sauces, Dips, and Condiments) also goes well with salmon. Steamed potatoes and a green salad are good accompaniments.*

....

YIELD 6 SERVINGS

....

4 pounds (1.8 kg) dressed salmon
Sea salt
Black pepper
1 onion, thinly sliced
5 sprigs of dill
2 tablespoons (30 ml) melted butter
Juice of 1 lemon
½ cup (125 ml) white wine

DIRECTIONS

Heat the oven to 375°F (190°C). Season salmon inside and out with salt and pepper to taste. Stuff the salmon body cavity with the onion and dill, place on a large sheet of foil, and brush both sides of the salmon with melted butter. Pour lemon juice and wine over and wrap loosely to enclose salmon completely. Place on a baking pan; bake for about 40 to 45 minutes. In the meantime make your choice of sauce. Remove baking pan from the oven; open foil, peel off skin on both sides of the salmon and discard. Place the fish on a platter and strain cooking liquid onto it. Serve a sauce on the side.

Baked Rainbow Trout

The trout is seasoned, wrapped in foil, and then cooked in a hot oven. The fish cooks in the trapped steam and preserves its own moisture, which combines with the seasonings to make a delicious natural sauce. It is dramatic to let guests slit open their own portion and enjoy the escaping aroma. Serve with mashed potatoes and vegetables. Sautéed mushrooms are exceptional with trout.

YIELD 4 SERVINGS

4 sheets of foil each, 10 inches (25.4 cm) square
1 tablespoon (15 ml) olive oil
4 dressed rainbow trout, about 10 ounces (284 g) each
Black pepper
Salt
2 ounces (57 g) melted butter
4 slices onion
4 sprigs fresh thyme
1 tablespoon (15 ml) white wine

DIRECTIONS

Heat the oven to 425°F (218°C). Brush one side of the foil squares with oil. Season trout body cavities with black pepper and salt to taste; place on foil squares. Brush trout with melted butter. Lay a slice of onion and a sprig of thyme on each trout, and pour wine over. Fold foil squares loosely over trout to form a package and crimp edges tightly. Place trout packages on a baking sheet, place in the oven, and bake for 18 to 20 minutes. Slit the packages and place on dinner plates, or open packages and place trout on dinner plates and spoon cooking juices on. Serve with mashed potatoes and sautéed mushrooms.

Spicy Cheese-crusted Mahimahi (DORADO)

This is a simple and easy yet elegant fish dish to serve with pasta and tomato sauce, especially for a crowd.

YIELD 6 SERVINGS

6 portions pasta
1 cup (250 ml) **Tomato Sauce** (see Sauces, Dips, and Condiments)
6 mahimahi fillets, about 5 ounces (142 g) each

Seasonings

3 teaspoons (15 ml) finely chopped garlic
1 tablespoon (15 ml) finely chopped onion
3 tablespoons (45 ml) chopped basil leaves
½ teaspoon (2.5 ml) cayenne pepper
½ teaspoon (2.5 ml) black pepper
1 teaspoon (5 ml) salt

Topping

½ cup (125 ml) chopped parsley
½ cup (125 ml) sour cream
½ cup (125 ml) grated Parmesan cheese
1 cup (250 ml) fresh bread crumbs

DIRECTIONS

Cook pasta and tomato sauce and keep warm to serve with fish. Heat the oven to 450°F (232°C). Pat the fish dry with paper towels; rub in seasoning ingredients with salt to taste and place in a baking pan. Mix ingredients for topping, spread on fish, and bake for 8 to 10 minutes. Serve with pasta and tomato sauce.

Baked Long-tail Red Snapper in a Salt Crust (ONAGA)

Do not be alarmed at the quantity of salt used to cover the fish. The salt crust is removed and the fish, when ready to serve, will not be too salty. If you use an attractive baking pan to bake the fish in, you may crack open and serve the fish tableside. Oven-roasted potatoes, broiled tomatoes, and cooked greens make lovely accompaniments for this elegant snapper. Nowadays markets are full of luscious greens: beet tops, kale, collard greens, and arugula. Most of these greens can be fast sautéed. Arugula leaves may be wilted and seasoned with a dash of lemon juice. Steamed buttered beans are a good choice too.

YIELD 4 SERVINGS

4 pounds (1.8 kg) dressed red snapper
4 cloves garlic, sliced
2 shallots, sliced
6 thyme sprigs
6 tarragon sprigs
4 pounds (1.8 kg) coarse sea salt
½ recipe **Sauce Beurre Blanc** (see Sauces, Dips, and Condiments)

DIRECTIONS

Heat the oven to 475°F (246°C). Pat fish dry with paper towels; stuff the body cavity with garlic, shallots, and half the herbs. Spread the bottom of a baking pan large enough to hold the fish with a thick layer of the salt. Place fish on salt and spread remaining thyme and tarragon on the fish. Cover completely with the balance of the salt and press, so salt sits tightly on the fish, enclosing it completely. Bake for 45 to 50 minutes. While fish is cooking, make sauce beurre blanc and keep warm. When fish is done, remove from oven and leave to rest for 5 minutes. Using a light-weight hammer, hit the salt crust lightly so it cracks open without touching the fish. Discard the broken salt crust on top while the fish is still in the pan on the bottom layer of salt. Using two serving spoons lift the top 2 fish fillets off the fish and place on 2 dinner plates. Turn fish over and lift the bottom two fillets off the bone and place on 2 more dinner plates. Serve accompanying vegetables and sauce beurre blanc.

Baked Gray Mullet with Roasted Red Bell Pepper Vinaigrette (ʻAMAʻAMA)

Baked Gray Mullet with Roasted Red Bell Pepper Vinaigrette ('AMA'AMA)

This method of baking fish is not limited to mullet; try with other fish as well. Be aware that the potential for parasitic infection is high in mullet, so cook thoroughly. Serve with pasta, a simple green salad, and hot crusty bread.

YIELD 4 SERVINGS

4 dressed gray mullet, about 12 to 14 ounces (340 to 397 g) each
Black pepper
Salt
½ cup (125 ml) red wine
2 teaspoons (10 ml) crushed red pepper
8 sprigs fresh basil, coarsely sliced
8 garlic cloves, thinly sliced
2 ounces (57 g) cold butter
1 lemon, thinly sliced and seeded

For Vinaigrette

2 red bell peppers
3 tablespoons (45 ml) olive oil
2 tablespoons (30 ml) balsamic vinegar
1 teaspoon (5 ml) lemon juice
1 teaspoon (5 ml) lemon zest

DIRECTIONS

Wash fish; pat dry with paper towels and sprinkle with pepper and salt to taste. Place fish in a baking dish; add red wine, crushed red pepper, basil, and garlic, and turn fish over to coat the other side. Leave to marinate for 15 minutes. Heat the oven to 475°F (246°C). Turn the fish in the marinade; cut up butter into bits and place on fish along with lemon slices; place in the oven and bake for 35 to 40 minutes, basting with the cooking liquid 2 to 3 times. For the vinaigrette, coat peppers with a teaspoon of olive oil, then cook on a hot grill to burn the skin. Peel and discard skins and seeds. Cut peppers into thin strips and toss together with remaining olive oil, balsamic vinegar, lemon juice, lemon zest, and salt and pepper to taste. Serve the fish in the baking dish, and the vinaigrette in a sauce boat.

Stuffed Baked Long-tail Red Snapper (ONAGA)

*The crusty baked fish has a stuffing of potato and herbs. To accompany fish serve a mixed green salad with a light dressing and crusty French bread. This is a great dish for a special meal. Dress and butterfly the fish leaving tail and head on. See **To butterfly a fish** (Preparing Fish for Cooking). If you are not confident to dress and butterfly the fish, have the fisherman do it for you. Sometimes I don't remove the fins of a red snapper; they look attractive after roasting.*

....

YIELD 4 SERVINGS

....

4 pounds (1.8 kg) red snapper, dressed and butterflied with the tail and head on
1 teaspoon (5 ml) black pepper
1 teaspoon (5 ml) cayenne pepper
⅛ teaspoon (0.63 ml) **turmeric**
Juice of 1 lemon
Salt

For stuffing

2 tablespoons (30 ml) vegetable oil
½ cup (125 ml) chopped onion
1 cup (250 ml) small diced potato

½ cup (125 ml) cold water
1 teaspoon (5 ml) ground **cumin**
1 teaspoon (5 ml) ground **coriander**
½ cup (125 ml) chopped mint
½ cup (125 ml) chopped cilantro
1 teaspoon (5 ml) black pepper
2 tablespoons (30 ml) melted butter
Juice of 1 orange, about ½ cup (125 ml)
½ cup (125 ml) white wine

DIRECTIONS

Pat fish dry with paper towels; rub in and out with black pepper, cayenne pepper, turmeric, lemon juice and salt to taste. Put in refrigerator. Heat oven to 375°F (190°C). For the stuffing, heat oil in a skillet and sauté onions to a gold color; add potatoes, water, cumin, and coriander. Cover skillet and cook on medium heat for 5 to 6 minutes or until potatoes are cooked through but not mushy. Mix in herbs with black pepper and salt to taste. Leave to cool. Stuff the fish with the cooled potato mixture; place the stuffed fish in a baking pan; press in toothpicks to keep fish fillet and stuffing in place. Brush with melted butter, pour orange juice and wine over, and bake for 40 to 45 minutes. While fish is cooking, baste with cooking liquid 3 to 4 times.

Stuffed Baked Long-tail Red Snapper (ONAGA)

Gray Snapper Tagine (UKU)

A tagine is a round, shallow earthenware dish with a tall, conical, hatlike lid. It is ovenproof and holds the heat. Because the tagine gives gentle heat, distributed evenly, it is good for cooking slow, long-simmered dishes. Besides these desired qualities, the tagine is attractive to serve the food in. It is common in Morocco to cook fish in a tagine. If you don't have a tagine, use a heavy-bottomed stainless steel pot or an earthenware casserole for this oven-simmered fish dish. Serve with **Couscous** *(see Accompanying Staples).*

YIELD 2 SERVINGS

3 to 4 pounds (1.4 to 1.8 kg) dressed gray snapper

Seasonings

1 tablespoon (15 ml) ground **cumin**
1 tablespoon (15 ml) ground **coriander**
1 teaspoon (5 ml) sugar
2 tablespoons (30 ml) olive oil
Salt

Other ingredients

2 teaspoons (10 ml) cayenne pepper
3 tablespoons (45 ml) paprika
1 tablespoon (15 ml) minced garlic
3 cups (725 ml) peeled, seeded and diced tomatoes
1 **Pickled Lemon** (see Sauces, Dips, and Condiments)

DIRECTIONS

Heat oven to 400°F (204°C). Wash fish and pat dry with paper towels. Score fish on both sides, making two 1-inch (2.5-cm) diagonal cuts. Rub seasonings and salt to taste inside body cavity and on the outside of the fish. Place fish in an earthenware dish. Mix cayenne, paprika, garlic, and tomatoes and spoon onto the fish. Remove excess salt from pickled lemon, cut into 6 wedges, and place around fish; cover dish tightly with foil and bake for 40 minutes. Remove foil and bake for 10 minutes more. Serve from the earthenware dish.

Baked Goatfish in Tomato Sauce (KŪMŪ)

Fish cooked whole is better than fillets because the moisture is preserved. Mixed spices cooked in oil release their natural fragrance and give the sauce an extraordinary depth of flavor. Serve with a rice dish and vegetables of your choice.

YIELD 2 SERVINGS

2 dressed goatfish with heads on, about 14 ounces (397 g) each
Sea salt
Juice of 1 lemon
3 tablespoons (45 ml) olive oil
1 teaspoon (5 ml) crushed **coriander** seeds
1 teaspoon (5 ml) **fennel** seeds
1 medium onion, thinly sliced
1 tablespoon (15 ml) sliced garlic
1 cup (250 ml) peeled, seeded, and chopped tomato
1 teaspoon (5 ml) crushed red pepper
2 tablespoons (30 ml) red wine vinegar
½ cup (125 ml) white wine
½ cup (125 ml) water or fish stock

DIRECTIONS

Heat the oven to 400°F (204°C). Pat fish dry with paper towels, place on a plate and sprinkle with salt and lemon juice to taste; rub well to season; cover and refrigerate. Heat oil in an oven-proof skillet with a tight-fitting lid; add spices and cook on high heat until spices splutter. Turn heat to low; add and sauté onions until they turn a light golden color. Add the rest of the ingredients and season with salt to taste. Cook on low heat about 5 minutes. Place fish in the sauce and sprinkle a little salt over the fish. Cover skillet tightly with lid and bake for 15 minutes. Spoon the sauce over once while cooking. Place a fish on each plate and spoon sauce over.

Simply Roasted Red Snapper (ONAGA)

Dressed fish with skin and head on is ideal for roasting. Make sure fish is well scaled and cleaned before roasting. The skin will encase the natural moisture and flavor of the fish and will become crisp and golden when done. Fatty fish such as salmon, striped, or black sea bass with their colorful skins are some fish you can roast. Basting with butter during roasting helps the skin to turn crisp and prevents fish from drying out. A 6-pound (2.7 kg) dressed, roasted red snapper will generously serve eight guests. Serve with vegetables and potatoes or salad.

YIELD 6 TO 8 SERVINGS

1 dressed red snapper, 6 pounds (92.7 kg)
Salt
Black pepper
¼ cup (60 ml) white wine
Handful dill sprigs
1 lemon, thinly sliced
¼ cup (60 ml) melted butter

DIRECTIONS

Heat the oven to 400° F (204°C). Pat fish dry with paper towels and generously season with salt and pepper. Place in a roasting pan; pour wine over and place the dill and lemon slices on the fish. Roast 45 to 50 minutes, basting with melted butter while fish is roasting. Serve with pan juices.

Honey-glazed Roast Gray Snapper with Peaches

(UKU)

This is an exotic preparation. Snapper takes well to this heavy glaze and pairs well with peaches and couscous. At end of cooking time there will be pan juices to spoon around the fish.

YIELD 4 SERVINGS

1 dressed gray snapper about 4 pounds (1.8 kg)
Salt
Black pepper
2 teaspoons (10 ml) finely chopped ginger
¼ cup (60 ml) honey
¼ cup (60 ml) balsamic vinegar
¼ cup (60 ml) dark soy sauce
2 tablespoons (45 ml) lime juice
1 teaspoon (5 ml) **chili paste**
2 ripe peaches peeled, halved, and seeds removed
¼ cup (60 ml) white wine
1 recipe **Couscous** (see Accompanying Staples)

DIRECTIONS

Heat oven to 375°F (190°C). Score fish, making two diagonal ½-inch (1.28 cm) cuts on both sides of the fish. Season with salt and pepper and rub fish all over with minced ginger. For the glaze combine honey, balsamic vinegar, soy sauce, lime juice, and chili paste in a pan and simmer on low heat. Cool and pour a tablespoon of the glaze on fish; place on a rack in a roasting pan and roast for 30 minutes. Brush with glaze generously and place peaches cut side down around the fish; pour white wine over peaches and brush the peaches with glaze. Cook for 15 minutes. While fish is roasting, make couscous and keep warm. Place fish and peaches on a platter and spoon the pan drippings on the fish. Serve with couscous.

Roasted Miso Salmon

Japanese flavoring ingredients add a special touch to this salmon dish. The salmon is marinated overnight; the marinade seasons the salmon and also draws out moisture from it.

YIELD 6 SERVINGS

1 teaspoon (5 ml) **shichimi**
¼ cup (60 ml) rice wine vinegar
2 tablespoons (30 ml) brown sugar
1 tablespoon (15 ml) minced ginger
2 tablespoons (30 ml) sherry
1 cup (250 ml) white **miso**
6 salmon fillets, 6½ ounces (184 g) each
1 tablespoon (15 ml) vegetable oil
8 ounces (227 g) shitake mushrooms, stems removed
    and cut into quarters
Salt
Black pepper
8 ounces (227 g) spinach leaves, washed and trimmed
4 ounces (113 g) halved cherry tomatoes

DIRECTIONS

For marinade, combine shichimi, vinegar, sugar, ginger, sherry, and miso in a pan, whisking till smooth; simmer over low heat for 35 minutes, stirring often. Pour into a glass or china dish and cool down completely. Place salmon on marinade, turn over to coat well, cover, and marinate overnight in refrigerator. Heat oven to 400° F (204°C). Lift salmon from the marinade and place on a rack in a roasting pan; roast for 3 minutes on each side or until just cooked through. For vegetables, heat oil in a sauté pan; add mushrooms, along with salt and black pepper to taste and sauté about 3 minutes. Fold in spinach and cherry tomatoes and cook a minute or two until spinach is just wilted. Serve the salmon with the vegetables and rice.

Roasted Long-tail Red Snapper

(ONAGA)

*Roasted red snapper enhanced with exotic spices is a treat. The aroma of the roasting fish is enticing, not to mention its soft, moist, and luscious flesh. Serve with **Saffron Rice** (see Accompanying Staples), mango chutney, and a green salad.*

YIELD 4 SERVINGS

1 dressed red snapper, about 4 pounds (1.8 kg)
Salt
4 ounces (113 g) butter
1 teaspoon (5 ml) coarsely crushed **coriander** seed
1 teaspoon (5 ml) **fenugreek** seed
4-inch (10 cm) piece of **cinnamon** stick, broken into 2 pieces
1 tablespoon (15 ml) sliced garlic
⅛ teaspoon (0.63 ml) of **saffron**
2 lemons, cut into 8 wedges each
1 cup (250 ml) mint sprigs
1 cup (250 ml) white wine

DIRECTIONS

Heat oven to 400°F (204°C). Score twice on both sides of the fish making ½-inch (1.28-cm) deep cuts about 2 inches (5 cm) long and 2 inches (5 cm) apart down the thickest part of the fish. Sprinkle salt all over the fish and inside the body cavity. Place in a roasting pan. Melt butter in a small pan, add coriander, fenugreek seeds, cinnamon, and garlic and fry for 30 seconds on medium heat. Remove from heat, add saffron and let the spiced butter cool down for 3 to 4 minutes. Stuff the body cavity of the fish with 6 lemon wedges, mint, and a spoon of spiced butter. Spoon the rest of the spiced butter on the fish and place remaining lemon wedges around the fish. Pour the wine into the roasting pan and roast for 40 to 45 minutes, basting fish with pan juices. Using two spatulas, remove fish onto a platter; arrange roasted lemon wedges around fish. Place cinnamon sticks on fish as a garnish. (Note: Cinnamon sticks are not to be eaten.)

Pan-cooked Pink Snapper Fillets with Greens ('ŌPAKAPAKA)

*This is very easy to make because both the snapper and the greens cook fast, yet it ends up very exotic mainly because of the special spice used. If **mizuna** is unavailable, you may use kale. Make sure you don't overcook the greens. It is simply put together. Mashed potatoes are a good starch to accompany the fish with greens.*

YIELD 6 SERVINGS

6 pink snapper fillets, 5 ounces (142 g) each
Salt
Black pepper
1 tablespoon (15 ml) olive oil
½ teaspoon (2.5 ml) **fenugreek** seeds
½ pound (227 g) spinach leaves, washed and trimmed
1 cup (250 ml) washed, shredded **mizuna** leaves
½ cup (125 ml) chopped green onion
½ cup (125 ml) white wine
⅛ teaspoon (0.63 ml) **turmeric**
8 lime slices, seeds removed
½ cup (125 ml) sour cream, whisked smooth

DIRECTIONS

Season fish with salt and pepper to taste. Heat olive oil in a skillet on high heat; add fenugreek seeds and stir for 30 seconds. Immediately turn heat to low and stir in greens, wine, and turmeric; place fish skin side down in the skillet and place lime slices around fish. Cover skillet and cook on low heat for 4 minutes. Use a spatula and turn the fish over; spoon the lime slices with the sauce over fish, cover, and cook for 4 minutes more. Place fish and greens with sauce on plates and spoon a dollop of sour cream on each portion of fish. Serve with mashed potatoes.

Swordfish with Penne Pasta and Spinach (SHUTOME)

Cubed swordfish is cooked fast in this dish. Make sure it is cooked through but not overcooked because overcooked swordfish can be tough and dry. This is a great pasta dish, and note that you can substitute any pasta you wish.

YIELD 4 SERVINGS

2 tablespoons (30 ml) olive oil
¾ pounds (340 g) swordfish fillets, cut into 1-inch (2.5 cm)
    cubes
Salt
1 tablespoon (15 ml) sliced garlic
1 teaspoon (5 ml) crushed red pepper
1 tablespoon (15 ml) chopped anchovies
1 red bell pepper, seeded and sliced
1 cup (250 ml) chopped tomato
½ cup (125 ml) white wine
½ cup (125 ml) cream
1 bunch spinach leaves, washed and trimmed
4 portions cooked penne pasta

DIRECTIONS

Heat oil in a sauté pan; add fish and season with salt to taste. Sear on high heat for 3 minutes, turn heat to low, add garlic, red pepper, anchovies, bell pepper, tomato, and wine; stir to deglaze pan, cover, and cook for 3 minutes. Add cream and fold in spinach leaves and pasta; cook for 4 minutes.

Simply Sautéed Pink Snapper Fillets (ʻŌPAKAPAKA)

Fillets of flat fish such as sole or fillets of round fish such as snapper are best to sauté. The golden crusty outside seals juices of the simply sautéed fish. Pick your preferred starch and vegetables or a salad.

YIELD 4 SERVINGS

4 snapper fillets with skin on, about 5 ounces (142 g) each
Salt
Black pepper
1 tablespoon (15 ml) olive oil
2 tablespoons (30 ml) flour
¼ cup (60 ml) white wine
2 tablespoons (30 ml) butter
1 tablespoon (15 ml) lemon juice
1 tablespoon (15 ml) chopped parsley
4 lemon slices

DIRECTIONS

Season fish with salt and pepper to taste. Place a sauté pan on high heat with olive oil. Dust skin side of the fish in flour and shake off excess; when olive oil is hot, place fish skin side down in the pan and sauté for 2 to 3 minutes until skin is crisp. Use a spatula and turn over fish once taking care not to break the fish. With the fish still in the sauté pan, tilt and drain off the fat. Pour wine into the sauté pan and cook 3 to 4 minutes. Remove fish and place on hot dinner plates with crispy skin side facing up. Place the sauté pan back on the heat; add butter and cook until butter foams and turns a light brown. Add lemon juice and parsley to foaming butter and quickly pour around fish. Do not pour on the fish, or the crispy skin of the fish will get soggy. Place a lemon slice on each portion of fish.

Broiled Swordfish in Tomato Sauce (SHUTOME)

*Swordfish is good when grilled. Make sure it is cooked through but not overcooked because it can be tough and dry when overdone. Serve with **Pasta with Chili and Garlic** (see Accompanying Staples)*

YIELD 6 SERVINGS

6 swordfish fillets, 5 ounces (142 g) each
Salt
Black pepper
2 tablespoons (30 ml) lemon juice
2 tablespoons (30 ml) olive oil
1 large onion, chopped fine
1 tablespoon (15 ml) minced garlic
2 sprigs thyme
1 cup (250 ml) white wine
2 cups (500 ml) peeled, seeded, and diced tomatoes
1 cup (250 ml) quartered, trimmed fresh or canned artichoke hearts
1 teaspoon (5 ml) crushed red pepper
1 tablespoon (15 ml) chopped parsley
¼ cup (60 ml) shredded Parmesan cheese

DIRECTIONS

Heat the grill. Season fish with salt, pepper, and lemon juice; marinate in refrigerator for 30 minutes. Heat oil in a skillet; add onion, garlic, and thyme and cook for 2 to 3 minutes. Add wine, tomatoes, artichoke hearts, and chili flakes; season with salt to taste and cook for 8 minutes; sprinkle with parsley. While artichokes are cooking, grill fish about 4 minutes on each side. Plate the grilled fish and spoon artichokes and tomato sauce around it; sprinkle with cheese.

Lemon-glazed Pink Snapper ('ŌPAKAPAKA)

The pink snapper is a gorgeous fish; when cooked it melts in the mouth. Any snapper will work well. Wine-enriched lemony pan sauce is ideal for the snapper. I often serve a risotto and steamed broccoli raab with the fish.

YIELD 6 SERVINGS

2 lemons sliced and preserved, see **Preserved Lemon Wheels** (see Sauces, Dips, and Condiments)

6 pink snapper fillets, 5 ounces (142 g) each

Salt

Black pepper

2 tablespoons (30 ml) olive oil

½ cup (125 ml) white wine

3 tablespoons (45 ml) lemon syrup (from the preserved lemon wheels)

2 ounces (57 g) cold butter

1 tablespoon (15 ml) chopped parsley

DIRECTIONS

Make preserved lemon wheels and place aside. Season fish with salt and pepper to taste. Heat oil in a skillet, and on high heat sear fish about 3 minutes on each side. Remove fish from pan and cover to keep it warm. To the skillet add the wine and lemon syrup. Cook down to 2 tablespoons (30 ml) to a glaze. Whisk in cold butter, and check for seasoning. Season the glaze with more salt and pepper if needed; spoon over fish. Sprinkle parsley on the fish and place a slice of preserved lemon on top of each portion.

Blackened Bigeye Tuna ('AHI)

The blackening spice mix I use to coat the tuna is very special because it gives a hint of East Asian curry flavor to the fish. Serve with **Basmati with Cumin Seed and Chives** *(see Accompanying Staples),* **Cucumber Raita** *(see Sauces, Dips, and Condiments), and chutney.*

YIELD 6 SERVINGS

6 tuna fillets, about 5 ounces (142 g) each
2 tablespoons (30 ml) olive oil

Spice mix
1 tablespoon (15 ml) ground **cumin**
1 tablespoon (15 ml) ground **coriander**
½ teaspoon (2.5 ml) ground **fenugreek**
1 tablespoon (15 ml) ground **fennel**
1 teaspoon (5 ml) paprika
1 tablespoon (15 ml) black pepper
½ tablespoon (7.5 ml) cayenne pepper
2 teaspoons (10 ml) salt

DIRECTIONS

Heat an iron skillet until red-hot. Brush the fish with olive oil and place aside. Mix the spices together with salt and spread on a plate; dip fish in the spices, coating both sides of each portion of fish. Place in the hot skillet and cook 2 minutes on each side.

Bigeye Tuna Steaks with Pearl Onions and Cashews ('AHI)

Tuna is able to match with strong spice flavors. Sweet pearl onions glazed in sugar and wine are perfect with the spicy tuna. You may use frozen pearl onions to avoid peeling the fresh. Serve tuna steaks with steamed asparagus and mashed potatoes.

YIELD 4 SERVINGS

24 small white pearl onions, boiled
4 tuna steaks, about 5 ounces (142 g) each
1 teaspoon (5 ml) ground **coriander**
1 teaspoon (5 ml) ground **cumin**
1 teaspoon (5 ml) ground **cinnamon**
1 teaspoon (5 ml) cracked black pepper
Salt
2 tablespoons (30 ml) olive oil
1 teaspoon (5 ml) sugar
½ cup (125 ml) white wine
½ cup (60 g) unsalted roasted cashew halves
1 tablespoon (15 ml) chopped parsley

DIRECTIONS

Peel the onions and place aside. Season fish with spices and salt to taste. Heat olive oil in a skillet and sear fish on high heat about 3 minutes on each side. Remove fish from the skillet onto a plate and keep warm. Add onions, sugar, wine, and cashews to the skillet, stirring constantly cook on low heat to a glaze. Place fish back in the skillet and simmer for 1 minute. Strew parsley over and serve hot.

Fruity Seared Yellowfin Tuna with Basil Sauce ('AHI)

Tuna is a hardy fish, dense and meaty when cooked. It is good to have it almost rare in the center at the end of the cooking time. I have spiced the tuna with red pepper to go with the pungent, rich, and creamy basil sauce.

YIELD 6 SERVINGS

6 tuna fillets, about 5 ounces (142 g) each
½ cup (125 ml) passion orange drink
2 teaspoons (10 ml) crushed red pepper
1 tablespoon (15 ml) balsamic vinegar
Salt
2 tablespoons (30 ml) olive oil

For basil sauce

1 cup (250 ml) white wine
1 shallot, chopped
1 cup (250 ml) cream
1 cup (250 ml) chopped basil leaves
4 ounces (113 g) butter
1 tablespoon (15 ml) lemon juice

DIRECTIONS

Place fish in a container, add passion orange drink, red pepper, balsamic vinegar, and salt to taste and rub into the fish; pour olive oil over and leave to marinate in refrigerator for 30 minutes. For basil sauce place white wine and shallots in a pan and cook until reduced to ½ cup (125 ml). Add cream and basil and simmer until reduced to ½ cup (125 ml). Strain this reduction and pour it back into the pan and bring to a simmer. Whisk in butter and season with salt and lemon juice to taste. Remove from heat immediately, strain the sauce and place aside. Heat a skillet to very hot and sear the fish for 3 minutes on each side for rare. Plate fish and drizzle with basil sauce.

Furikake-crusted Salmon

Furikake, *a seasoning blend, has an enticing taste of "ocean." The salmon is simply seasoned, coated in furikake, and cooked fast. When done, the salmon is crusty on the outside and meltingly soft inside. The creamy rich butter sauce and the pungent furikake meld perfectly and take the simple salmon to new heights. Mashed potatoes and steamed greens are good accompaniments.*

YIELD 6 SERVINGS

½ cup (125 ml) sake
¼ cup (60 ml) **mirin**
¼ cup (60 ml) light soy sauce
6 salmon fillets, about 6 ounces (170 g) each
1 recipe **Sauce Beurre Blanc** (see Sauces, Dips, and Condiments)
2 ounces (57 g) **furikake**
1 tablespoon (15 ml) olive oil

DIRECTIONS

Heat the oven to 400°F (294°C). Whisk together the sake, mirin, and soy sauce; pour over the salmon and mix to coat the salmon evenly. Make the beurre blanc and keep warm. Spread furikake on a plate and place salmon on the furikake; turn over to coat both sides. Heat olive oil in an oven-proof skillet and on very high heat; sear the salmon about 30 seconds on each side. Place skillet with the salmon in the oven and cook about 4 to 5 minutes or until salmon is cooked through. Transfer to hot plates. Serve with sauce beurre blanc.

Stir-fried Moonfish with Eggplant, Tomato, and Basil (OPAH)

Moonfish, low in fat, has a delicate fine taste. The eggplant, tomatoes, and basil in the stir-fry add bold flavors to the dish, complementing the fish. Salting the eggplant removes any strong taste.

YIELD 6 SERVINGS

3 Asian eggplants
Salt
1 pound (454 g) trimmed moonfish fillet
1 tablespoon (15 ml) lemon juice
¼ cup (60 ml) vegetable oil
2 tablespoons (30 ml) thinly sliced onion
1 tablespoon (15 ml) chopped ginger
1 tablespoon (15 ml) chopped garlic
1 teaspoon (5 ml) oyster sauce
1 teaspoon (5 ml) crushed red pepper
2 tomatoes, cut in large dice
½ cup (125 ml) basil leaves

DIRECTIONS

Cut the eggplants into ½-inch (1.28 cm) cubes, sprinkle with a teaspoon of salt, and set aside for 30 minutes. Cut fish into 1-inch (2.5 cm) cubes, season with salt and lemon juice and refrigerate. Rinse the eggplant to get rid of the salt and pat dry. Heat oil in a wok and fry the eggplant until crisp and cooked through, remove from the wok and place on paper towels to drain. Add ginger and garlic to the wok and stir-fry for 1 minute. Add fish and cook for about 5 to 6 minutes or until fish is cooked through. Add oyster sauce, crushed red pepper, fried eggplant, tomatoes, basil leaves and salt to taste. Stir-fry 2 to 3 more minutes. Serve hot with rice.

Hawaiian Sea Bass in Black Bean Sauce (HĀPUʻUPUʻU)

Sea bass is a lean fish. Its sweet firm flesh, coated in the oyster-flavored black bean sauce holds well in this recipe. Serve with steamed green vegetables and rice.

YIELD 4 SERVINGS

1½ pounds (680 g) sea bass fillet
1 tablespoon (15 ml) **salted black beans**
1 tablespoon (15 ml) peanut oil
1 tablespoon (15 ml) chopped ginger
1 tablespoon (15 ml) oyster sauce
1 tablespoon (15 ml) rice wine
1 teaspoon (5 ml) crushed red pepper
2 teaspoons (10 ml) sugar
¼ cup (60 ml) light chicken broth
2 tablespoons (30 ml) sliced green onion

DIRECTIONS

Cut the fish into 1-inch (2.5 cm) cubes and refrigerate. Rinse black beans under running water and mash roughly with a fork. Place a wok on high heat and add oil; when very hot, add and stir-fry the fish until it turns opaque. Add black beans, ginger, oyster sauce, rice wine, crushed red pepper, and sugar; cover and simmer for 2 minutes. Stir in chicken broth and stir-fry until fish is done; sprinkle with green onions. Serve with rice.

Long-tail Red Snapper Curried in Yogurt Sauce

(ONAGA)

This mild fish preparation includes yogurt, which yields a thick, velvety sauce that coats the cooked fish. Spices not only flavor the dish but also give it an appetizing golden hue. Handle snapper fillets gently; they are fragile and can flake when being moved around in the pan. Also take care not to overcook the fish. Serve this simple dish with rice and cooked vegetables.

YIELD 6 SERVINGS

6 red snapper fillets, 5 ounces (142 g) each
2 tablespoons (30 ml) lemon juice
Salt
3 tablespoons (45 ml) olive oil
½ cup (125 ml) finely sliced onions
1 **serrano chili**, thinly sliced
1 cup (250 ml) thinly sliced tomato
2 teaspoons (10 ml) **curry powder**
½ teaspoon (2.5 ml) paprika
¼ teaspoon (1.25 ml) **turmeric**
1 cup (250 ml) plain yogurt
¼ cup (60 ml) water

DIRECTIONS

Season the fish with lemon juice and salt to taste; refrigerate. Heat olive oil in a pan, add onions and green chili and cook on low heat until onions are soft. Add tomato, curry powder, paprika, and turmeric and cook for 4 minutes. Add fish and cook on low heat for 3 minutes, using a spatula to turn the fish over. Whisk together the yogurt and water, add to the fish with salt to taste, and simmer for 4 to 5 minutes.

Chili-fried Cod (PACIFIC COD)

*Cod has a mild, delicate flavor, and its firm white flesh flakes easily when cooked. The spice paste is cooked first and then fish is added to avoid overcooking and flaking. At the end of its short cooking time the fish gets coated in the spicy **tamarind** sauce. As its name indicates, this is a hot dish; you may cut down on chilies to your taste.*

....

YIELD 4 SERVINGS

....

1½ pounds (680 g) cod fillet, skin removed
1 pinch of **turmeric**
Salt
12 dried red chilies
5 shallots
3 garlic cloves
3 slices fresh ginger
1 teaspoon (5 ml) **shrimp paste**
¼ cup (60 ml) water

To fry

2 tablespoons (30 ml) peanut oil
¼ cup (60 ml) water
1 beefsteak tomato, cut into 8 wedges
1 medium onion, thinly sliced
2 teaspoons (10 ml) sugar
¼ cup (60 ml) **tamarind** juice to taste

DIRECTIONS

Cut fish into 2-inch (5 cm) cubes; add turmeric and salt to taste, mix, and leave to marinate in refrigerator. Grind chilies, shallots, garlic, ginger, and shrimp paste in a blender, adding enough water to make a smooth paste. Heat oil in a wok; add the ground spice paste and stir-fry on moderate heat for 3 to 4 minutes. Fold in marinated fish; add water with salt to taste and the rest of the ingredients; continue to stir-fry for 4 to 5 minutes or until fish is cooked through. Serve with rice.

Goanese-style Hawaiian Sea Bass Curry (HĀPUʻUPUʻU)

Goa has a rich tradition of cooking with spices in unique ways, such as combining roasted coconut in their spice mixes. Many spices are used in a harmonious blend; this delicious fish curry has a long list of ingredients, but it is not all that difficult to make, and the results are worth the trouble. To begin, assemble the list of ingredients in order of use as directed. As usual the best accompaniments with curry are rice and chutney.

YIELD 6 SERVINGS

2½ pounds (1.1 kg) sea bass fillet
Juice of 2 lemons
Salt

Spice paste

1 cup (250 ml) grated fresh coconut
10 whole dry red chilies
2 tablespoons (30 ml) ground **coriander**
1 tablespoon (15 ml) ground **cumin**
½ teaspoon (2.5 ml) **turmeric**
1 teaspoon (5 ml) black pepper
½ cup (125 ml) water

For the curry

2 tablespoons (30 ml) vegetable oil
2 medium onions, sliced thin
2 teaspoons (10 ml) chopped ginger
4 green chilies, sliced
¼ cup (60 ml) **tamarind** juice
2 cups (500 ml) coconut milk
½ cup (125 ml) water

DIRECTIONS

Clean and cut the fish into 2-inch (5 cm) slices, mix with lemon juice and salt to taste; refrigerate for 30 minutes. Heat a skillet on medium heat; add the grated coconut, using a wooden spoon to move it around, and roast to a dark brown color. Use a blender to grind the browned coconut and the rest of the ingredients for the spice paste, adding enough water to thin down; grind till the mixture is smooth. For the curry, heat oil in a pan and sauté the onions to a golden color; stir in the ginger, green chilies, and ground spice paste. Sauté for a few minutes until the spices start to smell fragrant. Add the rest of the ingredients; stir to combine to a smooth consistency. Bring to a slow simmer. Add and fold the fish in so it is barely covered with the sauce; continue to simmer uncovered on low heat for 10 minutes or until fish is cooked. Check for seasoning and add more salt if needed.

Hawaiian Sea Bass and Pineapple Curry (HĀPUʻUPUʻU)

*There are many blends of **curry powders** available today. Chef Cooray's Curry Powder is one of the popular brands available. Use the Curry Powder for Shrimp for this delicious fish curry. Serve with **Yellow Rice** (see Accompanying Staples) and **Fresh Mint Chutney** (see Sauces, Dips, and Condiments) as accompaniments.*

YIELD 6 SERVINGS

2 pounds (907 g) sea bass fillet
2 tablespoons (30 ml) olive oil
1 onion, finely chopped
1 teaspoon (5 ml) finely chopped ginger
1 teaspoon (5 ml) finely chopped garlic
1 tablespoon (15 ml) hot **curry powder**
1 cup (250 ml) pineapple chunks
1 cup (250 ml) coconut milk
½ cup (125 ml) water
Salt
½ cup (125 ml) roughly chopped roasted cashew nuts

DIRECTIONS

Slice fish into 2-inch (5 cm) thick pieces and refrigerate. Heat oil in a sauté pan; add onion, ginger, and garlic and cook on medium heat until onions are soft. Turn heat to low; add curry powder and stir for 2 to 3 minutes. Place fish in the sauté pan, add pineapple, coconut milk, and water, with salt to taste; sprinkle cashew nuts. Simmer on low heat for 8 minutes, shaking the pan occasionally.

Curried Scads with Okra (AKULE)

This fish dish partners well with rice. If you do not like okra, you may substitute beans, snap peas, or spinach. This is a family dish using whole scads, so you need to be careful about the bones in the fish. Of course you can substitute any fish fillets you like.

YIELD 3 SERVINGS

6 dressed scads, 10 ounces (280 g) each
Salt

Seasoning mix

1 tablespoon (15 ml) **tamarind** juice
4 garlic cloves, thinly sliced
2 red **serrano chilies**, sliced
2 green serrano chilies sliced
2 tablespoons (30 ml) **curry powder**
1½ cups (375 ml) water

For curry

2 tablespoons (30 ml) vegetable oil
1 onion, thinly sliced
15 **curry leaves** (optional)
10 small okra, stems and tails trimmed
1 tablespoon (15 ml) lime juice
1½ cup (375 ml) coconut milk
2 large tomatoes, cut into wedges

DIRECTIONS

Rub the fish inside and out with salt, then rinse thoroughly. For the seasoning mix, whisk together the tamarind juice, garlic, serrano chilies, curry powder, and water and place aside. Heat oil in a pan; add onion, curry leaves, okra, and lime juice, and stir around in the pan; cook till the onions and okra are cooked, about 3 minutes. Add the seasoning mix, bring to a simmer and add the coconut milk. Add tomatoes and fish; season with salt to taste and simmer on low heat, uncovered, till fish is cooked, about 15 minutes.

Marlin and Spinach Curry (KAJIKI)

You may serve this easy-to-prepare fish dish with pasta. The delicate angel hair pasta is particularly good with this curry.

YIELD 4 SERVINGS

1½ pounds (680 g) swordfish fillet
¼ teaspoon (1.25 ml) **turmeric**
Salt
2 tablespoons (30 ml) olive oil
¼ cup (60 ml) chopped onion
1 large tomato, peeled and finely chopped
1 teaspoon (5 ml) chopped ginger
1 teaspoon (5 ml) chopped garlic
1 teaspoon (5 ml) ground **coriander**
1 teaspoon (5 ml) ground **cumin**
⅛ teaspoon (0.63 ml) ground **cinnamon**
A pinch of grated **nutmeg**
1 cup (250 ml) water
1 bunch washed spinach, leaves trimmed
½ cup (125 ml) cream
4 servings cooked angel hair pasta

DIRECTIONS

Cut fish into 1-inch (2.5 cm) cubes; toss with turmeric and a teaspoon of salt. Heat oil in a sauté pan; add onion and sauté to a golden brown color. Add fish and on high heat sauté for 5 minutes to seal in juices of the fish. Stir in the tomato, ginger, garlic, and spices, and cook for 3 minutes. Add water, cover pan, and let simmer until fish is done, about 5 minutes. Add spinach and stir in cream, season with salt to taste and simmer for 5 minutes. Serve with angel hair pasta.

Wahoo with Onion and Mustard Sauce (ONO)

*Fish fillets or fish cubes are both good curried in this manner. Mustard is the vital ingredient in this dish; it gives a slight tang and a silky texture to the onion-laced sauce that envelops the fish. Back home we always used a piece of **goraka** when we cooked fish. It gives the fish a rich, tangy taste that is very special. Vegetables and rice are good side dishes.*

YIELD 4 SERVINGS

4 wahoo fillets, 5 ounces (140 g) each
Sea salt
Black pepper
¼ teaspoon (1.25 ml) **turmeric**
4 tablespoons (60 ml) olive oil
2 medium onions, sliced ⅛- inch (3.2 mm) thick
1 teaspoon (5 ml) sugar
2 teaspoons (10 ml) chopped ginger
2 teaspoons (10 ml) chopped garlic
1 bulb **lemongrass**, bruised
½ cup (125 ml) white wine
1 cup (250 ml) water
1 tablespoon (15 ml) vinegar
2 teaspoons (10 ml) ground **coriander**
1½ tablespoons (22.5 ml) Dijon country mustard
¾ cup (175 ml) cream or coconut milk

DIRECTIONS

Season fish with salt and black pepper and rub in the turmeric, which gives a nice golden blush to fish when cooked. Heat 2 tablespoons (30 ml) oil in a skillet, and on high heat sear fish about 3 minutes on a side; remove to a plate and set aside. Add the remaining oil to the skillet. Add onion, sprinkle with sugar, and sauté on medium heat to a golden color; set aside with the fish. Add the ginger, garlic, and lemongrass to the skillet; stir in wine, water, vinegar, and coriander and simmer for 5 minutes. Whisk together the mustard and cream or coconut milk; add to skillet and season with salt to taste. Place the seared fish in the sauce in the skillet, cover, and simmer for 3 to 4 minutes. Pick out and discard the lemongrass; add the reserved onion back to the skillet. Place fish on a hot platter, spoon onion with sauce over fish.

Devilled Swordfish (SHUTOME)

This is a very hot and spicy dish. You may substitute tuna for the dish. Devilled fish can be served with rice or with a salad and a glass of beer to accompany.

YIELD 4 SERVINGS

1½ pounds (680 g) swordfish fillet

Seasoning for fish

2 teaspoons (10 ml) salt
1 teaspoon (5 ml) black pepper
1 teaspoon (5 ml) Worcestershire sauce
1 teaspoon (5 ml) chopped garlic
1 teaspoon (5 ml) chopped ginger

For stir-frying

2 tablespoons (30 ml) oil
1 stalk of **lemongrass**, crushed
1 teaspoon (5 ml) paprika
1 teaspoon (5 ml) crushed red pepper
1 teaspoon (5 ml) Dijon country mustard
1 tablespoon (15 ml) white wine vinegar
¼ cup (60 ml) water
1 onion, halved and sliced ¼ inch (0.64 cm) thick
15 **curry leaves** (optional)
1 red jalapeño pepper, seeded and sliced
1 green jalapeño pepper, seeded and sliced
Juice of half a lemon

DIRECTIONS

Pat fish dry with paper towels and cut into 1-inch (2.5 cm) cubes. Add salt, pepper, Worcestershire sauce, garlic, and ginger and mix to coat the fish. Heat oil in a wok, and on high heat add lemongrass and fish and stir-fry for 2 to 3 minutes. Add paprika, crushed red pepper, mustard, vinegar, and water and stir-fry for 2 to 3 minutes. Turn heat to low; cover wok and cook for 4 minutes. Add onions, curry leaves, and peppers and stir-fry on high heat for 2 to 3 minutes or until the onions are wilted. Season with lemon juice to taste.

Devilled Swordfish (SHUTOME)

Curried Wahoo Steaks (ONO)

*This is a simple curry that can be made with any fish. Wahoo is one of my favorite fish, but you could use any firm-fleshed fish like swordfish or mahimahi. **Goraka** when available can be added when cooking fish. It gives a special tangy flavor to the dish. Rice is the best accompaniment to serve with fish curry.*

YIELD 4 SERVINGS

4 wahoo steaks, 6 ounces (170 g) each
Salt

For sauce

1 tablespoon (15 ml) vegetable oil
1 medium onion, chopped fine
15 **curry leaves** (optional)
1 teaspoon (5 ml) chopped ginger
2 jalapeño peppers, seeded and sliced
1 tablespoon (15 ml) **curry powder**
A large pinch **turmeric**
½ teaspoon (2.5 ml) cayenne pepper
1 cup (250 ml) water
1 cup (250 ml) seeded, chopped tomatoes
1 cup (250 ml) coconut milk
Juice of ½ lemon
Salt

DIRECTIONS

Season both sides of the fish steaks with salt and place aside. Heat oil in a skillet; add onion, curry leaves, and ginger and cook on medium heat till onions turn a light gold color. Add jalapeño peppers, curry powder, turmeric and cayenne and stir on low heat for a minute. Add the water, stir in the tomatoes, and add the fish. Turn heat to very low; cover skillet and cook for 5 minutes. Turn the fish over, add coconut milk, and simmer for 4 minutes; season with lemon juice and salt to taste.

Hot Hawaiian Sea Bass Curry (HĀPUʻUPUʻU)

Using a bone-in fish, cut into big chunks, especially sea bass, makes the sauce rich and the fish tastier. Make sure that the sea bass is devoid of scales before using. Note that **fish sauce** *is salty, so no extra salt is used. You may omit the fish sauce and use salt or use both in combination. Rice is the accompaniment for this curry.*

YIELD 4 SERVINGS

2 pounds (907 g) sea bass fillet, cut into 2-inch (5 cm) pieces

Curry Sauce

1 onion, sliced

¼ cup (60 ml) **palm sugar**

2 stalks **lemongrass**, crushed

1 tablespoon (15 ml) chopped garlic

1 tablespoon (15 ml) chopped ginger

1 cup (250 ml) whole basil leaves

1 cup (250 ml) diced tomatoes

¼ cup (60 ml) **fish sauce**

1 cup (250 ml) water

2 cups (500 ml) coconut milk

2 tablespoons (30 ml) **Thai red curry paste**

¼ teaspoon (2.5 ml) **turmeric**

2 fresh hot green chilies

DIRECTIONS

Rinse fish and refrigerate. Place onion, palm sugar, lemongrass, garlic, ginger, basil, tomatoes, and fish sauce in a pan; add water and bring to a simmer. Cook on medium heat for 10 minutes; stir in coconut milk, curry paste, and turmeric and simmer for 10 minutes, stirring often. Remove and discard lemongrass; add green chilies and fish. Cover pan and simmer on low heat for 8 to 10 minutes.

Curried Short-tail Red Snapper ('EHU)

*The short-tail red snapper with its sweet flesh is ideal for this curry that does not use coconut milk. If snapper is not available to you, you can substitute a fish of your choice. Rice or naan bread and a **Cucumber Raita** (see Sauces, Dips, and Condiments) are good accompaniments.*

YIELD 2 SERVINGS

1 dressed short-tail red snapper, 2 to 2½ pounds (907 grams to 1.1 kg)
½ teaspoon (2.5 ml) **turmeric**
Salt

For sauce

2 tablespoons (30 ml) peanut oil
2 medium onions, thinly sliced
1 teaspoon (5 ml) finely chopped ginger
3 tablespoons (45 ml) **garam masala**
1 teaspoon (5 ml) cayenne pepper
2 jalapeño peppers, sliced
2 large tomatoes, peeled, seeded, and chopped
1½ cups (375 ml) water
Juice of 1 lemon

DIRECTIONS

Pat the fish dry with paper towels. Score the fish, making two diagonal cuts 1 inch (2.5 cm) deep and 2 inches (5 cm) long on each side. Rub inside and out with turmeric and salt to taste and refrigerate. Use a skillet large enough to hold the fish. Heat the oil in the skillet; add onion and cook on moderate heat to a light golden color. Add ginger, garam masala, and cayenne; cook on low heat for 2 to 3 minutes, stirring constantly. Stir in the jalapeño pepper and tomatoes, add water, and simmer uncovered for 5 minutes. Place fish in the sauce, cover skillet, and simmer for 6 minutes on low heat. Season with lemon juice and more salt if needed; turn fish over, cover, and simmer for 8 more minutes or until fish is cooked through.

Fried Short-tail Red Snapper in Thai Curry Sauce

('EHU)

Curries range from simple to sophisticated, and they cannot fail to delight curry lovers. This is a simple Thai-style fish curry that is served with rice.

YIELD 2 SERVINGS

3 pounds (1.4 kg) dressed red snapper

For the sauce

1 tablespoon (15 ml) peanut oil
1 tablespoon (15 ml) chopped onion
1 teaspoon (5 ml) chopped garlic
1 teaspoon (5 ml) chopped ginger
1 tablespoon (15 ml) **fish sauce**
3 **Kaffir lime** leaves
1 cup (250 ml) water
1 cup (250 ml) coconut milk
3 tablespoons (45 ml) **Thai green curry paste**
Juice of 1 lime

For frying the fish

2 tablespoons flour (30 ml)
2 cups (500 ml) peanut oil

DIRECTIONS

Score the fish, making two diagonal cuts ½ inch (1.28 cm) deep and 2 inches long (5 cm) on each side of the fish. For the sauce, heat the tablespoon of peanut oil in a skillet and cook the onions, garlic, and ginger until the onions start to caramelize. Add the fish sauce, lime leaves, water, coconut milk, and 2 tablespoons (30 ml) curry paste and stir until smooth. Simmer on low heat for 5 to 6 minutes; season with lime juice, strain, and reserve to pour on the fish. Pat fish dry with paper towels. Rub in the remaining curry paste and dust lightly with flour. Heat the 2 cups (500 ml) oil in a wok and on moderately high heat fry the fish about 6 to 8 minutes on each side. Remove fish onto a platter. Pour reserved sauce on the fish.

Singapore-style Wahoo Fish Head Curry (ONO)

*It is not often that one is bold enough to try a fish head curry, let alone make it! Because the head of a fish can accumulate toxins, use your discretion if you ever wish to make fish head curry. The best fish to use for this is wahoo, followed by snapper. The recipe has a long list of ingredients, but it is easily put together. The sauce is enriched with **tamarind** juice, which has a chocolate-like yet sour taste. At the end, the sauce is also seasoned with lemon juice to taste. These are the nuances of flavoring that make Asian curries so special. Fish head curry is often served with rice; however, many people enjoy picking the meat off the fish head and savoring the vegetables, so at the end little or none of the rice is eaten.*

YIELD 4 SERVINGS

1 wahoo head, 3 to 3½ pounds
(1.4 to 1.6 kg), split into two,
cleaned and washed
Salt
1 lemon, halved

For the sauce
½ cup (125 ml) peanut oil
2 teaspoons (10 ml) **black mustard
seed**
1 teaspoon (5 ml) **fenugreek**
1 teaspoon (5 ml) **cumin** seed
2-inch (5 cm) piece of **cinnamon
stick**
1 cup (250 ml) finely chopped
shallots
1 tablespoon (15 ml) chopped
garlic
1 tablespoon (15 ml) chopped
ginger

15 dried red chilies, ground to a
fine powder; or 2 tablespoons (30
ml) cayenne pepper
2 tablespoons (30 ml) ground
coriander
1 tablespoon (15 ml) ground **fennel**
½ teaspoon (2.5 ml) **turmeric**
6 cups (1½ L) water

Vegetables and seasoning
2 medium red onions, quartered
3 tomatoes, quartered
½ pound (227 g) okra, stems
trimmed
½ cup (125 ml) **tamarind** juice
20 **curry leaves**
2 cups (500 ml) coconut milk
Juice of 1 lemon
Salt

DIRECTIONS

Rinse the fish head, then rub it with salt and half the lemon; rinse again in running water. Pat dry and refrigerate. In a deep braising pan big enough for the fish head, heat oil on medium heat; add black mustard seed, fenugreek, cumin, and cinnamon and fry until the mustard seeds start to splutter. Add shallots, garlic, and ginger and cook for 5 minutes. Add ground red chilies, coriander, fennel, and turmeric and stir well to combine. Add water and on high heat cook for 10 minutes. Add fish head, onions, tomatoes, okra, and tamarind juice; lower heat and simmer for 35 minutes, turning fish head over once during cooking time. Add curry leaves and coconut milk and simmer 20 minutes. Season with lemon juice and salt to taste

GRILLS AND BARBECUES

Grilling is a dry-heat cooking technique with the food cooked by heat from beneath the food. Barbecuing is a form of grilling in which the food is basted with a barbecue sauce during cooking. Appearance, texture, and flavor are three important areas when gauging grilled items.

The equipment used to grill may be an ordinary wood-burning grill or a brazier fitted with a grill or a spit. Charcoal, electric, or gas may also be used as a heat source. Grill racks must be thoroughly cleaned to prevent food from sticking to the rack and ruining its appearance. It is also important to know which grill area is hotter so items can be moved from hotter to cooler spots on the grill to prevent unnecessary charring of the item.

Dry heat does not have a tenderizing effect on the food; however, marinating or basting during the grilling process helps to keep the food moist.

The desired smoky flavor of grilled food is a result of the flaring up of the juices and the fats that are rendered as it cooks. To introduce special flavors to grills, mesquite, grapevines, and aromatic herbs can be used.

Fish is easy to overcook because of its delicate texture. It takes time to master this technique. Grills and barbecues involve marinades and rich tangy sauces, and it is important to use utensils and equipment of **nonreactive** material.

Spicy Grilled Pink Snapper with Spinach Raita (ʻŌPAKAPAKA)

Grilled Bigeye Tuna with Curry Butter (ʻAHI)

Simply Grilled Teriyaki-glazed Butterfish (PACIFIC BUTTERFISH)

Miso-glazed Grilled Butterfish (PACIFIC BUTTERFISH)

Spicy Grilled Jackfish (PĀPIO)

Grilled Gray Snapper (UKU)

Grilled Whole Long-tail Red Snapper (ONAGA)

Grilled Herrings (PACIFIC HERRINGS)

Stuffed Grilled Jackfish (PĀPIO)

Jackfish Grilled in Banana Leaves (PĀPIO)

Grilled Bigeye Tuna with Tamarind Sauce (ʻAHI)

Grilled Scad and Tomatoes with Pesto (AKULE)

Chutney-marinated Grilled Yellowfin Tuna (ʻAHI)

Grilled Wahoo with Green Peppercorn Vinaigrette (ONO)

Grilled Bigeye Tuna with Cucumber Salad (ʻAHI)

Grilled Marlin on Fennel Salad with Orange and Red Onion (KAJIKI)

Herb-crusted Grilled Bigeye Scad (AKULE)

Grilled Mackerel Scad with Berry Sauce (ʻŌPELU)

Simply Barbecued Gray Snapper Fillets (UKU)

Spicy Barbecued Gray Snapper (UKU)

Barbecued Swordfish with Avocado Salad (SHUTOME)

Spicy Grilled Pink Snapper with Spinach Raita ('ŌPAKAPAKA)

*This recipe can be prepared using any white fish. The skin on the fish should be left on. When the fish is grilled, the skin will be crisp and the flavor of the fish will shine through the simple spice combination in the light marinade. Serve with rice and **Spinach Raita** (see Sauces, Dips, and Condiments). The addition of a chutney of your choice will make the spicy fish even better.*

YIELD 4 SERVINGS

4 fish fillets, 5 ounces (142 g) each

For marinade

1 teaspoon (5 ml) black pepper
½ teaspoon (2.5 ml) cayenne pepper
1 teaspoon (5 ml) ground **cumin**
1 teaspoon (5 ml) ground **coriander**
1 teaspoon (5 ml) chopped ginger
1 teaspoon (5 ml) chopped garlic
1 teaspoon (5 ml) lemon juice
1 teaspoon (5 ml) salt

For basting

3 tablespoons (45 ml) melted butter

DIRECTIONS

Pat the fish dry with paper towels. Combine the ingredients for the marinade and rub all over the fish. Refrigerate for at least 1 hour. Cook on a very hot grill 4 to 5 minutes on each side, brushing with melted butter.

Grilled Bigeye Tuna with Curry Butter ('AHI)

Fish that is firm-textured and with a pronounced flavor like tuna is just right for this recipe. Care must be taken not to overcook the tuna; it is at its best when underdone. Curry butter can be made in a larger quantity, then frozen and used when needed.

YIELD 4 SERVINGS

4 tuna fillets, 5 ounces (142 g) each

Marinade

1 tablespoon (15 ml) olive oil
Juice of 1 lime
1 teaspoon (5 ml) chopped ginger
Salt
Black pepper

Curry butter

2 teaspoons (10 ml) olive oil
1 tablespoon (15 ml) finely chopped onion
1 tablespoon (15 ml) finely chopped **curry leaves** (optional)
2 teaspoons (10 ml) **curry powder**
1 tablespoon (15 ml) mango chutney
4 ounces (113 g) unsalted butter, softened to room temperature

Garnish

1 lime cut into 4 wedges

DIRECTIONS

Pat fish dry with paper towels and place in a dish; add olive oil, lime juice, and ginger with salt and pepper to taste. Place in the refrigerator. Heat oil in a pan, add onion and curry leaves and sauté till the onions are a golden color. Add curry powder and chutney and cook for 2 minutes on low heat. Cool the mixture and add the softened butter, stirring to combine well. Spoon onto a piece of foil and roll into a log shape; refrigerate and use as needed. Heat the grill until very hot; grill fish for 2 to 3 minutes on each side. Top each fillet with a slice of curry butter and serve with a wedge of lime.

Simply Grilled Teriyaki-glazed Butterfish

(PACIFIC BUTTERFISH)

Try the following simple teriyaki-glazed grilled fish. Rice and a steamed green vegetable are the ideal accompaniments to this simple yet tasty grilled fish.

YIELD 4 SERVINGS

¼ cup (60 ml) soy sauce
¼ cup (60 ml) **mirin**
¼ cup (60 ml) sake
1 tablespoon (15 ml) brown sugar
¼ cup (60 ml) rice vinegar
1 tablespoon (15 ml) finely chopped ginger
4 butterfish fillets, 5 ounces (142 g) each

DIRECTIONS

Preheat the grill. Mix the soy sauce, mirin, sake , brown sugar, and vinegar in a small pan and bring to a simmer. Add the ginger and set aside to cool. Pour the soy sauce mix on the fish and marinate for 15 minutes. Grill for 6 minutes on each side, brushing the fish with the marinade. Serve hot off the grill.

Miso-glazed Grilled Butterfish

(PACIFIC BUTTERFISH)

*Rice is great with grilled butterfish, and a cooked green vege-
table is a complement to this delicious fish dish. Butterfish is
delicate and absorbs the flavors of the marinade well. When
done right the flesh is supple and easily breaks into juicy flakes.
You may also broil butterfish.*

YIELD 6 SERVINGS

6 butterfish fillets, about 6 ounces (170 g) each
1 teaspoon (5 ml) **shichimi**
1 cup (250 ml) **miso**
½ cup (113 g) teriyaki sauce
¼ cup (60 ml) brown sugar
1 tablespoon (15 ml) finely chopped ginger
½ cup (125 ml) sake

DIRECTIONS

Season the fish with shichimi; place in a dish and pour miso
over to coat the fish; cover and refrigerate overnight. In a pan
whisk together the teriyaki sauce, sugar, ginger, and sake; place
on medium heat and reduce to about ½ cup (125 ml); remove
from heat. Heat the grill. Remove fish from marinade and
wipe off excess marinade with paper towels. Place fish on the
reduced teriyaki sauce and move around to coat the fish evenly.
Place on the grill and cook on medium heat for about 5 minutes
on each side.

Spicy Grilled Jackfish (PĀPIO)

Coconut milk has a sweet flavor and will enrich and enhance all other flavors in the marinade. This sweet and spicy fish needs rice as an accompaniment.

YIELD 4 SERVINGS

1 jackfish, about 5 pounds (2.3 kg), dressed
½ cup (125 ml) chopped onion
2 cloves garlic
1 **serrano chili**
1 stalk **lemongrass**, finely sliced
½ cup (125 ml) water
1 teaspoon salt
2 teaspoons (10 ml) cayenne pepper
⅛ teaspoon (0.63 ml) **turmeric**
1 **Kaffir lime** leaf, finely shredded
Juice of 2 limes
1 tablespoon (15 ml) olive oil
1 cup (250 ml) coconut milk
1 teaspoon (5 ml) brown sugar

DIRECTIONS

Score fish, making two diagonal cuts ½ inch (1 cm) deep, 2 inches (5 cm) long, and 2 inches (5 cm) apart on both sides of the fish. Place the onion, garlic, serrano chili, and lemongrass in a blender; add water and blend to a smooth paste. Remove to a bowl; add salt, cayenne pepper, turmeric, shredded lime leaf, and lime juice; mix. Spoon half of the seasoning mix over the fish and rub inside and out to season. Heat oil and stir in the balance of the seasoning mix. Stir in the coconut milk and sugar and cook on low heat for a few minutes until sauce thickens. Place aside to serve with fish. Grill the fish on medium heat 20 minutes on each side. Serve reserved sauce with the fish.

Grilled Gray Snapper (UKU)

The sweet and spicy nuances imparted to this fish are one of the trademarks of Chinese cooking. Serve rice and a vegetable stir fry with this delicious grilled fish.

YIELD 4 SERVINGS

1 gray snapper, about 3 pounds (1.4 kg), dressed
2 tablespoons (30 ml) soy sauce
2 tablespoons (30 ml) **hoisin sauce**
2 tablespoons (30 ml) finely chopped ginger
2 tablespoons (30 ml) chopped green onion
2 tablespoons (30 ml) sherry
1 tablespoon (15 ml) brown sugar
1 tablespoon (15 ml) **chili paste**

DIRECTIONS

Clean and pat the fish dry with paper towels. Score the fish, making 2 diagonal cuts, 1 inch (2.5 cm) deep, 2 inches (5 cm) long, and 4 inches (10 cm) apart, on each side. Place in a glass or china dish. In a bowl whisk the rest of the ingredients; pour over the fish to coat both sides. Cover and refrigerate overnight. Grill on a moderately hot, well-oiled grill for 20 minutes on each side.

Grilled Whole Long-tail Red Snapper (ONAGA)

Tamarind imparts a sweet piquancy and blends beautifully with the spices to create a rich, spicy glaze on the grilled fish. The aroma of fish grilled this way is tantalizing.

YIELD 4 SERVINGS

1 snapper, about 3 pounds (1.4 kg), dressed
2 tablespoons (30 ml) finely chopped ginger
1 teaspoon (5 ml) ground **cumin**
½ teaspoon (2.5 ml) cayenne or 2 ground dried red chilies
2 tablespoons (30 ml) **tamarind** juice
2 tablespoons brown sugar
Salt
Black pepper
2 tablespoons (30 ml) olive oil
8 pineapple rings
6 sprigs mint
6 lime wedges

DIRECTIONS

Score the fish, making two diagonal cuts 1 inch (2.5 cm) deep, and 2 inches (5 cm) long, and 2 inches (5 cm) apart on each side; rub in the combined ginger, cumin, cayenne or ground red chilies, tamarind, brown sugar, salt, and pepper all over the fish. Marinate for 1 hour. Grill over a hot grill for 35 to 45 minutes, turning the fish over once, brushing with the oil often. Place the pineapple rings on the grill, brush with oil, and cook about 2 to 3 minutes on each side. When fish is done place on a platter, strew with mint, and place grilled pineapple and lime on top.

Grilled Herrings (PACIFIC HERRINGS)

Sardines may also be grilled in this manner. Small fish such as herrings and sardines must be eviscerated, cleaned, and washed before cooking. See To eviscerate fish (Preparing Fish for Cooking). The fish is simply seasoned; it needs a flavorful dip like Chermoula or Aïoli (see Sauces, Dips, and Condiments).

YIELD 4 TO 5 SERVINGS

24 herrings, fresh or frozen and thawed
2 tablespoons (30 ml) chopped mint
2 tablespoons (30 ml) chopped cilantro
2 tablespoons (30 ml) olive oil
2 tablespoons (30 ml) sea salt

DIRECTIONS

Eviscerate the fish, brush off the scales, rinse, and pat dry with paper towels. Heat the grill. Stuff the belly of each fish with mint and cilantro. Brush with olive oil; lightly roll in sea salt, and grill on high heat about 4 to 5 minutes on each side.

Stuffed Grilled Jackfish (PĀPIO)

*All the bones of the fish are removed in the process of butterfly-ing. **To butterfly a fish**, see Preparing Fish for Cooking. Serve grilled fish with a green salad or a tomato salad dressed in vin-aigrette.*

YIELD 8 SERVINGS

1 jackfish, 6 to 7 pounds (2.7 to 3.2 kg), dressed and
   butterflied
Salt
2 tablespoons Worcestershire sauce
4 tablespoons (60 ml) olive oil
¼ cup (60 ml) chopped onion
2 teaspoons (10 ml) chopped garlic
1 cup (260 ml) chopped tomatoes
8 pitted black olives, chopped
2 anchovy fillets, mashed
¼ cup (60 ml) chopped parsley
¼ cup (60 ml) toasted almonds
1½ cups (375 ml) fresh bread crumbs
Black pepper

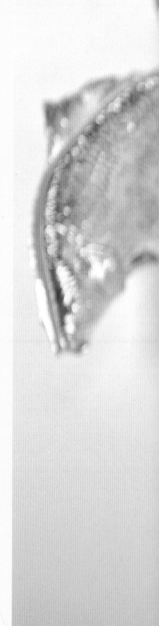

DIRECTIONS

Season the fish inside out with salt and Worcestershire sauce. Heat the grill. To make the stuffing, heat 2 tablespoons of olive oil and sauté onions and garlic over medium heat. Add toma-toes, olives, anchovies, parsley, and almonds and cook for 2 to 3 minutes. Remove from heat and fold in the breadcrumbs, season with salt and pepper to taste. Stuff the fish and bring the fillets together; press to form the shape of the fish. Stick in a few tooth-picks to hold the fish in place. Brush the fish occasionally with the remaining olive oil and grill on moderate heat for 20 minutes on each side. Any extra stuffing may be heated up and served beside the grilled fish.

Jackfish Grilled in Banana Leaves (PĀPIO)

Smothered in a minty coconut paste, this is a very special fish dish you may serve for an outdoor event or for the centerpiece of a buffet. You need a large banana leaf with the mid-rib removed to enclose the fish. Warming the leaf will make it flexible and wrapping easy. If you have no access to banana leaves, use foil. Rice and vegetables or potatoes and salads are all suitable accompaniments for this aromatic fish.

YIELD 5 SERVINGS

1 jackfish, about 5 pounds (2.3 kg), dressed, cleaned, and washed
2 teaspoons (10 ml) **garam masala**
⅛ teaspoon (0.63 ml) **turmeric**
1 teaspoon (5 ml) black pepper
Sea salt

For mint paste

1 packed cup (225 g) mint leaves
½ cup (120 g) cilantro leaves
1 cup (225 g) freshly grated coconut or ½ cup (120 g) shredded dry coconut
4 jalapeño peppers, sliced
2 shallots, sliced
1 tablespoon (15 ml) chopped ginger
Juice of 1½ lemons
2 teaspoons (10 ml) sugar
1 banana leaf, warmed over heat
2 tablespoons (30 ml) vegetable oil

DIRECTIONS

Pat the fish dry with paper towels. Rub garam masala, turmeric, and pepper with salt to taste all over and inside the belly cavity of the fish. For the mint paste, in a blender grind the mint, cilantro, coconut, jalapeño pepper, shallots, and ginger. Add lemon juice, sugar, and salt to taste and continue to blend to a smooth paste. Apply all over fish and place fish on the banana leaf. Pour olive oil over the mint-paste-covered fish and enclose in the banana leaf. Cook over a charcoal grill on moderate heat for 20 minutes on each side. Place on a serving platter, open the banana leaf, and let guests help themselves.

Grilled Bigeye Tuna with Tamarind Sauce ('AHI)

This simple yet exotic grilled tuna needs a rice dish, a yogurt salad, or steamed vegetables such as string beans to accompany. For those who like it hot, serve with a small bowl of **Harissa** *(see Sauces, Dips, and Condiments).*

YIELD 4 SERVINGS

2 tablespoons (30 ml) **tamarind** paste (to taste)
½ cup (125 ml) water
3 cloves garlic, finely chopped
2 teaspoons (10 ml) finely chopped ginger
2 teaspoons crushed red pepper
2 tablespoons (30 ml) sugar
Salt
4 tuna fillets, 6 ounces (170 g) each
1 tablespoon (15 ml) olive oil

Garnish
2 tablespoons (30 ml) chopped mint leaves

DIRECTIONS

Prepare the tamarind sauce: place tamarind paste, water, garlic, ginger, red pepper and sugar in a pan with salt to taste. Simmer on moderate heat for 5 minutes. Cool. Pat the fish dry with paper towels and place in a dish; spoon 2 tablespoons (30 ml) of the tamarind sauce on the fish to season. Place the seasoned fish on a piece of foil, drizzle the olive oil over the fish, and place the foil with the fish on a hot grill. Grill for about 4 minutes. Brush the fish with some of the remaining sauce; turn the fish over on the foil and brush again with the sauce; cook for 4 more minutes. Place the fish on a platter and pour the sauce collected on the foil around the fish and scatter mint on.

Grilled Scad and Tomatoes with Pesto

(AKULE)

*Use large dressed scads and prepare the fish for cooking as explained in To **butterfly a fish** (see Preparing Fish for Cooking). After the fish is butterflied it is easy to prepare and can be part of a great outdoor family meal.*

YIELD 2 SERVINGS

4 scads 10 ounces (280 g) each, butterflied
⅛ teaspoon (0.63 ml) **turmeric**
1 teaspoon (5 ml) finely chopped garlic
1 teaspoon (5 ml) black pepper
Juice of 1 lime
Salt
1 tablespoon (15 ml) olive oil
2 tomatoes, trimmed and halved

For the pesto

1 cup (250 ml) basil leaves
¼ cup (60 ml) walnuts
¼ cup (60 ml) Parmesan cheese
¼ cup (60 ml) olive oil

DIRECTIONS

Place the butterflied fish opened out like a book on a work surface. Mix turmeric, garlic, black pepper, lime juice, and salt to taste, rub all into the fish, and refrigerate for 30 minutes. Turn the grill on. For the pesto, puree basil and walnuts in a food processor, add cheese, gradually drizzle in the oil, and process till well emulsified. Cook fish on the hot grill for 4 to 5 minutes on each side while brushing with oil. Grill tomatoes and place beside fish. Spoon the pesto lightly on fish and tomatoes.

Chutney-marinated Grilled Yellowfin Tuna ('AHI)

*The fish is so flavorful with its chutney marinade that you need a rice dish such as **Citrus-flavored Herbed Rice** (see Accompanying Staples) and more chutney to complement the dish.*

YIELD 6 SERVINGS

6 tuna fillets, 6 ounces (170 g) each
1 teaspoon (5 ml) ground **cumin**
2 teaspoons (10 ml) crushed red pepper
Black pepper
Salt
2 tablespoons (30 ml) red wine
¼ cup (62 ml) mango chutney
2 ounces (57 g) melted butter
1 tablespoon (15 ml) lime juice
1 tablespoon (15 ml) snipped chives

DIRECTIONS

Heat the grill. Pat fish dry with paper towels, place in a glass or enamel dish, sprinkle with the cumin, red pepper, black pepper, and salt to taste, and rub into the fish. Mix wine and chutney together and pour on the fish; refrigerate for 30 minutes. Grill over moderate heat for 4 to 5 minutes on a side while brushing with melted butter. Place on a serving dish, drizzle with lime juice, and scatter chives on.

Grilled Wahoo with Green Peppercorn Vinaigrette (ONO)

This is an easy-to-make fish dish, complete with its own vege-tables and a flavorful vinaigrette. It is best served with baked potatoes or a potato salad.

YIELD 4 SERVINGS

4 wahoo steaks, 5 ounces (142 g) each
Salt
Black pepper
2 tablespoons (30 ml) olive oil
12 asparagus spears, trimmed
1 red onion, sliced ¼ inch (0.64 cm) thick into 4 slices
4 tomato slices, ¼ inch (0.64 cm) thick
2 tablespoons (30 ml) olive oil
1 tablespoon (15 ml) white wine vinegar
1 tablespoon (15 ml) Dijon country mustard
1 tablespoon (15 ml) honey
1 tablespoon (15 ml) crushed green peppercorns

DIRECTIONS

Preheat grill. Season fish with salt and pepper to taste. Brush with oil and grill about 3 minutes on each side. Season vegetables with salt and grill, brushing with oil. For vinaigrette, whisk remaining ingredients in a bowl and season with salt. Arrange the grilled vegetables on a platter and drizzle with vinaigrette; place grilled fish on the vegetables.

Grilled Bigeye Tuna with Cucumber Salad ('AHI)

Here is another grilled fish that is easy to prepare. In small portions this can be a starter to a meal; in larger portions it can be an entrée.

YIELD 4 SERVINGS

1 seedless cucumber, peeled and thinly sliced
Salt
1 jalapeño pepper, seeded and thinly sliced
1 tablespoon (15 ml) thinly sliced shallots
Black pepper
Juice of 1 lime
2 tablespoons (30 ml) thick coconut milk
4 tuna steaks, 4 ounces (113 g) each
½ teaspoon (2.5 ml) cayenne pepper
1 tablespoon (15 ml) chili sauce
1 tablespoon (15 ml) tomato ketchup
1 teaspoon (5 ml) Worcestershire sauce
1 tablespoon (15 ml) light soy sauce
1 tablespoon (15 ml) olive oil

DIRECTIONS

Preheat grill. Prepare cucumber salad: mix cucumber with a teaspoon of salt and set aside for 10 minutes; place in a strainer and squeeze out the liquid. Place cucumber in a bowl; add jalapeño pepper, shallots, black pepper, and lime juice to taste. Mix in the coconut milk and spoon onto a platter. Season fish with cayenne pepper, chili sauce, ketchup, Worcestershire sauce, soy sauce, and salt to taste. Grill the fish on high heat, brushing with oil, for 3 to 4 minutes on each side or until charred to a reddish brown. Place on cucumber salad.

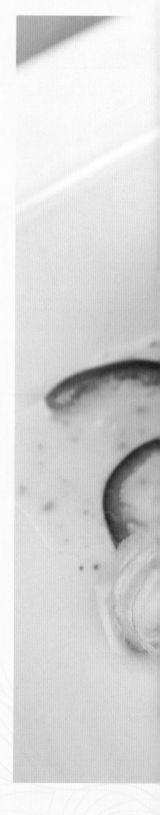

Grilled Marlin on Fennel Salad with Orange and Red Onion (KAJIKI)

*Mahimahi can be substituted for marlin in this recipe. The fresh **fennel** in the salad dressing makes a tasty sauce for fish. Crispy french fries are good as a side dish.*

YIELD 4 SERVINGS

4 marlin fillets, 5 ounces (142 g) each
¼ teaspoon (1.25 ml) crushed red pepper
1 teaspoon (5 ml) orange zest
1 tablespoon (15 ml) cider vinegar
Salt
1 tablespoon (15 ml) olive oil, reserve for grilling fish

For fennel salad
1 **fennel** bulb, thinly sliced and soaked in cold water
1 small red onion, thinly sliced and soaked in cold water
1 orange, peeled and segmented
Juice of 1 orange
Juice of 1 lemon
1 tablespoon (15 ml) rice wine vinegar
1 teaspoon (5 ml) cracked black pepper

DIRECTIONS

Season fish with crushed red pepper, orange zest, vinegar, and salt to taste. Marinate in refrigerator for 30 minutes. Heat the grill. Strain fennel and onion from the soaking water; discard the water and place fennel and onion in a bowl along with the orange. Whisk together orange juice, lemon juice, rice wine vinegar, cracked pepper with salt to taste, pour on the fennel mix and toss. Grill fish for 4 to 5 minutes on each side, brushing occasionally with olive oil. Spoon fennel salad onto plates and place grilled fish on each salad.

Herb-crusted Grilled Bigeye Scad

(AKULE)

Fish grilled whole is moist as long as it is not overdone. Serve with baked potatoes and sour cream and a green salad. The sour cream gives a luscious taste to the moist, flaky, arugula-pesto-crusted fish. You may use any other fish; however, my favorite is red snapper.

YIELD 2 SERVINGS

2 scads, 12 ounces (375g) each, dressed
2 teaspoons (10 ml) sea salt
2 teaspoons (10 ml) cracked black pepper
4 tablespoons (60 ml) olive oil

For pesto crust
2 cups (500 ml) arugula leaves, roughly chopped
2 jalapeño peppers, seeded and minced
½ cup (125 ml) shredded Parmesan cheese
½ cup (125 ml) chopped pistachio nuts
½ cup (125 ml) dry bread crumbs

DIRECTIONS

Heat the grill. Pat fish dry with paper towels; rub inside and out with salt, pepper, and 1 tablespoon (15 ml) olive oil. For the pesto crust, in a bowl mix together arugula, peppers, cheese, pistachios, bread crumbs, and the rest of the olive oil. Press the pesto evenly and firmly onto both sides of the fish. Place fish in a hinged grill and place on the grill for 12 minutes on each side or until the crust is golden brown. Check for doneness and continue to cook a few more minutes if needed.

Grilled Mackerel Scad with Berry Sauce ('ŌPELU)

*Serve this plain grilled fish with **Spiced Quinoa** (see Accompanying Staples). The oil-fried spices in the quinoa burst with flavor and aroma and partner well with simply grilled fish. A cooked green vegetable or a green salad is a perfect match for grilled fish.*

YIELD 4 SERVINGS

¼ pound (113 g) poha berries or gooseberries
1 cup (250 ml) water
1 tablespoon (15 ml) finely chopped onion
2 tablespoons (30 ml) white wine vinegar
½ cup (125 ml) white wine
¼ teaspoon (2.5 ml) ground **cinnamon**
Pinch of grated **nutmeg**
Pinch of cayenne pepper
Salt
2 tablespoons (30 ml) sugar or more to taste
4 mackerel scad, dressed, about 12 ounces (340 g) each
Juice of 1 lemon
Black pepper
2 tablespoons (30 ml) olive oil

DIRECTIONS

Wash berries, place in a small pan with water, and cook for 2 minutes. Strain berries and discard cooking water. Mash berries and pass through a sieve. Place berry pulp in a saucepan with onions, vinegar, wine, spices, a pinch of salt, and sugar to taste. Cook on low heat for 10 minutes until sauce is shiny and set aside. Score the fish, making diagonal cuts 1 inch (2.5 cm) long and about 2 inches (5cm) apart on both sides of each fish. Season the fish with lemon juice, black pepper, and salt to taste; rub in the olive oil. Grill for 5 to 7 minutes on each side until crisp and golden brown. Serve with berry sauce.

Simply Barbecued Gray Snapper Fillets (UKU)

*Try this simple barbeque recipe. You can make the barbeque sauce and store in the refrigerator, it is handy to use as needed. You may also barbecue dressed snapper using this sauce; it is perfect for a crowd when served with **Yellow Rice** (see Accompanying Staples) and a vegetable salad such as coleslaw.*

YIELD 4 TO 6 SERVINGS

6 gray snapper fillets, 8 ounces (227 g) each
1 tablespoon (15 ml) olive oil
Salt

Barbecue sauce

1 tablespoon (15 ml) vegetable oil
½ cup (125 ml) diced onion
1 tablespoon chopped garlic
5 dry chipotle chilies, ground
1 cup (250 ml) diced pineapple
1 tablespoon (15 ml) **tamarind** paste
½ cup (125 ml) tomato ketchup
½ cup (125 ml) chili sauce
¼ cup (60 ml) soy sauce
¼ cup (60 ml) apple cider vinegar
1 tablespoon (15 ml) Worcestershire sauce
Juice of 1 orange
Juice of 1 lemon
½ cup (125 ml) brown sugar

DIRECTIONS

Brush the fish with oil and season with salt to taste; refrigerate until ready to use. Heat the barbecue grill. For the barbecue sauce, heat the vegetable oil in a saucepan, add onions and garlic, and sauté until caramelized. Add remaining ingredients and simmer on low heat for 30 minutes. Puree in a blender until smooth. Cool the sauce and store in a sterilized jar in the refrigerator. (To prevent contamination spoon out some sauce to use as needed.) Sear the fish on the hot barbeque grill for 2 minutes on each side. Then brush with the barbecue sauce and barbecue on low heat for 4 minutes on each side. Brush with the sauce a few times while the fish is on the grill.

Spicy Barbecued Gray Snapper (UKU)

*It takes effort **to butterfly a fish** (see Preparing Fish for Cooking), but it is worth all the work. Baked potatoes with sour cream and a simple green salad are delicious with spicy fish.*

YIELD 4 SERVINGS

1 dressed gray snapper, about 3 pounds (1.4 kg), washed
    and butterflied
2 tablespoons (30 ml) vinegar
¼ teaspoon (1.25 ml) **turmeric**
1 teaspoon (5 ml) black pepper
Salt

Seasonings

1 tablespoon (15 ml) ground **coriander**
2 teaspoons (10 ml) ground **cumin**
1 teaspoon (5 ml) ground **cinnamon**
1 teaspoon (5 ml) cayenne pepper
1 teaspoon (5 ml) finely chopped ginger
1 teaspoon (5 ml) finely chopped garlic
1 tablespoon (15 ml) finely chopped onion
1 tablespoon (15 ml) cold butter

For basting

2 tablespoons (30 ml) melted butter
2 tablespoons (30 ml) chili sauce

DIRECTIONS

Heat the barbecue grill. Season the fish with vinegar, turmeric, black pepper, and salt to taste. Mix together the ingredients for the seasoning. Open up the fish on a work surface and spread the seasoned cold butter on the two fillets; press the two buttered sides of the fillets together. Mix the melted butter and chili sauce together in a bowl. Barbecue the fish on low heat about 10 minutes each side while brushing with the butter-chili sauce until fish is cooked through.

Barbecued Swordfish with Avocado Salad (SHUTOME)

This dish may be part of an outdoor barbecue. A salad such as coleslaw is good with the fish.

YIELD 4 SERVINGS

4 swordfish fillets, 5 ounces (142 g) each
1 jalapeño pepper
4 cloves garlic
1 tablespoon (15 ml) chopped cilantro
1 tablespoon (15 ml) cider vinegar
2 tablespoons (30 ml) tomato sauce
2 teaspoons (10 ml) soy sauce
1 teaspoon (5 ml) brown sugar
Juice of 1 orange
Salt
4 ripe tomatoes, sliced
2 avocados, peeled, seeded, and sliced
½ cup (125 ml) basil leaves, shredded
¼ cup (60 ml) olive oil
1 tablespoon (15 ml) balsamic vinegar
Black pepper

DIRECTIONS

Pat the fish dry with paper towels and place in a glass or enamel dish. Place the pepper, garlic, cilantro, vinegar, tomato sauce, soy sauce, brown sugar, and orange juice in a blender container, add salt to taste, and blend to a smooth puree. Pour over the fish and let marinate for 30 minutes. Heat the barbecue grill. Arrange tomatoes, avocado, and basil leaves on a platter and drizzle with olive oil and balsamic vinegar. Sprinkle salt and pepper to taste. Grill the fish on high heat 3 to 4 minutes on each side and place the barbequed fish on the salad.

CURED AND SMOKED

In ancient times fishing communities brined fish in seawater and left them on the shore to ferment or dry. Similarly, hunting communities hung meats over smoldering or smoking fires to smoke and dry them. Preserved thus, these items added the necessary proteins and minerals to otherwise skimpy diets.

Salt is one of the basic and common ingredients used to preserve foods. Preserved foods, cured or smoked, are very different from fresh food. Salt-cured foods will have a harsh flavor unless sugar or sweeteners, such as honey, maple syrup, or corn syrup, are added to the curing mix to mellow it. Herbs and spices are often used to enhance flavor and give the food a special character. Smoke helps not only to dry and preserve foods, but also to give these foods special enticing flavors and aromas.

Cured Marlin with Fruit Salsa (KAJIKI)

Gravlax

Salted Salmon

Cured Wahoo (ONO)

Grilled Cured Wahoo with Minty Fruit Relish (ONO)

Smoked Marlin (KAJIKI)

Smoked Marlin with Jicama and Fruit Salad (KAJIKI)

Pan-smoked Skipjack Tuna with Roasted Bell Pepper Salad (AKU)

Pan-smoked Skipjack Tuna (AKU)

Spice-smoked Wahoo (ONO)

*Smoked Wahoo with Pea Sprouts, Orange, Goat Cheese,
    and Lemon-honey Dressing* (ONO)

Spice-smoked Wahoo with Citrus Relish (ONO)

Teriyaki-smoked Gray Snapper Fillets (UKU)

Teriyaki-smoked Gray Snapper Fillets with Grilled Fruit (UKU)

CURING FISH

Curing is an important process for items that are to be smoked. Curing also allows the product to marinate briefly with salt and any other spices and herbs used. Cured foods may also be broiled, grilled, or steamed. All utensils and equipment used for curing fish must be of nonreactive material.

Cured Marlin with Fruit Salsa (KAJIKI)

This recipe is to cure a 4 to 5 pound (1.8 to 2.3 kg) fillet. Once the fish is cured, slice the number of servings you need and grill as stated in the recipe. The balance of the cured fish may be wrapped in parchment paper and refrigerated for later use.

YIELD 4 SERVINGS

4 to 5 pounds (1.8 to 2.3 kg) marlin fillets

For curing

¾ cup (185 ml) kosher salt
¾ cup (185 ml) brown sugar
2 tablespoons (30 ml) cracked peppercorns
½ teaspoon (2.5 ml) crushed red pepper

For grilling

2 tablespoons (30 ml) olive oil
1 tablespoon (15 ml) honey
1 cup (250 ml) **Fruit Salsa** (see Sauces, Dips, and Condiments)

DIRECTIONS

Pat fish dry with paper towels. Mix curing ingredients and rub into the fish; place fish on a piece of cheesecloth in a glass or enamel container and cover loosely with plastic wrap. Place a kitchen weight on the plastic wrap to press on the fish. Refrigerate overnight. Wash the fish and dry completely with paper towels. Slice four portions roughly 4 ounces (110 g) each; grill for 3 to 4 minutes on each side while brushing a few times with olive oil and honey. Serve with fruit salsa.

Gravlax

Gravlax is salmon that has been cured for one to three days in salt, sugar, and aromatics such as dill. In this recipe the salmon is salt-cured. The skin of the salmon is kept on during curing but is not meant to be eaten. Traditionally, gravlax is served with sour cream, chopped hard-cooked egg, chopped onion, capers, lemon wedges, and toast points.

YIELD 2½ POUNDS (1.1 KG); 15 TO 20 SERVINGS

1 fresh salmon fillet with the skin, about 3 pounds (1.4 kg)

6 ounces (170 g) kosher salt

8 ounces (227 g) brown sugar

1 teaspoon (5 ml) crushed dill seed

½ cup (125 ml) chopped fresh dill

2 tablespoons (30 ml) cracked black peppercorns

Zest of 1 lemon

2 teaspoons (10 ml) oil

DIRECTIONS

Place the salmon fillet on a cutting board; pick and discard the bones; place on a piece of cheesecloth large enough to wrap the salmon completely. In a bowl mix salt, sugar, dill seed, fresh dill, peppercorns, lemon zest, and oil; sprinkle evenly on the salmon and wrap in the cheesecloth. Place the wrapped salmon in hotel pan and place another pan directly on top. Place a kitchen brick about 2 pounds (907 g) in weight on the top pan to weigh down and press the salmon. Refrigerate for 2 days, turning over once. On the third day unwrap the salmon, scrape off the salt and the seasonings, and wipe off excess moisture thoroughly with paper towels. You may slice the gravlax and serve right away or you may wrap it in parchment paper and store in an airtight container and refrigerated for up to 5 days. To serve, slice gravlax very thin, avoiding slicing the skin. Arrange on a platter and serve with traditional accompaniments

Salted Salmon

1 pound (450 g) salmon fillet with
   the skin (pin bones removed)
¼ cup (60ml) sea salt
4 cups (1 L) cold water

DIRECTIONS

Place the salmon in a glass or enamel
dish, sprinkle with sea salt, cover, and
refrigerate overnight. Drain off and discard the collected liquid and pour the
cold water over the salmon. Cover and
refrigerate for 2 days. Again, drain off
and discard the collected water. Remove
the salmon skin (it peels off easily) and
discard. Wash away excess salt from
the salmon in 3 changes of fresh water.
Refrigerate and use the salted salmon as
needed.

Cured Wahoo (ONO)

*Cured fish may be used for grilling, bak-
ing, or steaming. It may be used in spreads
for sandwiches and canapés. Cured fish
has a tendency to be salty; therefore care
should be taken when seasoning items
like spreads. Mahimahi and swordfish
may be cured in this manner.*

YIELD 2 POUNDS (907 G)

3 pounds (1.4 kg) wahoo fillets, cut
   into slices 2 inches (5 cm) thick

Curing mix
Juice of 1 lemon
Zest of 1 lemon
5 ounces (142 g) kosher salt
5 ounces (142 g) granulated sugar
1 tablespoon (15 ml) crushed black
   pepper
1 tablespoon (15 ml) crushed
   coriander seed
½ tablespoon (7.5 ml) crushed
   fennel seed

DIRECTIONS

Pat fish with paper towels and place on
a piece of cheesecloth large enough to
wrap fish completely. For the curing mix,
mix together lemon juice and zest, salt,
sugar, and spices and press on top of the
fish evenly. Wrap fish loosely in cheesecloth and place in a glass or enamel dish;
refrigerate for 3 days. On the third day,
scrape off the curing mix and wipe dry.
The fish may be wrapped and refrigerated and used for cooking as required.

Grilled Cured Wahoo with Minty Fruit Relish (ONO)

The glaze on the cured fish is piquant; the addition of the minted fruit gives a taste combination that complements smoked fish. When cooking, make sure the cured fish does not sit too long on the grill or it will dry out. Serve with a bowl of horseradish-flavored sour cream.

4 SERVINGS

1 pound (454 g) **Cured Wahoo** fillet (see recipe this section)
¼ teaspoon (1.25 ml) cayenne pepper
1 tablespoon (15 ml) honey
2 tablespoons (30 ml) lime juice
1 tablespoon (15 ml) olive oil
6 butter lettuce leaves
6 mint sprigs

Fruit relish

6 strawberries, cut into small dice
2 kiwi, peeled and cut into small dice
1 cup (250 ml) small diced pineapple
½ cup (125 ml) chopped fresh mint
2 teaspoons (10 ml) honey
1 tablespoon (15 ml) rice wine vinegar
Salt

DIRECTIONS

Heat the grill. Wash the cured fish thoroughly to remove excess salt; pat dry with paper towels; cut into 4 slices, roughly 4 ounces (110 g) each. Mix cayenne pepper, honey, and lime juice and brush on fish. Place on a hot grill; brush with olive oil and cook for 2 to 3 minutes on each side. Place lettuce and mint on plates and place grilled fish on top. In a bowl mix the fruit relish ingredients together with salt to taste and spoon around fish.

SMOKING

Usually foods to be smoked first undergo a process known as curing. Smoking adds flavor and color to foods. The smoky flavor of the food is a desired quality. Hardwoods such as apple, cherry, hickory, oak, and mesquite are traditional and quite commonly used. Whole spices, citrus peelings, exotic herbs, and teas can also be used in smoking, these give a special flavor and are popular today.

Smoked Marlin (KAJIKI)

The sliced marinated marlin is slowly smoke-roasted on a barbecue grill. Make sure the heat is not too high. Smoking on too high heat will cook away the moisture, making the fish dry and shrunken.

YIELD 2 POUNDS (907 G)

3 pounds (1.4 kg) marlin fillet sliced 2 inches (5 cm) thick
¼ cup (60 ml) soy sauce
2 tablespoons (30 ml) finely chopped ginger
2 tablespoons (30 ml) finely chopped onion
2 tablespoons (30 ml) finely chopped garlic
2 tablespoons (30 ml) finely chopped green onion
2 tablespoons (30 ml) brown sugar
2 tablespoons (30 ml) olive oil

DIRECTIONS

Place fish in a glass or enamel dish. Add soy sauce, ginger, onion, garlic, green onion, sugar, and oil and mix to coat fish. Marinate in the refrigerator overnight or for at least 10 hours. Remove fish from marinade and discard the juices collected in the dish. Place fish on a barbecue grill, cover, and smoke on very low heat for 15 to 20 minutes. Cool, wrap in parchment paper, and refrigerate. Use as needed.

Smoked Marlin with Jicama and Fruit Salad (KAJIKI)

This salad goes well with other smoked fish too. Sometimes if you are short on smoked fish, flake the fish instead of dicing and toss with the jicama salad. It makes an awesome starter.

YIELD 6 SERVINGS

1 pound (454 g) smoked marlin
1 small head iceberg lettuce broken into bite-size pieces
1 small jicama, peeled and cut into small dice
1 orange, segmented
1 cup (250 ml) diced pineapple
1 jalapeño pepper, seeded and chopped
1 tablespoon (15 ml) rice wine vinegar
1 teaspoon (5 ml) sugar
Juice of 1 lemon
½ teaspoon (2.5 ml) crushed black peppercorns
½ teaspoon (2.5 ml) crushed red pepper
Salt

DIRECTIONS

Cut the smoked fish into small dice. Place lettuce on a chilled platter. Mix jicama, orange, pineapple, jalapeño pepper, rice wine vinegar, sugar, lemon juice, black and red pepper and salt to taste. Mix in the smoked fish and spoon on the lettuce.

Pan-smoked Skipjack Tuna with Roasted Red Bell Pepper Salad (AKU)

*This is a satisfying salad that is not too heavy and makes a fine first course. When served with **Pan-smoked Skipjack Tuna** (see recipe this section) it makes a light luncheon dish.*

YIELD 4 SERVINGS

2 cups (500 ml) arugula leaves
1 tablespoon (15 ml) olive oil
2 red bell peppers
2 tomatoes, peeled, seeded, and diced
¼ cup (60 ml) pitted black olives
2 anchovy fillets, chopped
1 teaspoon (5 ml) finely chopped garlic
1 tablespoon (15 ml) chopped capers
¼ cup (60 ml) chopped parsley
1 tablespoon (15 ml) lemon juice
Salt
½ cup (125 ml) shaved Parmesan cheese
8 ounces (230 g) smoked skipjack tuna, sliced

DIRECTIONS

Trim arugula, arrange on a platter, and refrigerate. Brush peppers with olive oil and place on grill, turning often to let the skins burn. Peel and discard skins and seeds; cut the peppers into strips. Place in a bowl with the rest of the ingredients and toss with salt to taste; spoon on the chilled arugula and sprinkle with the cheese. Serve with smoked sliced tuna.

Pan-smoked Skipjack Tuna (AKU)

*Smoked sliced tuna can be used in salads or in appetizers. For **pan smoking** see Cooking Methods. Wrap the smoked tuna in parchment paper and keep refrigerated until ready to use.*

YIELD 2 POUNDS (907 G)

3 pounds (1.4 kg) skipjack tuna fillet
Salt
Coarse ground black pepper
2 tablespoons (30 ml) olive oil
A handful of rosemary sprigs for smoking
¼ cup (60 ml) water

DIRECTIONS

Slice the tuna 2 inches (5 cm) thick. Season with salt and pepper to taste. Rub in the 2 tablespoons (30 ml) of olive oil and set aside. Place smoker over a heat source, add the rosemary to the pan and sprinkle with the water; place the rack in the pan and cover tightly with the lid. Let the rosemary smoke for 10 minutes. Open the smoker, place the fish on the rack, close the lid firmly and smoke on very low heat for 20 to 25 minutes.

Spice-smoked Wahoo (ONO)

*Spice-smoked fish is very aromatic. The **curry leaves** add an exotic aroma.*

YIELD 6 SERVINGS

3 pounds (1.4 kg) wahoo fillet, sliced 2 inches (5 cm) thick
1 tablespoon (15 ml) lemon zest
1 tablespoon (15 ml) orange zest
½ teaspoon (2.5 ml) sea salt
1 teaspoon (5 ml) crushed black peppercorns
3 tablespoons (15 ml) olive oil
1 tablespoon (15 ml) **cloves**
Handful of **curry leaves** (optional)
Handful of **cinnamon** sticks (soaked in water for 20 minutes or more)
¼ cup water (60 ml)

DIRECTIONS

Pat the fish dry with paper towels. Sprinkle fish with lemon and orange zest, salt and pepper. Drizzle olive oil over and refrigerate overnight. Place the cloves, curry leaves, and the soaked cinnamon in the smoker bottom pan and sprinkle with the water. Place the rack in the smoker and cover firmly with the lid. Place the smoker on a heat source. Let the aromatics smoke for 10 minutes. Remove fish from the refrigerator and pat dry. Open the smoker, place the fish on the rack, close lid firmly, and smoke on very low heat for 15 to 20 minutes. Cool, wrap in parchment paper, and refrigerate.

Smoked Wahoo with Pea Sprouts, Orange, Goat Cheese, and Lemon-honey Dressing (ONO)

You can substitute other vegetables for the pea sprouts to suit your taste. The combination of flavors in this salad is in harmony with the dressing and the smoked fish. Care should be taken not to over-salt the salad, because smoked fish is slightly salty.

YIELD 4 SERVINGS

6 ounces (170 g) **Spice-smoked Wahoo** (see recipe this section)
¼ cup (60 g) pea sprouts
2 oranges, peeled and segmented
2 tablespoons (30 ml) honey
½ cup (120 ml) heavy cream
2 tablespoons (30 ml) lemon juice
¼ teaspoon (1.25 ml) crushed red pepper
Black pepper
Salt
4 ounces (113 g) goat cheese, crumbled

DIRECTIONS

Flake the fish and place in a salad bowl with the pea sprouts and orange segments. Whisk the honey and cream together and add the lemon juice, crushed red pepper, and black pepper and salt to taste. Whisk till smooth, pour on the salad, and toss to coat the salad ingredients. Sprinkle crumbled goat cheese on top.

Spice-smoked Wahoo with Citrus Relish (ONO)

The citrus relish is a good partner to the lemony smoked fish. The sour cream is the taste component that brings all the flavors together.

YIELD 6 SERVINGS

6 portions **Spice-smoked Wahoo** (see recipe this section)
½ cup (125 ml) sour cream
1 orange, segmented
1 lemon, segmented
¼ cup (60 ml) chopped pickles
1 jalapeño pepper, seeded and chopped
1 tablespoon (15 ml) capers
¼ cup (60 ml) chopped red onion
Salt

DIRECTIONS

Heat the smoked fish on a grill. Reserve the sour cream in a bowl. For the relish toss the rest of the ingredients with salt to taste. Serve the relish and sour cream with the smoked fish.

Teriyaki-smoked Gray Snapper Fillets (UKU)

Wahoo, swordfish, or mahimahi may be used in this recipe in place of the gray snapper. Once the fish is smoked it can be wrapped and refrigerated for later use.

YIELD 3 POUNDS (1.4 KG)

4 pounds (1.8 kg) gray snapper fillets
1 cup (250 ml) teriyaki sauce
Juice and zest of 1 orange
Juice of 1 lemon
2 whole green onions, chopped
1 tablespoon (15 ml) chopped ginger

DIRECTIONS

Pat the fish dry with paper towels and place in a glass or ceramic dish. Combine the teriyaki sauce, orange juice and zest, lemon juice, green onion, and ginger; pour on the fish and refrigerate overnight. Remove fish from the marinade and pat dry. Discard marinade. Smoke the fish on very low heat, covered, over a barbecue grill. Cool, wrap in parchment paper, and refrigerate or freeze.

Teriyaki-smoked Gray Snapper Fillets with Grilled Fruit (UKU)

Both sweet and tart fruits go well with the teriyaki flavor, better still when they are grilled. Present the smoked and grilled fish fillet on a platter with the fruit for guests to help themselves.

YIELD 5 SERVINGS

1 pound (454 g) **Teriyaki-smoked Gray Snapper Fillets** (see recipe in this section)

1 orange, sliced, with the skin

½ pineapple, peeled, cored, and sliced ½ inch (1.28 cm) thick

2 peaches, halved, seed removed

2 tablespoons (30 ml) olive oil

Juice of 1 orange

1 tablespoon (15 ml) rice wine vinegar

1 tablespoon (15 ml) honey

Salt

DIRECTIONS

Briefly grill the smoked fish to heat up and place aside. Place the fruit on the very hot grill. Whisk together olive oil, orange juice, rice wine vinegar, honey, and a pinch of salt and brush on the fruit while grilling. Place the fish and the grilled fruit on a platter and serve.

ACCOMPANYING STAPLES

Saffron rice

Yellow rice

Basmati Rice with Cumin Seed and Chives

Spinach Rice

Citrus-flavored Herbed Rice

Spiced Quinoa

Lentils with Brown Rice

Hot Brown Lentils

Wasabi Mashed Potatoes

Roasted Whole Red Potatoes

Devilled Potatoes

Mashed Potatoes with Black Mustard Seeds

Roasted Garlic Mashed Potatoes

Herbed Hot Noodles

Pasta with Chili and Garlic

Couscous

SAUCES, DIPS, AND CONDIMENTS

Hollandaise Sauce

Sauce Beurre Blanc

Wasabi Buerre Blanc

Tomato Sauce

Cocktail Sauce

Tartar Sauce

Rémoulade Sauce

Chili Crème Fraiche

Rouille

Aïoli

Anchovy Dip

Roasted Garlic

Garlic Butter

Pickled Lemons

Preserved Lemon Wheels

Harissa

Chermoula

Tomato and Apricot Chutney

Fresh Mint Chutney

Fruit Salsa

Spinach Raita

Cucumber Raita

Cucumber Relish

Marinated Cucumber

Tomato Relish

Tomato and Onion Relish

ACCOMPANYING STAPLES

Most fish dishes need an accompanying staple such as rice, lentils, potatoes, pasta, or couscous to make a wholesome meal; some fish dishes need only a salad or vegetables. Some need sauce, pickles, and relishes to give that extra kick. Most of the entrée recipes have suggestions for the accompanying staple, or you may pick one from the variety in this section.

Saffron Rice

*When cooking rice, especially **basmati** rice, it is best to follow the instructions given on the bag of rice.*

YIELD 6 SERVINGS

3 tablespoons (45 ml) butter
1 tablespoon (15 ml) chopped onion
1½ cups (375 ml) **basmati rice**, washed and drained
A pinch of **saffron** threads soaked in 1 tablespoon (15 ml) hot water
4 whole **cloves**
4 **cardamom** pods bruised
2-inch (5 cm) piece of **cinnamon** stick
1 teaspoon (5 ml) salt
2 cups (500 ml) water

DIRECTIONS

Melt butter in a pot; add the onion and cook on medium heat to a golden brown. Stir in the rice, saffron, and spices with salt to taste. Add water, place on high heat, and bring to a boil. Stir the rice once, turn heat to very low, and cover the pot with a tight-fitting lid. Cook for 25 minutes. Remove from heat and let sit unopened for 5 minutes. Open, remove and discard the spices (which would have settled on top), and fluff the rice with a fork. Serve hot.

Rice is the commonest grain and has become a big part of diets around the world. There are many kinds of rice and many styles of cooking rice. In this section you will find a selection of recipes that are good accompaniments for simple to grand fish dishes.

Yellow Rice

*This is a quick and easy recipe for fragrant rice enriched with coconut milk. The golden hue in the rice is created by the addition of **turmeric**.*

YIELD 6 SERVINGS

2 tablespoons (30 ml) butter or vegetable oil
1 tablespoon (15 ml) chopped onion
6 **cloves**
8 **cardamom** pods, bruised
1 teaspoon (5 ml) **turmeric**
1-inch (2.5 cm) piece of **cinnamon** stick
1½ teaspoons (7.5 ml) salt
1½ cups (375 ml) long grain rice, washed and drained
2 cups (500 ml) coconut milk
¾ cup (185 ml) water

DIRECTIONS

Melt butter or heat vegetable oil in a pot; add onion and sauté to a golden brown. Add the spices, salt, and rice and stir until the rice is well coated with the spices. Add coconut milk and water and bring to a slow simmer. Reduce heat to low, cover pot tightly, and cook for 25 minutes. Remove the pot of rice from the heat and leave the rice to rest unopened for 5 minutes. Uncover the pot, remove and discard the spices that have settled on top of the rice, and gently fluff the rice with a fork. Serve hot.

Basmati Rice with Cumin Seed and Chives

YIELD 6 SERVINGS

2 cups (500 ml) **basmati rice**,
washed and drained

3 tablespoons (45 ml) butter

1-inch (2.5 cm) piece of **cinnamon**
stick

¼ teaspoon (1.25 ml) **cumin** seed

2 tablespoons (30 ml) chopped
onion

2 teaspoons (10 ml) chopped ginger

Juice of 1 lemon

2 teaspoons (10 ml) salt

4 cups (1 L) cold water

½ cup (125 ml) chopped chives

DIRECTIONS

Melt the butter in a pot; add spices and onions and cook for about 2 minutes until the onions turn a light golden color. Add the ginger, lemon juice, and salt. Stir in the rice and water and bring to a slow simmer; cover the pot tightly and cook on low heat for 25 minutes. Remove pot of rice from heat, fold in the chives, cover pot, and leave the rice to rest unopened for 5 minutes. Fluff the rice gently with a fork; remove and discard the cinnamon stick. Serve hot.

Spinach Rice

YIELD 6 SERVINGS

2 tablespoons (30 ml) butter

1 tablespoon (15 ml) chopped
onion

1 teaspoon (5 ml) **cumin** seed

¼ teaspoon (1.25 ml) **turmeric**

2 ½ cups (625 ml) water

1 teaspoon (5 ml) salt

1 ½ cups (375 ml) **basmati rice**,
washed and drained

Zest of 1 lemon

2 cups (500 ml) packed fresh
spinach leaves

DIRECTIONS

Melt the butter in a pot; add onion and cumin and cook till the onions turn a golden color. Add turmeric, water, salt, and rice; stir and bring to a slow simmer. Cover the pan tightly and cook on low heat for 25 minutes. Add and gently fold in the lemon zest and spinach. Cover and continue to cook for 2 more minutes. Allow the rice to rest for 5 minutes. Fluff gently with a fork and serve hot.

Citrus-flavored Herbed Rice

YIELD 6 SERVINGS

2 tablespoons (30 ml) butter
¼ teaspoons (1.25 ml) **turmeric**
1-inch (2.5 cm) piece of **cinnamon** stick
1½ cups (375 ml) long-grain rice, washed and drained
2 cups (500 ml) water
Juice of 1 lemon
Juice of 1 orange
Salt
¼ cup (60 ml) chopped green onion
¼ cup (60 ml) chopped cilantro
¼ cup (60 ml) chopped mint

DIRECTIONS

Melt the butter in a pot; add turmeric and cinnamon stick; add the rice and stir to combine and color with the turmeric. Add water, citrus juices, and salt to taste. Bring to a simmer, cover pot tightly, and cook for 25 minutes. Remove the pot from heat and fold in herbs, cover pot and leave unopened for 5 minutes. Fluff the rice gently with a fork; remove and discard the cinnamon stick. Serve hot.

Spiced Quinoa

Quinoa is a grain that was the staple of the ancient Incas. This ivory-colored bead-shaped grain is high in protein content and is prepared similar to rice. I use spices and nuts to counter the bland taste of this grain. Washed quinoa should be dried on a kitchen towel or on paper towels before use.

YIELD 4 SERVINGS

1 cup (250 ml) **quinoa**, washed and dried
2 tablespoons (30 ml) olive oil
1 tablespoon (15 ml) chopped onion
1 teaspoon (5 ml) **fenugreek** seeds
1 teaspoon (5 ml) **cumin** seeds
½ teaspoon (2.5 ml) **turmeric**
1 teaspoon (5 ml) crushed red pepper
¼ cup (60 ml) chopped almonds
Salt
2½ cups (625 ml) water
1 tablespoon (15 ml) chopped mint

DIRECTIONS

Heat a skillet, add the dry quinoa, and move around with a wooden spoon; let the grains toast for about 8 minutes. Set aside. Heat oil in a sauté pan; add onions, fenugreek, and cumin and cook until the spice seeds start to splutter. Stir in the turmeric, chili flakes, almonds, and toasted quinoa with salt to taste. Add the water, stir, and bring to a boil. Reduce heat to low, cover the sauté pan with a tight-fitting lid, and cook for 20 minutes. Add mint, fluff with a fork, cover, and set aside for 5 minutes before serving.

LEGUMES

Lentils are legumes, a rich source of fiber and full of nutrients. They cook fast and make a good partner to simply cooked fish.

Lentils with Brown Rice

YIELD 6 SERVINGS

4 ounces (113 g) red lentils, washed
2 cups (500 ml) water
1 cup (250 ml) cooked brown rice
2 tablespoons (30 ml) olive oil
½ cup (125 ml) chopped onion
1 teaspoon (5 ml) crushed **coriander** seed
1 cup (250 ml) small diced tomatoes
Salt
Black pepper
1 tablespoon (15 ml) butter
1 tablespoon (15 ml) dried mint

DIRECTIONS

Wash lentils and place in a saucepan; cover with water and cook until the lentils are soft to the touch, about 20 minutes. Strain off the cooking water and reserve the lentils along with the cooked rice. Heat olive oil in a pan; fry the onions to a golden color, add the coriander, and cook for a few seconds. Add the tomatoes; fold in lentils and rice with salt and pepper to taste and cook 2 to 3 minutes; spoon into a serving bowl. In a small sauté pan heat the butter to a deep hazel brown color, add the mint leaves, and when sizzling pour over the lentils and rice. (This procedure takes only a few seconds; be careful not to burn the butter.)

Hot Brown Lentils

YIELD 6 SERVINGS

8 ounces (227 g) brown lentils
3 tablespoons (45 ml) olive oil
3 green onions, sliced (green and the white parts)
1 teaspoon (5 ml) chopped ginger
1 teaspoon (5 ml) chopped garlic
1 teaspoon (5 ml) ground **cumin**
½ teaspoon (2.5 ml) crushed red pepper
2 tablespoons (30 ml) chopped mint
Juice of half a lemon
Salt
Black pepper

DIRECTIONS

Wash lentils and soak overnight (soaking helps them cook faster). Discard the soaking water, cover with fresh water, and cook for 30 to 35 minutes or until the lentils are soft to the touch. Drain off the cooking water and reserve the lentils. Heat oil in a sauté pan; add onion, ginger, garlic, cumin, and red pepper and cook for 2 to 3 minutes. Stir in the lentils, mint, lemon juice, and salt and pepper to taste. Keep moving the lentils in the pan and cook on low heat for 3 to 4 minutes to combine all the flavors.

POTATOES

Next to rice, potatoes remain a popular starch and an important staple. They add variety and interest to meals especially when fish is the center of the plate. They can be prepared in many ways. Here you will find some recipes that are easy to prepare.

Wasabi Mashed Potatoes

YIELD 6 SERVINGS

2 pounds (907 g) russet potatoes,
    peeled and diced
Water
1 ounce (30 g) butter
½ cup (125 ml) cream
½ cup (125 ml) milk
¼ cup (60 ml) **wasabi** powder,
    mixed to a paste with
    1 tablespoon (15 ml) water
Salt

DIRECTIONS

Place potatoes in a saucepan, cover with water, place on high heat, and cook for 20 to 25 minutes until the potatoes are soft. Drain potatoes and place in a bowl. Place butter, cream, and milk in a pan, bring to a simmer, and pour over the potatoes. Add the wasabi and salt to taste and beat the potatoes to a smooth consistency. Serve hot.

Roasted Whole Red Potatoes

YIELD 6 SERVINGS

1½ pounds (680 g) medium red
    potatoes, unpeeled
2 tablespoons (30 ml) olive oil
10 garlic cloves peeled
4 sprigs of thyme
½ cup (125 ml) water
Black pepper
Salt

DIRECTIONS

Preheat oven to 300°F (149°C). Wash the potatoes and place in a baking pan. Add all the ingredients with pepper and salt to taste. Roast for 40 to 45 minutes, occasionally moving potatoes around in the pan. Test for doneness by piercing the potatoes with a knife. The water should have evaporated, and the potatoes should be soft inside, crisp and golden on the outside. Serve hot.

Devilled Potatoes

YIELD 6 SERVINGS

1½ pounds (680 g) baking potatoes
Water
3 tablespoons (45 ml) olive oil
1 sprig **curry leaves** (optional)
2 medium onions, thinly sliced
4 garlic cloves, thinly sliced
1 teaspoon (5 ml) crushed red
   pepper
¼ teaspoon (2.5 ml) paprika
¼ teaspoon (2.5 ml) **turmeric**
Salt

DIRECTIONS

Place potatoes in a pan, cover with cold water, and cook until soft. Peel and cut into 1-inch (2.5 cm) cubes. Heat oil in a skillet; add curry leaves, onions, and garlic and sauté on medium heat until the onions turn a light golden color. Stir in the crushed red pepper, paprika, and turmeric. Cook for 1 minute. Add and mix in the potatoes with salt to taste. Cook on medium heat for 10 minutes, turning and folding the potatoes using a spatula.

Mashed Potatoes with Black Mustard Seeds

YIELD 6 SERVINGS

1½ pounds (680 g) baking potatoes
Water
2 tablespoons (30 ml) olive oil
2 medium onions thinly sliced
1 sprig **curry leaves** (optional)
1½ teaspoons (7.5 ml) **black
   mustard** seeds
½ teaspoon (2.5 ml) **cumin** seeds
⅛ teaspoon (0.63 ml) **turmeric**
Salt

DIRECTIONS

Place potatoes in a pan, cover with water, and cook until the potatoes are soft. Peel and mash the potatoes (the mash should be rough, not smooth). Heat oil in an oven-proof skillet; add onions and sauté until the onions are a light golden color. Add curry leaves, mustard, and cumin seeds; cook for 2 minutes until the seeds start to splutter. Stir in turmeric and cook for 1 minute. On high heat, add and fold in the potatoes with salt to taste. Using a spatula keep moving the potatoes around in the skillet to combine with the onions and the spices. Place the skillet in a hot oven and bake for 15 minutes. At the end of cooking time the potatoes should be spice coated and still a rough mash.

Roasted Garlic Mashed Potatoes

YIELD 6 SERVINGS

2 pounds (907 g) russet potatoes, peeled and diced
Water
1 tablespoon (15 ml) **Roasted Garlic** (see recipe this section)
1½ cups (375 ml) milk
1 tablespoon (15 ml) butter (optional)
Salt
Black pepper

DIRECTIONS

Preheat the oven to 350°F (176°C). Place potatoes in a pan, cover with water, place on high heat, and cook for 15 to 20 minutes until the potatoes are soft. Drain the potatoes; place in a bowl, and add the mashed roasted garlic. Place milk and butter in a pan; bring to a simmer and add to the potatoes with salt and pepper to taste; beat the potatoes to a smooth consistency. Serve hot.

Pasta is also a popular starch that is used to accompany seafood. Pasta should be cooked "al dente" meaning "firm to the bite." The following recipes are easy to make.

Herbed Hot Noodles

SERVES 4

8 ounces (227 g) fine-cut noodles
4 cups (1 L) water
2 tablespoons (30 ml) olive oil
2 tablespoons (30 ml) sliced onion
5 whole green chilies
1 teaspoon (5 ml) chopped garlic
½ cup (125 ml) finely sliced green onion
½ cup (125 ml) chopped cilantro
½ cup (125 ml) chopped tomatoes
Lemon juice
Black pepper
Salt

DIRECTIONS

Cook noodles in boiling water, strain and set aside. Heat olive oil in a skillet; add onions, chilies, and garlic and cook until the onions are soft. Add the rest of the ingredients with pepper and salt to taste. Toss in the noodles, combine with the seasonings in the skillet and serve on a platter.

Pasta with Chili and Garlic

YIELD 5 SERVINGS

1 pound (454 g) fettuccine, cooked
¼ tablespoon (60 ml) olive oil
6 garlic cloves, thinly sliced
3 hot **chili peppers**, seeded and sliced
1 cup (250 ml) canned crushed plum tomatoes
½ cup (125 ml) finely chopped celery
1 tablespoon (15 ml) chopped basil
¼ cup (60 ml) chopped parsley
1 teaspoon (5 g) sugar
Salt
Black pepper

DIRECTIONS

Strain the cooked pasta and place aside. Place a sauté pan on moderate heat; add the olive oil, garlic, and chili peppers and cook until the garlic turns to a light gold color. Add tomatoes, celery, and herbs and season with sugar, and salt and pepper to taste. Simmer on low heat for 20 minutes. Add pasta and toss to combine all the flavors.

Couscous

Couscous is hard wheat ground semolina, moistened and rolled into grains. The cooked dish served with a rich stew is also known as couscous and is the national dish of Morocco. Instant packaged couscous is available in supermarkets. This precooked product is easy to cook too. Here is a recipe that is light and matches well with fish.

YIELD 6 SERVINGS

2 cups (500 ml) couscous
2 cups (500 ml) boiling water
1 tablespoon (15 ml) olive oil
1 tablespoon (15 ml) chopped onion
1 teaspoon (5 ml) ground **cumin**
2-inch (5 cm) piece of **cinnamon** stick
Salt
¼ cup (60 ml) chopped parsley
½ cup (125 ml) roasted cashew nuts, coarsely chopped
2 tablespoons (30 ml) butter

DIRECTIONS

Place couscous in a bowl and gradually add the boiling water; stir, making sure all the grains are soaked in the water; cover tightly and set aside for 10 minutes. Heat olive oil in a pan; add onion and cook for 2 to 3 minutes. Add cumin and cinnamon; stir in the couscous, season with salt to taste, and cook on low heat for 5 minutes. Remove from heat and fold in the parsley, cashew pieces, and butter; pick and discard the cinnamon stick. Serve hot.

SAUCES, DIPS, AND CONDIMENTS

A sauce is a flavorful liquid, well-seasoned, thickened or unthickened, used to enhance other foods. Some fish recipes in this book suggest sauces be served with them. Sauces add flavor and give excitement to the food. The sauces in this section can be used to make the fish dish of your choice a big part of a fine meal.

Dips are flavorful thick "sauces," usually served cold although certain dips can be served hot. Dips add flavor to food, especially fried fish.

The pickles, compotes, chutneys, and salsas below also add taste to fish dishes. They can also replace rich sauces for fish dishes.

Hollandaise Sauce

YIELD 1 CUP (250 ML)

4 egg yolks
1 tablespoon (15 ml) hot water
½ pound (227 g) unsalted butter, diced small
A pinch of cayenne pepper
1 teaspoon (5 ml) lemon juice

DIRECTIONS

Use a double boiler to make hollandaise. Pour water about 1 inch (2.5 cm) deep into the bottom pan of the double boiler; place on low heat and bring the water to a slow simmer. Place the top pan of the double boiler over the pan of simmering water and add the egg yolks and the cold water. Start whisking the egg yolks and continue until the yolks are smooth. To the egg yolks add a spoonful of butter and whisk until the butter is absorbed. Continue adding the butter and whisking after each addition until all the butter is used. Continue to whisk until the sauce is thick and fluffy. Whisk in cayenne pepper, lemon juice, and salt to taste. The sauce should be used within an hour.

Sauce Beurre Blanc

*Sauce beurre blanc is a simple French sauce, made with wine, butter, and cream and seasoned with shallots. Because it is an emulsified butter sauce, care must be taken when preparing it to prevent it from "breaking," meaning the fat and the liquid will separate if the sauce is cooked on too high heat or too low heat. This sauce cannot be reheated either as reheating can cause it to break. It is best to prepare the sauce close to serving time. Hold the sauce in a **bain-marie** and serve the sauce hot or warm. If the sauce gets cold, the fat will congeal and the sauce will not be usable.*

YIELD 1½ CUPS (325 ML)

1 cup (250 ml) white wine
1 teaspoon (5 ml) white wine vinegar
1 tablespoon (15 ml) chopped shallots
1 cup (250 ml) cream
1 pound (454 g) unsalted butter, chilled and cut up into ¼-inch (0.64 cm) cubes
Salt
Black pepper
1 to 2 teaspoons (5 to 10 ml) lemon juice

DIRECTIONS

Place wine, vinegar, shallots, and cream in a saucepan, and on medium heat reduce to 1 cup (250 ml). Briskly whisk in the chilled butter cubes in small quantities and season with salt, pepper, and lemon juice to taste. The sauce should be emulsified and thick once the last piece of butter is incorporated into the sauce. Remove from the heat, strain, and serve hot or warm.

Wasabi Beurre Blanc

YIELD 1½ CUPS (325 ML)

1 cup (250 ml) white wine
1 teaspoon (5 ml) white wine
    vinegar
1 tablespoon (15 ml) chopped
    shallots
1 cup (250 ml) cream
1 pound (454 g) unsalted butter,
    chilled and cut up into ¼-inch
    (0.64 cm) cubes
1 to 2 teaspoons (5 to 10 ml) lemon
    juice
1 tablespoon (15 ml) moistened
    wasabi
2 teaspoons (10 ml) light soy sauce
Salt

DIRECTIONS

Place wine, vinegar, shallots, and cream in a saucepan, and on medium heat reduce to 1 cup (250 ml). Briskly whisk in the chilled butter cubes in small quantities and whisk in lemon juice, wasabi, and soy sauce. Check for seasoning and add a little salt if needed. Remove from heat, strain, and serve hot or warm.

Tomato Sauce

YIELD 1¼ CUPS (310 ML)

1 tablespoon (15 ml) olive oil
1 large onion, chopped
3 cups (325 ml) canned crushed
    plum tomatoes
1 garlic clove, crushed
1 sprig parsley, chopped
2 sprigs thyme
1 bay leaf
½ teaspoon (2.5 ml) crushed red
    pepper
1 to 2 teaspoons (5 to 10 ml) sugar,
    to taste
1 tablespoon (15 ml) Worcestershire
    sauce
½ cup (125 ml) white wine
Salt
Black pepper

DIRECTIONS

Heat olive oil in a pan; add onions and sauté on high heat until they are soft. Add the rest of the ingredients and simmer uncovered for 30 to 35 minutes on moderate heat; season with salt and pepper to taste. Remove and discard thyme and bay leaf and pass the sauce through a food mill.

Cocktail Sauce

YIELD 1 ½ PINT (325 ML)

2 cups (500 ml) tomato ketchup
½ cup (125 ml) chili sauce
¼ cup (60 ml) prepared horseradish
2 teaspoons (10 ml) Worcestershire sauce
1 teaspoon (5 ml) Tabasco sauce
1 tablespoon (15 ml) lemon juice

DIRECTIONS

Combine the ingredients in a bowl and mix till well combined. Refrigerate. Serve cold.

Tartar Sauce

YIELD 1 ½ PINTS (325 ML)

2 cups (500 ml) mayonnaise
1 tablespoon (15 ml) finely chopped gherkins
1 tablespoon (15 ml) finely chopped red onion
1 tablespoon (15 ml) coarsely chopped capers
1 tablespoon (15 ml) finely chopped parsley
1 tablespoon (15 ml) finely chopped celery
2 teaspoons (10 ml) Worcestershire sauce
2 teaspoons (10 ml) vinegar
¼ teaspoon (1.25 ml) black pepper

DIRECTIONS

Combine all the ingredients in a bowl and mix well. Keep refrigerated, covered, until ready to use.

Rémoulade Sauce

Rémoulade sauce is a French mayonnaise-based sauce; it is close to a tartar sauce except it is strikingly seasoned with mustard and anchovies. This sauce is especially good with seafood.

YIELD 1 PINT (500 ML)

- 1 pint (500 ml) **tartar sauce** (see On the Side)
- 1 tablespoon (15 ml) anchovy paste
- 1 tablespoon Dijon country mustard
- 1 teaspoon (5 ml) Tabasco sauce

DIRECTIONS

Make the tartar sauce, add and mix in the anchovy paste, mustard, and Tabasco. Keep refrigerated until ready to use.

Chili Crème Fraîche

Crème fraîche is a cultured dairy product similar to sour cream, tangy but thinner in texture. This product is available commercially. Crème fraîche has a rich taste, and mixed with a hot sauce or spices and herbs it makes a fine addition to any dish it partners.

YIELD 1 CUP (125 ML)

- 1 tablespoon (15 ml) **sriracha**
- 1 cup (125 ml) crème fraîche
- Salt
- 2 teaspoons (10 ml) finely chopped basil
- 2 teaspoons (10 ml) finely chopped green onion

DIRECTIONS

Add sriracha to the créme fraîche, stir, and season with salt to taste; fold in basil and green onion. Keep chilled until ready to serve.

Rouille

Rouille is a garlicky, spicy-hot sauce thickened with bread, egg yolks, and olive oil and seasoned with vinegar or lemon juice. This French preparation is very much like a mayonnaise, yet pasty, and is used as a topping to liven up fish stews and soups.

YIELD 1½ CUPS (325 ML)

- 1 thick slice of white bread, crust removed
- 2 ounces (60 ml) heavy cream
- 4 egg yolks
- 1 tablespoon (15 ml) finely chopped garlic
- 1 tablespoon (15 ml) hot water
- 6 ounces (177 ml) olive oil
- ½ teaspoon (2.5 ml) cayenne pepper
- Salt
- Black pepper
- 2 teaspoons (10 ml) lemon juice

DIRECTIONS

Place bread in a bowl; pour the cream over and let the bread soak. Place the egg yolks, garlic, and water in the bowl of a food processor. Squeeze the bread to remove most of the cream; discard the cream and add the soaked bread to the egg yolks; process while drizzling the olive oil in a steady stream. Add cayenne and salt and pepper to taste and process a second or two more with lemon. Keep refrigerated until ready to use.

Aïoli

Aïoli is a condiment, a home-made mayonnaise laden with garlic. It originated in the Provence region of France.

YIELD 1½ CUPS (325 ML)

- 4 egg yolks
- 1 tablespoon (15 ml) hot water
- 1 tablespoon (30 ml) finely minced garlic
- 2 cups (500 ml) olive oil
- Salt
- 1 tablespoon (15 ml) lemon juice

DIRECTIONS

Place egg yolks and water in the bowl of a food processor and process for a few seconds. Add the garlic and process for a few seconds. Add the olive oil in a steady stream as you process for a few seconds, adding salt and lemon juice to taste. Store the aïoli in the refrigerator until ready to use.

Anchovy Dip

....
YIELD 1½ CUPS (325 ML)
....

6 anchovy fillets
¼ cup milk
1 teaspoon (5 ml) chopped shallots
1 teaspoon (5 ml) chopped garlic
1 teaspoon (5 ml) chopped green
   onion
1 tablespoon (15 ml) capers
1 tablespoon (15 ml) chopped
   pickles
½ cup (125 ml) chopped parsley
1 teaspoon (5 ml) black pepper
¼ cup (60 ml) lemon juice
1 cup (250 ml) olive oil

DIRECTIONS

Place anchovy fillets in milk for 20 minutes. Remove anchovies from the milk
and wipe off the salt; add the fillets to
the other ingredients and process in a
food processor, drizzling in the olive oil
in a stream. When the ingredients are
blended, spoon the dip into a bowl. The
dip should be chunky, not overblended
to a puree.

Roasted Garlic

*Choose plump garlic bulbs and use
them unpeeled for roasting. Roasting
removes the bitterness and brings out
the sweetness in them. Roasted mashed
garlic may be used to enrich condiments and sauces. Sometimes it is
served on toast.*

....
YIELD ¾ CUP (185 ML)
....

4 garlic bulbs
½ teaspoon (2.5 ml) salt
3 tablespoons (45 ml) olive oil
1 tablespoon water (15 ml) water

DIRECTIONS

Preheat the oven to 350°F (175°C). Slice
about ¼ inch (6 mm) off the leaf sides of
the garlic bulbs. Place in a roasting pan
and sprinkle with salt and olive oil. Pour
the water into the roasting pan; this will
create a little moisture and prevent the
garlic from browning too much. Cover
roasting pan and roast for 30 to 35 minutes. Remove from the oven, cool, peel,
and mash. Use right away or refrigerate
and use as needed. Once refrigerated,
the roasted garlic must be used within
a day or two.

Garlic Butter

Garlic butter is a compound butter. Compound butters are made by adding a variety of seasoning and flavoring ingredients to softened butter and then whisking to a light and fluffy consistency. The butter is then enclosed in foil or parchment paper and rolled into log shapes kept handy in the freezer. These butter logs are sliced when ready to use and placed on simply grilled or broiled fish; the butter melts over the fish and coats it like a sauce.

YIELD 2 POUNDS (907 G)

2 pounds (907 g) unsalted butter at room temperature
¼ cup (60 ml) Worcestershire sauce
½ cup (125 ml) minced garlic
1 teaspoon (5 ml) salt
1 teaspoon (5 ml) black pepper
1 tablespoon (15 ml) sherry
1 tablespoon (15 ml) lemon juice
1 tablespoon (15 ml) chopped parsley
1 tablespoon (15 ml) anchovy paste or anchovies mashed to a paste

DIRECTIONS

Place butter in a mixing machine with the rest of the ingredients. Mix till light and fluffy. Divide into 8 portions. Roll up each portion in foil or parchment paper and twist the two ends of each roll to make the roll airtight. Freeze and use as needed. Garlic butter keeps well in the freezer for 2 months.

Pickled Lemons

Pickles are foods that are preserved in a seasoned vinegar or citrus solution. Pickles are also seasoned and aromatized with herbs and spices and are commonly served as a condiment. The pickled lemon given here may be used in preparing the famous Moroccan dish **Fish Tagine** *(see recipe for* **Snapper Tagine** *in Entrées). Pickled lemon can also be chopped up and served as a condiment.*

YIELD 20 TO 24 SERVINGS

6 large lemons
1 tablespoon (15 ml) salt
1 tablespoon (15 ml) **cumin** seeds
½ teaspoon (2.5 ml) cracked black peppercorns
2-inch (5 cm) piece of **cinnamon** stick
6 lemons, juiced and juice refrigerated

DIRECTIONS

Wash and wipe the lemons with a kitchen towel. Make 4 cuts lengthwise at the flower end on each lemon to allow the wedges to open out like a flower yet still stay attached at the stem end. Mix salt, cumin, and peppercorns, and stuff the lemons, gently pressing the wedges back together like an almost closed flower. Place in a sterilized glass jar, add the piece of cinnamon stick, cover the jar tightly and refrigerate for 3 days. On the third day, place the refrigerated lemon juice in a pan and bring to a boil. Remove the jar of salted lemons from the refrigerator and pour in the boiled lemon juice. Cool and cover the jar tightly. Place in the refrigerator and invert the jar every 2 to 3 days to mix the flavors; keep refrigerated for 1 month. Keep refrigerated and use as required.

Preserved Lemon Wheels

Preserves are made from fresh or dried fruits cooked in sugar syrup, sometimes enhanced with spices that can be hot and spicy. These lemon slices may be used as a garnish. The syrup may be used to enrich sauces or to glaze broiled or grilled fish.

YIELD 1 PINT (500 ML)

4 lemons, sliced ⅛ inch (3.2 millimeter) thick
2 cups (500 ml) cold water
1 tablespoon (15 ml) salt
¾ cup (185 ml) sugar
½ cup (125 ml) honey
1½ cups (325 ml) water
4 whole **cloves**
½-inch (1.28 cm) piece of **cinnamon** stick

DIRECTIONS

Place the sliced lemons in a bowl, cover with the 2 cups (500 ml) of cold water, sprinkle with salt, and set aside for 30 minutes. Place sugar, honey, and water in a stainless steel saucepan and add the spices. Place on medium heat and bring to a slow simmer. Lower heat and simmer for 10 minutes. Drain the lemon slices from the salted water (discard the salted water); wash in fresh water and add to the syrup. Simmer for 20 minutes until the lemon wheels turn transparent. Cool and put all lemon slices and the syrup into a sterilized jar. Cover tightly and refrigerate. Use as required.

Harissa

This is a hot and spicy condiment. It is simple yet adds a fiery flavor and interest to bland food.

YIELD 1 CUP (250 ML)

24 hot dried red chilies
½ cup (125 ml) water
1 tablespoon (15 ml) **coriander** seed
1 tablespoon (15 ml) **cumin** seed
4 garlic cloves, sliced
1 teaspoon (5 ml) salt
¼ cup (60 ml) olive oil

DIRECTIONS

Stem the chilies and soak in the water for 30 minutes; drain off and discard water. Heat a skillet and dry roast the coriander and cumin seeds till crisp; using a spice grinder, grind them to a fine powder. Using a mortar and pestle, pound the garlic, softened chilies, and roasted ground spices with salt to a smooth paste. Pour the olive oil in a stream and continue to pound in a rolling motion, until the mixture is emulsified and smooth. Spoon into an airtight jar and refrigerate. Keeps well for 2 to 3 weeks.

Chermoula

This is an interesting condiment that can be spooned over stews or used as a dip for fried fish; it can also be used as a marinade before the fish is dipped in flour and deep-fried.

YIELD ¾ CUP (185 ML)

¼ cup (60 ml) olive oil
2 tablespoons (30 ml) vinegar
Juice of 1 lemon
1 teaspoon (5 ml) ground **cumin**
1 teaspoon (5 ml) paprika
1 teaspoon (5 ml) cayenne pepper
1 fresh red chili, seeded and finely
   chopped
½ cup (125 ml) finely chopped
   cilantro
½ cup (125 ml) finely chopped mint
1 tablespoon (15 ml) minced garlic
Salt

DIRECTIONS

Place olive oil, vinegar, and lemon juice in a bowl and whisk together; add the rest of the ingredients with salt to taste and continue to whisk until all are well combined. Use fresh.

Tomato and Apricot Chutney

Chutney is an Indian condiment made with fruit or vegetables, cooked or sometimes uncooked, in a mix of vinegar, sugar, and spices. Chutney flavors range from mild to hot. Chutnies are very popular today.

....

YIELD 2 CUPS (500 ML)

....

2 tablespoons (30 ml) olive oil

½ teaspoon (2.5 ml) **cumin** seeds

½ teaspoon (2.5 ml) **fennel** seeds

½ teaspoon (2.5 ml) **black mustard** seeds

½ teaspoon (2.5 ml) crushed red pepper

4 cloves garlic, finely chopped

1 tablespoon (15 ml) finely chopped ginger

½ cup (125 ml) sugar

½ cup (125 ml) white vinegar

Salt

1½ pounds (680 g) plum tomatoes, cut into small dice

½ cup (125 ml) dried apricots, cut into small dice

DIRECTIONS

Heat the oil in a sauté pan and on medium heat fry cumin, fennel, and black mustard seeds. When mustard seeds star to pop, add crushed red pepper flakes, garlic, and ginger. Turn heat to low and cook for a few seconds. Add sugar, vinegar, and salt to taste and bring to a simmer. Stir in tomatoes and apricots and cook on low heat for 40 minutes until the chutney is thick. Cool and place in a sterilized jar. Cover and refrigerate. The chutney keeps well up to one month.

Fresh Mint Chutney

YIELD ¾ CUP (185 ML)

1 cup (250 ml) mint leaves
½ cup (125 ml) plain yogurt
1 teaspoon (5 ml) chopped shallots
1 teaspoon (5 ml) chopped ginger
1 green chili, seeded and
    chopped
2 tablespoons (30 ml) lemon juice
2 tablespoons (30 ml) water
1 teaspoon (5 ml) sugar
Salt

DIRECTIONS

Place all the ingredients in a food processor with salt to taste, and process till smooth. Cover and refrigerate. Keeps for a day or two.

Fruit Salsa

Salsa is a cold "sauce" made with fruit or vegetables, flavored with onions and herbs and seasoned with vinegar, citrus juice, and salt. Salsas may be hot, medium, or mild.

YIELD 2 CUPS (500 ML)

½ peeled, cored, and diced fresh
    pineapple
1 cup (250 ml) diced strawberries
½ peeled, diced mango
¼ cup (60 ml) diced onion
2 jalapeño peppers, seeded and
    chopped
1 tablespoon (15 ml) chopped
    ginger
½ cup (125 ml) chopped mint
2 tablespoons (30 ml) orange juice
Juice of 2 limes
Salt

DIRECTIONS

Combine all the ingredients in a bowl with a pinch of salt. Refrigerate and serve chilled.

Spinach Raita

*Raita is an Indian salad, yogurt or curd based, with fruit or vegetables and enhanced with spices such as **cumin**, **black mustard seed**, and spice mixes like **garam masala**.*

YIELD 4 SERVINGS

3 cups (750 ml) spinach leaves, washed and trimmed
1 teaspoon (5 ml) butter
½ teaspoon (2.5 ml) **cumin**
½ teaspoon (2.5 ml) **fenugreek**
½ teaspoon (2.5 ml) **black mustard seed**
¼ teaspoon (1.25 ml) crushed red pepper
¼ teaspoon (1.25 ml) black pepper
½ teaspoon (2.5 ml) salt
1½ cups (325 ml) yogurt

DIRECTIONS

Place the spinach in a sauté pan and place on high heat. (The pan does not need any fat or water. There is enough moisture in the spinach to allow the spinach to wilt.) Use a pair of tongs and move the spinach around in the hot pan until it wilts, about a minute; set aside. Heat butter in a small sauté pan and fry the cumin, fenugreek, and mustard seeds until the seeds start to pop. Immediately remove the pan from the heat and stir in red and black pepper and salt and let cool. Whisk the yogurt and stir into the spices along with the wilted spinach leaves. Serve warm or cold.

Cucumber Raita

YIELD 4 SERVINGS

. . . .

2 cucumbers

Salt

½ cup (125 ml) plain yogurt

½ teaspoon (2.5 ml) ground **cumin**

1 tablespoon (15 ml) chopped fresh
dill

1 tablespoon (15 ml) lemon juice

½ teaspoon (2.5 ml) black pepper

½ teaspoon (2.5 ml) sugar

DIRECTIONS

Peel cucumbers, cut each in half lengthwise, and scoop out and discard the
seeds if any. Slice thinly, sprinkle with a
teaspoon of salt, and set aside for half an
hour. Place the cucumber in a strainer
and push out all the liquid. Discard the
liquid; set aside the cucumbers. Put the
rest of the ingredients into a bowl and
whisk till smooth. Add the cucumber
and toss with salt to taste. Refrigerate
until ready to use.

Cucumber Relish

*Relish is a cooked or uncooked "sauce"
made with cooked or uncooked fruits
or vegetables, with seasonings varying
from mild to hot.*

. . . .

YIELD 1 CUP (250 ML)

. . . .

1 seedless cucumber, peeled and
thinly sliced

1 teaspoon (5 ml) minced ginger

1 **serrano chili**, thinly sliced

1 teaspoon (5 ml) chopped cilantro

3 tablespoons (45 ml) rice wine
vinegar

2 teaspoons (10 ml) sugar

Salt

Lime juice

DIRECTIONS

Toss all together with salt and lime juice
to taste.

Marinated Cucumber

Marinated cucumber tastes like a pickle and goes well with spicy food, especially satay.

YIELD 6 SERVINGS

2 medium cucumbers
Salt
½ cup (125 ml) white wine vinegar
2 tablespoons (30 ml) sugar

DIRECTIONS

Peel the cucumbers. Cut them in half lengthwise and remove and discard the seeds. Slice the cucumber diagonally into thin slices. Place the cucumber slices in a bowl and sprinkle generously with salt. Let sit for about 15 minutes, then place in a colander and squeeze out liquid. Place the cucumber slices in a salad bowl, add the vinegar and sugar to taste, and mix well. Leave to marinate for half an hour before serving.

Tomato Relish

YIELD 4 SERVINGS

1 cup (250 ml) diced tomatoes
1 tablespoon (15 ml) chopped cilantro
2 tablespoons (30 ml) chopped mint
1 teaspoon (5 ml) crushed red pepper
1 tablespoon (15 ml) **fish sauce**
1 jalapeño pepper, chopped
Juice of 1 lemon
½ teaspoon (2.5 ml) sugar
Salt

DIRECTIONS

Mix all the ingredients in a glass bowl with salt to taste. Refrigerate for an hour before serving.

Tomato and Onion Relish

YIELD 4 SERVINGS

1 large beefsteak tomato, cored, halved, and seeded

½ red onion, sliced very fine and soaked in water for 10 minutes

½ cup (125 ml) shredded basil leaves

¼ teaspoon (1.25 ml) crushed red pepper

½ teaspoon (2.5 ml) cracked black pepper

1 tablespoon (15 ml) cider vinegar

1 tablespoon (15 ml) lemon juice

Salt

DIRECTIONS

Slice tomatoes very thin and place in a bowl. Drain water from the onion, squeeze out the excess water, and add the onions to the tomatoes. Add basil, red and black pepper, vinegar, and lemon juice; season with salt to taste and mix well to combine. Serve immediately after mixing.

THE BASICS

STOCKS

Fish Stock

Fish Fumet

Court Bouillon

Nage

BATTERS

Simple Batter for Fish

Hot Beer Batter

STOCKS

Fish stock is a colorless liquid, clear and full of flavor and aroma extracted by slowly simmering fish bones with the addition of water, vegetables, and herbs for additional flavor. Fish stock and fish fumet are very similar, but wine and/or lemon juice is added for a fumet, and the result is more pronounced flavor. Court bouillon is a flavored liquid made with water, wine, vegetables, and seasonings. It is known as a "short" broth, simple and fast to produce. It is usually prepared fresh, unlike a stock, which takes time to prepare. A nage is an aromatic court bouillon, reduced and enriched with cream and butter and served as a light sauce for fish.

Fish bones are the most important ingredient in a fish stock; they add flavor and richness. Fish bones and trimmings of lean fish make the best stocks. Fish heads and bones from fatty fish like salmon and tuna are not commonly used to make stock. If you use fish heads for stock, the gills must be removed and discarded and the heads must be thoroughly washed under running water before use. Another basic ingredient for a fish stock is vegetables; the vegetables should be diced small or sliced thin so that all their flavors can be extracted during the short cooking time specified for stock. Herbs and spices are tied up in a **sachet** and added to enhance the flavor and aroma of the stock.

Making a good fish stock starts with cutting the fish bones into 2-inch (5 cm) pieces. The bones must be thoroughly washed under running cold water to ensure they are devoid of any blood, scales, or other impurities. Impurities can result in a cloudy, strong-flavored fish stock. The stock should not be cooked for more than 40 minutes once it starts to simmer, as specified in the recipe, because flavors begin to break down after a period of time. Skim and discard the scum that comes to the surface. Do this often, otherwise the scum will break up and mix into the stock or fumet. Take care not to boil the stock; boiling will break up the impurities and fats into minute particles and blend with the liquid, resulting in a cloudy stock. Always keep the bones covered with water while cooking; bones exposed to air will turn a dark color and in turn will discolor the liquid. Fish stock and fumet may be held in the refrigerator for two to three days or kept frozen for a month.

Fish Stock

YIELD 1 TO 1½ QUARTS (0.95 TO 1.4 L)

2 leeks, thinly sliced

1 medium onion, cut into small
  dice

2 celery stalks, thinly sliced

4 ounces (113 g) mushrooms, thinly
  sliced

4 parsley stems

4 pounds (1.8 kg) fish bones, washed
  and cut into 2-inch (5 cm) pieces

3 quarts (2.8 L) cold water

Sachet

1 bay leaf

2-inch (5 cm) piece of **cinnamon**
  stick

1 teaspoon (5 ml) black
  peppercorns, crushed

DIRECTIONS

Place all the ingredients in a stock pot.
Bring to a simmer. Skim the surface of
the stock as often as necessary. Simmer
for 35 to 40 minutes. Strain the stock
through a strainer lined with cheesecloth. Cool and refrigerate the stock.
Freeze the stock if not used within 3 to
4 days. Use in soups, stews, and sauces
as called for in recipes. Add salt as
needed.

Fish Fumet

*A fish stock and a fish fumet can be
used interchangeably when cooking
fish. Instead of the water in the fumet,
you may substitute fish stock to cook the
fumet. This results in a richer fumet.*

YIELD 1 QUART (0.95 L)

1 tablespoon butter or olive oil

2 leeks, washed and sliced

1 onion, thinly sliced

2 celery stalks, thinly sliced

4 parsley stems

4 pounds (1.8 kg) fish bones, washed
  and cut into 2-inch (5 cm) pieces

1 cup (250 ml) dry white wine

2 quarts (1.9 L) cold water

1 lemon, thinly sliced

2-inch (5 cm) piece of **cinnamon**
  stick

1 teaspoon (5 ml) black
  peppercorns

DIRECTIONS

Heat butter or olive oil in a stockpot;
add the vegetables and fish bones. Cover
the stockpot, and on low heat, allow
the vegetables and fish bones to sweat
for 5 minutes. Pour in the wine and
water. Add the rest of the ingredients
and bring to a simmer. Cook for 35 to
40 minutes, skimming frequently. Strain
through a strainer lined with a cheesecloth. Cool and refrigerate. Use as called
for in recipes. Add salt as needed.

Court Bouillon

A court bouillon is a simple preparation often used to poach fish. It is made like a stock with water, wine or vinegar, vegetables, and seasonings simmered together to impart their flavors and aroma.

YIELD 1 QUART (0.95 L)

2 quarts (1.9 L) water

1 ounce (28 g) vinegar

1 lemon, juiced and strained

1 teaspoon (5 ml) salt

2 leeks, thinly sliced

2 celery stems, thinly sliced

1 medium onion, cut into small dice

½ tsp (2.5 ml) crushed black peppercorns

1 small bay leaf

3 parsley stems

1-inch (2.5 cm) piece of **cinnamon** stick

DIRECTIONS

Combine all the ingredients in a pan and bring to a slow boil. Reduce heat and bring to a slow simmer. Cook for 40 minutes and strain. Use as called for in recipes.

Nage

The flavorful nage is made by reducing the liquid fish is cooked in, with additional herbs and aromatic vegetables like leeks. This flavorful liquid is strained, and for the final touch butter and cream or a sauce beurre blanc is whisked in. This smooth, thin luscious sauce is served in a pool under cooked fish as in **Braised Goatfish** (see Entrées).

YIELD 6 OUNCES (177 ML)

4 cups (1L) water

2 cups (500 ml) dry white wine

¼ cup (60 ml) white vinegar

2 tablespoons (30 ml) chopped shallots

1 cup (250 ml) chopped tomatoes

1 cup (250 ml) sliced leeks

1 cup (250 ml) sliced celery

½ cup (125 ml) chopped onion

1 teaspoon (5 ml) crushed black peppercorns

1 sprig of fresh thyme

1 bay leaf

Salt

DIRECTIONS

Place all the ingredients in a saucepan and simmer for an hour. Strain and use to cook fish as required.

BATTERS

Batters are fairly thick mixtures containing a starch such as flour and a liquid such as water, beer, or milk, with or without the addition of egg. Batters are used to dip food in before deep-frying. They give a protective coating to fried food, help to preserve moisture and flavor, and above all give a desirable crispness to the finished product.

Simple Batter for Fish

YIELDS 2 CUPS (500 ML)

1 cup (250 ml) all-purpose flour
Salt
¼ teaspoon (1.25 ml) cayenne
   pepper
1 tablespoon (15 ml) olive oil
1 to 1¼ cup (250 to 310 ml) water or
   milk
1 teaspoon (5 ml) chopped parsley
2 egg whites

DIRECTIONS

Sift the flour into a bowl, add salt and cayenne pepper. Gradually add the oil and water or milk, and whisk vigorously until smooth. Stir in the parsley. Cover the bowl of batter and leave at room temperature for 1 hour. Beat the egg whites to soft peaks. Fold into the batter and use immediately.

Hot Beer Batter

YIELD 3 CUPS (750 ML)

5 ounces (142 g) self-rising flour
1 ounce (28 g) rice flour
½ teaspoon (2.5 ml) cayenne
   pepper
Salt
2 tablespoons (30 ml) olive oil
1 cup (250 ml) beer
2 egg whites

DIRECTIONS

Place flours and cayenne in a bowl with salt to taste. Drizzle in the olive oil and the beer and whisk briskly with a wire whisk. Whisk till the batter is smooth and lump free. Cover the batter and set aside for 1 hour. In a separate bowl whisk the egg whites to soft peaks and fold into the batter and use immediately.

Which Fish Is This?
Common Names and Substitutions

Many people are often confused as to which fish they are actually buying. The same fish can go by a variety of names, and many similar-looking fish are actually separate species within a family. This makes identifying fishes properly a difficult task. Various colloquial names are given to the same fish, or the same name is used to refer to a number of different fishes. Adding to the confusion, some fishes are referred to by foreign names. The following list of commonly available fishes gives both American and Hawaiian names as well as common names used around the world. It offers comprehensive information and suggestions for substitutions that will help simplify the selection of fish. For ease of use, the list is organized alphabetically by common American or Western name. The descriptions follow the order of the common names as listed. The key below gives a handy outline of common and local names.

COMMON NAME	LOCAL NAME	COMMON NAME	LOCAL NAME
Anchovy	*Nehu*	Mullet	*'Ama'ama*
Bass or Sea Bass		Salmon, Atlantic	
Black Cod		Salmon, Pacific	
Butterfish		Scad	*Akule*
Cod		Sea Bass or Grouper	*Hāpu'upu'u*
Dorado	*Mahimahi*	Smelt	
Goatfish	*Kūmū*	Snapper, Gray	*Uku*
Halibut		Snapper, Long-tail Red	*Onaga*
Herring		Snapper, Pink	*'Ōpakapaka*
Jackfish	*Ulua*	Snapper, Short-tail Red	*'Ehu*
Kingfish	*Ono*	Swordfish	*Shutome*
Mackerel Scad	*'Ōpelu*	Threadfin	*Moi*
Marlin	*Kajiki*	Trout	
Moonfish	*Opah*	Tuna	*'Ahi*

LOCAL NAME	COMMON NAME	LOCAL NAME	COMMON NAME
'Ahi	Tuna	*Nehu*	Anchovy
Akule	Scad	*Onaga*	Long-tail Red Snapper
'Ama'ama	Mullet	*Ono*	Kingfish
'Ehu	Short-tail Red Snapper	*Opah*	Moonfish
Hāpu'upu'u	Sea Bass or Grouper	*'Ōpakapaka*	Pink snapper
Kajiki	Marlin	*'Ōpelu*	Mackerel Scad
Kūmū	Goatfish	*Shutome*	Swordfish
Mahimahi	Dorado	*Uku*	Gray Snapper
Moi	Threadfin	*Ulua*	Jackfish

Anchovy or Nehu (*Encrasicholina purpurea*)

COMMON NAME: Hawaiian anchovy

SUBSTITUTION: Smelts

QUALITY, FLAVOR, AND PREPARATION: Anchovies are small fish you can gut through the head. Take hold of the head with your thumb and forefinger and pull out the gills along with the guts (viscera) by twisting the head; discard. Larger anchovies can be gutted with the head on. After gutting, fish should be washed thoroughly by rinsing in a colander with cold running water, then drained and patted dry using a towel. Larger anchovies like those from the Mediterranean may be gutted and grilled or broiled. The smaller ones may be tossed lightly in seasoned flour, deep-fried and served with a dipping sauce such as cocktail sauce. Because fish such as anchovies, herrings, and sardines have bones that are soft and harmless when cooked, they are edible and are good sources of calcium. Anchovies make a good appetizer or side dish as in an Asian meal, but they are hardly ever served as an entrée. They are delicious and soft textured when cooked. Available fresh or frozen, a quarter pound of anchovies makes an appetizer portion.

CHARACTERISTICS AND HABITAT: Anchovy or *nehu* is in the family Engraulidae, the anchovy fish family that has approximately 139 species in many oceans around the world. It is an important tuna bait fish in Hawai'i. Anchovies are small, frail fishes of the shoreline areas; they also frequently inhabit the waters of bays and estuaries. Anchovies gather in large schools at which time they are captured in nets and used for bait. Their eggs hatch in a few days and grow rapidly into their adult form. They have silvery heads, compressed bodies with round full bellies, and widely forked tails. About four inches long, their bodies are a silvery greenish or brownish color with wide longitudinal silvery white stripes running horizontally on each side of their bodies from head to tail.

Bass

BLACK SEA BASS (*Centropristis striata*)
CHILEAN SEA BASS (*Dissostichus eleginoides*)
STRIPED SEA BASS (*Morone saxatilis*)

COMMON NAMES: Black sea bass: black fish, black Will; Chilean sea bass: white sea bass; striped sea bass: rock bass, striper

SUBSTITUTION: Sablefish, grouper

QUALITY, FLAVOR, AND PREPARATION: The flesh of sea bass is firm, lean and white in color. It has a sweet flavor when very fresh and is suitable to many cooking methods. The beauty of the fishes, especially the black bass, is in its skin, so it is at its best when cooked whole to show off the skin.

Dressed with the head on, steamed Chinese style is one of the best methods of cooking sea bass. Bass weighing around 2 pounds (907 g) or less cooked whole make a perfect single serving. Be sure to scale, eviscerate, and rinse before steaming, grilling, poaching, or baking. Bass have simple bone structures; the flesh can be lifted off the bone easily when cooked. These fishes have become popular menu items in major cities around the world. The black bass is often sold whole. Chilean bass is mainly available in fillet form, fresh and frozen. Farmed hybrid freshwater striped bass is freely available and is a good product although not on par with the wild bass.

CHARACTERISTICS AND HABITAT:

BLACK SEA BASS (*Centropristis striata*)
The black sea bass belongs to the family Serranidae, a large family of marine and freshwater fishes. Black sea bass are protogynous hermaphrodites, meaning that they are born as females and reverse their sex as they age and grow larger. This usually happens between the ages of two and four years. They are bottom fish and live in shallow coastal waters; in the winter they migrate offshore and are found in areas with hard substrates and rocks. They prey on crabs, mussels, clams, shrimp, and isopods. They are known to live as long as twenty years. The black skin of the black sea bass has a light coloring under the scales, and the black spiny fins have white markings.

CHILEAN SEA BASS (*Dissostichus eleginoides*)

The term "Chilean sea bass" comes from the fact that the fish was first commercially harvested in Chilean waters. Now the fish are caught off the coasts of Argentina, South Africa, and Australia. Chilean sea bass is not a sea bass at all; it is the Patagonian toothfish and belongs to the family Nototheniidae. This slow-growing species lives up to forty-five years and grows up to 35 pounds (16 kg). Because of their size they yield large fillets, and their snow-white flesh is firm. They are very much in demand for their rich oily flavor. They are highly regarded in Japan and China and much in demand in the United States, but the flow of fish to the latter country is affected by the conditions in the two Asian markets.

STRIPED SEA BASS (*Morone saxatilis*)

Striped bass belong to the Moronidae family and are native to the Atlantic coast of North America. They live in both saltwater and freshwater, where they spawn. This fish is one of the most beautiful fishes, shading from steely blue to olive green above with a silvery white belly and horizontal stripes along the sides. Their flesh has a fine texture and delicious taste. The fish grow up to about 125 pounds (56.7 kg), but the average size caught is around 50 pounds (22.6 kg). Farm-raised bass are available at weights ranging from 2 to 3 pounds (907 g to 1.4 kg). In certain places the striped bass is mainly reserved for sport fishing. Farmed freshwater striped bass is freely available and is a good product although not on a par with the wild bass.

Black Cod or Sablefish (*Anoplopoma fimbria*)

COMMON NAMES: Alaska cod, butterfish

SUBSTITUTION: Butterfish, Pacific cod, Atlantic cod

QUALITY, FLAVOR, AND PREPARATION: When cooked the flesh of sablefish is white with velvety, soft-textured flakes. Its rich, sweet-buttery flavor is due to its high fat content and recalls its other name, butterfish.

    Sablefish is marketed whole, as well as in fillets, steaks, and chunks in fresh or frozen form. It is also available smoked and cured. The fillets and steaks are best when grilled, broiled, or baked, and the chunks are best when roasted.

CHARACTERISTICS AND HABITAT: Sablefish is in the family Anoplomatidae. Also known as Alaska cod, black cod, and butterfish, it is actually neither a cod nor a butterfish. It is a sleek fish, ranging in color from blue black to gray with almost furry skin and pearly white flesh. Sablefish range in size from 10 to 80 pounds (4.5 to 36 kg). They are found in the North Pacific and are mostly caught in the cold Alaskan waters by trawlers and fish traps.

Butterfish or Pacific Butterfish (*Peprilus simillimus*)

COMMON NAMES: Pacific pompano, Pacific pomfret, California pompano

SUBSTITUTION: Atlantic butterfish, pompano, pomfret, sablefish, halibut

QUALITY, FLAVOR, AND PREPARATION: The butterfish gets its name from its very high fat content. Both species of butterfish have a mild, pleasing flavor and a very delicate texture. Because of its high fat content butterfish is best when panfried or broiled. Butterfish are available dressed, pan-dressed, and butterflied. As their flesh is oily, they are ideal for smoking. When cooked, the gray color flesh turns flaky and white.

CHARACTERISTICS AND HABITAT: Pacific butterfish is in the family Stromateidae and is a close relative of the Atlantic butterfish also known as American butterfish (*Peprilus triacanthus*). Atlantic butterfish in a salted form was first introduced to the Hawaiian Islands by New England whaling crews. In *lau lau*, a favorite Hawaiian dish, the essential components are salted butterfish and pork, which are wrapped in taro leaves and steamed. A Hawaiian luau is not complete without *lau lau*. Pacific butterfish are around 6 to 9 inches in length (15 to 23 cm), ½ to 1 pound (227 to 454 g) in weight. They are a silvery bluish color with a prominent forked tail.

Atlantic Cod (*Gadus morhua*)
Pacific Cod (*Gadus macrocephalus*)

COMMON NAMES: Atlantic: codfish, cod; Pacific cod: brown cod, true cod

SUBSTITUTION: Sablefish, butterfish

QUALITY, FLAVOR, AND PREPARATION: The more mature fish have firmer flesh; the younger fish have softer, flakier flesh. All fish of the cod family become tender when cooked and have large V-shaped flakes. Consequently, the butter or a sauce can embed itself between the flakes. Cod freezes well, and much of the Pacific cod is marketed mainly frozen and sold as "true cod" to distinguish it from "black cod," the market name for sablefish. It is marketed dressed, in fillets, and in steaks, fresh or in frozen form.

Cod may be poached in an oven, steamed, braised, or stewed. Cod are delicious deep-fried, broiled, and baked and are equally good in salad preparations. The flesh is low in fat but high in calories. Cod is also available salted, smoked, and canned. Salt-cured cod is delicious sautéed or baked and served with a sauce or in soups and stews. Though salt-cured, it should not taste too salty. To pick the best salt-cured cod, make sure the flesh is white and the skin dark and intact. Salt-cured cod should be soaked at least 12 hours and the water changed 4 to 5 times before preparation.

CHARACTERISTICS AND HABITAT: The cod belongs to the Gadidae family and includes both Atlantic and Pacific cod, haddock, pollock, hake, whiting, and many other fishes. Cod has a long history as a food fish. The early colonists made a fortune from this abundant fish. Cod was salt cured then, and it still remains very popular in most European countries. The Atlantic cod lives on both sides of the Atlantic, but now most are caught off Iceland and Norway. The Pacific cod comes from the northern part of the Pacific Ocean. It is similar to the Atlantic cod but smaller in size and not so plentiful. The skin color of the cod ranges from gray to olive green and brown shading to shiny white at the belly, and it has a white lateral line running from head to tail and a hooked, fleshy barbell under the jaw. The average cod taken is around 10 to 15 pounds (4.5 to 6.8 kg).

Dorado or Mahimahi (*Coryphaena hippurus*)

COMMON NAMES: *Mahimahi:* dorado, dolphinfish, dolphin

SUBSTITUTION: *Ono*, swordfish, sea bass, grouper, halibut

QUALITY, FLAVOR, AND PREPARATION: *Mahimahi* is available in fillet form with or without the coarse skin. The skin should be removed before cooking. The almost flaky light pink flesh turns white and firm textured when cooked. *Mahimahi* is available in fillets or steaks. It has a delicate, luscious, sweet flavor and can be cooked in many different ways. It can be broiled or grilled in fillet or steak form, sautéed, blackened, or stir-fried. As with all lean fish, care should be taken not to overcook. To preserve the moisture and avoid dryness, it should be cooked only until the meat flakes when tested with a fork, and no longer.

CHARACTERISTICS AND HABITAT: *Mahimahis* of the Coryphaenidae family. It is a very active, fast-growing, warm water, open ocean fish. The name "dolphin" is confusing since it is also the name of the aquatic mammal, the porpoise. Dorado is the Spanish name for this fish. It is one of the most gorgeous among fishes, colored with iridescent shades of sea green and emerald on its silvery purplish blue skin. It is a brilliant yellow on its flat-sided body and belly. Once dead, it quickly becomes plain dull gray in color. It swims at such terrific speed it can flush its prey up into the air and catch them as they fall back. The male *mahimahi* has a blunt, square, heavy-looking forehead and approaches 70 pounds (31.8 kg). The female has a more rounded forehead and weighs much less. The preferred market size of the fish is over 15 pounds (6.8 kg). In Hawai'i, most of these fish are caught by trollers and are between 10 to 30 pounds (4.5 to 13.6 kg). *Mahimahi* is caught year round with the peak being late spring and early fall. The local catch is seasonal, and is in high demand. A common sport fish in Hawai'i, *mahimahi* is one of the best-known restaurant fare and remains a tourist favorite among the other excellent Hawai'i fishes prepared for the table.

Goatfish or Kūmū (*Parupeneus porphyreus*)

COMMON NAMES: Surmullet, white-spot goatfish, white-saddle goatfish

SUBSTITUTION: Mullet, any fish in the goatfish family

QUALITY, FLAVOR, AND PREPARATION: Goatfish are available whole and are best when cooked whole. They must be drawn and thoroughly cleaned before cooking. This delicate fish is best when steamed or grilled. It may also be deep-fried or filleted and poached. The larger *kūmū* is excellent when braised. Care should be taken not to overcook this delicate, soft-fleshed fish.

CHARACTERISTICS AND HABITAT: Goatfish or *kūmū*, of the family Mullidae, are among the most prized fishes in Hawai'i, and they played an important role in early Hawai'i sacrificial ceremonies. *Kūmū* are found only in Hawai'i. Goatfish include other well-known species such as *weke* and *moana*. Members of this colorful family are easily recognizable by the pair of whiskers or barbels attached to the tips of their lower jaws. The body of the *kūmū* is purplish red; one of its most distinguishing features is the dark diagonal line running through its eye from the snout towards the dorsal fin. This fish grows to almost 16 inches (41 cm) in length, but most caught are around 7 to 8 inches (18 to 20 cm) in length. They are reef fish and are common in the shallow waters year round.

Halibut

PACIFIC HALIBUT (*Hippoglossus stenolepis*)
ATLANTIC HALIBUT (*Hippoglossus hypoglossus*)

COMMON NAMES: Atlantic halibut: topknot, flounder; Pacific halibut: Alaska long-line halibut

SUBSTITUTION: Sablefish

QUALITY, FLAVOR, AND PREPARATION: Halibut has pure white flesh with a fine grain and firm texture; it is lean and mild tasting. It is light and low in fat and lends itself to just about any kind of recipe from broiling, grilling, and steaming to braising and stir-frying. Because of its firm texture it holds its shape and is a favorite for skewering on brochettes for grilling. It is marketed in fillet or steak forms. Halibut was traditionally the fish eaten on Christian holy days. Today halibut cheeks are a sought-after delicacy!

CHARACTERISTICS AND HABITAT:

ATLANTIC HALIBUT (*Hippoglossus hippoglossus*)
Atlantic halibut is a close relative of the Pacific halibut, but commercial production is less than Pacific halibut. Atlantic halibut is extensively farmed in Norway and Scotland.

PACIFIC HALIBUT (*Hippoglossus stenolepis*)
Pacific halibut is a flatfish from the family Pleuronectidae. There are two flounder families: the right-eyed Pleuronectidae and the left-eyed Bothidae family. The California halibut, *Paralichthys californicus*, is a left-eyed flounder. All flatfish belonging to the order Pleuronectiformes have both of their eyes on the same side of their head. When the halibut is born its eyes are on both sides of its head, and it swims like most other fishes. When it is about 6 months old, one eye migrates to the other side of its head, making it look like a flounder. At the same time this eye moves, the body flattens; the side with the stationary eye develops a blackish gray pigment, while the other side remains off-white. Halibut live in the North Atlantic and North Pacific and grow to be as much as 500 pounds (227 kg), but the average weight is about 15 to 20 pounds (6.8 to 9 kg). Generally only female halibut grow to a significant size; males rarely grow more than 50 pounds (22.6 kg). Halibut spend most of their time in the bottom of the ocean, but move up to feed. They feed on any sea animal they can fit into their mouths, among them crab, salmon, cod, pollock, herring, and flounder.

Herring

ATLANTIC HERRING (*Clupea harengus*)
PACIFIC HERRING (*Clupea pallasii palasii*)

COMMON NAMES: Atlantic herring: sardine, American sardine, brit, labrador herring; Pacific herring: sardine, California herring, kara herring, eastern herring

SUBSTITUTION: Mackerel scad

QUALITY, FLAVOR, AND PREPARATION: This relatively small fish is not very popular in the United States in fresh form. It is preferred in many of its prepared forms, such as cured and smoked herring also known as kippers, as pickled herring, and as canned sardines. Rollmops are herring fillets marinated in vinegar and salt enhanced with aromatics. In the Mediterranean and France, the plump sardines are char grilled. They are excellent when lightly oiled, rolled in sea salt, and grilled. Their oily flesh keeps them moist and succulent. Both herrings and sardines are full of minerals and calcium, especially if the soft bones are eaten. The fish must be eviscerated, the fish scales brushed off, and the fish then rinsed and patted dry before any preparation. They can be eviscerated through the head. Fresh herrings are scarce in Hawaiian fish markets, but frozen or chilled whole herrings are sometimes available.

CHARACTERISTICS AND HABITAT:

ATLANTIC HERRING (*Clupea harengus*)

The Atlantic herring in the family Clupidae is one of the most abundant species of fish on the planet. They are found in vast areas on both sides of the Atlantic Ocean and are known to be great schoolers, congregating in huge groups often numbering hundreds of thousands and traveling the open oceans. The Atlantic herring fishery has been an important part of the New England and Canadian economy. One reason for this is that the fish habitat is relatively close to the coast, in the cold waters of the Gulf of Maine and Gulf of St. Lawrence. Atlantic herring are in general a fragile fish. They have a fairly slender, elongated body and rounded belly covered with large loose scales that come off easily when the fish comes into contact with any foreign matter. It is deep blue or blue green above with silver sides and underbody. When its large mouth is closed, the lower jaw protrudes beyond the upper lip, creating a small pointed snout.

PACIFIC HERRING (*Clupea pallasii pallasii*)

The Pacific herring are also in the Clupidae family. This species is named after Peter Simon Pallas, a well-known German naturalist and explorer. Pacific herring are found widely along the North American California coast, from Baja California north to Alaska and the Bering Sea. The Pacific herring is considered a keystone species because of its high productivity and interactions with a large number of predators and prey. Pacific herring often serves as food for many other marine species, including salmon, marine mammals, and seabirds. In addition it is an important bait fish. Notably, herring do not die after spawning but can breed in successive years, and their near-shore spawning cycle is a boon to the multimillion-dollar fishing industry. The average Pacific herring reaches about 9 inches (23 cm) in length and 1¼ pounds (635 g) in weight but sometimes grows larger. It is a shiny fish with bluish green to olive green coloration on the back, silver white sides and belly. It has a deeply forked tail. Unlike other members of this family, Pacific herring do not have scales on heads or gills. The young of the herring, when they are 3 to 6 inches (7.6 to 15 cm) in length, are known as sardines. Most of the U.S. harvest comes from Washington, California, and Alaska.

Jack or White Ulua, Ulua Aukea (*Caranx ignobilis*)

COMMON NAMES: Jackfish, *pāpio*, giant trevally

SUBSTITUTION: Grouper, any snapper, pompano

QUALITY, FLAVOR, AND PREPARATION: Jacks have clear white flesh, dense and somewhat coarse. The flavor of jackfish is rich and more pronounced than the flesh of snapper or grouper. Fish over 10 pounds (4.5 kg) are popular for restaurant dishes and are sold whole so that buyers can assess the product quality. Jackfish is also available in fillet form and can be sautéed, baked, or poached. The smaller jack with head on can be prepared similarly. Both may be smoked or dried. Jacks are sometimes implicated in ciguatera poisoning.

CHARACTERISTICS AND HABITAT: Jack or white *ulua* of the Carangidae family are found in both shallow and deep water and caught year round. They are fast and depend on their speed to attack and kill their prey. Even the small jacks, less than 10 pounds (4.5 kg) and called *pāpio* by their Hawaiian name, are fearless fighters. The fish can be found in schools or as solitary individuals. Jack caught in Hawaiian waters typically weigh from 10 to 40 pounds (4.5 to 18 kg) and can get up to 176 pounds (80 kg). They are taken by hook-and-line gear as well as trolling and spearing.

Kingfish, Ono (*Acanthocybium solandri*)

COMMON NAMES: Kingfish or *ono*: wahoo, tigerfish, oceanic barracuda

SUBSTITUTION: Mahimahi, seabass, snapper, halibut, mackerel

QUALITY, FLAVOR, AND PREPARATION: Wahoo with its flaky pinkish white flesh and delicate flavor is a Hawaiian favorite; in fact, the word "'ono" means "delicious." When cooked the meat turns to a creamy off-white color and a firm texture. As with other lean fish, care should be taken not to overcook. The fish may be steamed, sauetéed, grilled, broiled, or baked. *Ono* is usually available in fillet form with its thin skin on. *Ono* may be cooked with or without the skin, but in either case the scaly skin on the corselet and lateral line should be removed.

CHARACTERISTICS AND HABITAT: *Ono* of the Scombridae family are tropical and subtropical water fish. They are a close relative of the king mackerel. The *ono* has a long, slender body, a sharp, pointed head with a close-set mouth, and dark blue color on the back with irregular dark purplish gray bars on the sides. It has no scales, except for the scaly corselet and lateral lines. It is an open ocean game fish, swimming in oceans in many parts of the world. *Ono* are a fast-swimming migratory fish known for their fighting ability. They are caught by trolling and longline fishing. The size of the fish caught in Hawai'i is around 10 to 30 pounds (4.5 to 13.6 kg); however, they grow to almost 100 pounds (45 kg) or more in weight. In Hawai'i the peak season is during the summer and up to fall.

Mackerel Scad or 'Ōpelu (*Decapturus* spp)

COMMON NAMES: Scad, *'ōpelu-mama*

SUBSTITUTION: Mackerel, *akule*

QUALITY, FLAVOR, AND PREPARATION: Like the bigeye scad, the mackerel scad is available in fish markets in many countries around the world. Whole mackerel scad can be deep-fried, but tossing them lightly in flour before frying seals in the flavor of the soft meat. It is delicious biting into the soft meat enclosed in the crispy crust. Care should be taken when eating whole fried mackerel scad. Unlike anchovies and smelts that have soft edible bones, these fish have a few bones that you should avoid eating. Dressed mackerel scad may also be cooked wrapped in foil on a hot grill.

CHARACTERISTICS AND HABITAT: The mackerel scad of the Carangidae family has a cigar-shaped body. It is silvery blue on the upper third of the body shading to a silvery white below, with a dark spot on the gill cover. Mackerel scad inhabit the coastal waters of the Hawaiian Islands and swim mostly in schools on the surface and in mid-water. They are caught with handlines at and nets during both day and night. They grow to about 12 inches (35 cm), but most are caught when they are about 8 inches (10.2 cm).

Marlin and Spearfish

COMMON NAMES: Blue marlin or *kajiki*: Pacific blue marlin, spearfish, *a'u*; shortbill spearfish: shortbill, spearfish, *hebi*; striped marlin or *nairagi*: barred marlin, *a'u*

SUBSTITUTION: Swordfish, spearfish, tuna, mahimahi

QUALITY, FLAVOR, AND PREPARATION: Of all marlin species, the striped marlin is considered the best because of its tenderness. Marlin is available mostly in steak form, trimmed of its inedible rough skin. With its medium fat content, firm texture, and mild flavor, it is often used for **sashimi**. Its firm texture makes it a favorite for broiling and grilling. It can also be stir-fried, poached, or grilled or broiled on skewers. Marlin can be smoked and takes well to freezing.

CHARACTERISTICS AND HABITAT: Marlins are billfish of the tropical and subtropical oceans in the family Istiophoridae. An open ocean fish, they are impressive fighters and one of the most sought-after big game fish. They use the sharp bill projecting from the upper jaw to disable their prey. In Hawai'i the special attraction for game fishing is the abundance of Pacific blue marlin. The Kona Coast in Hawai'i is well known for its bill-fishing tournaments that bring in sport fishermen from all over the world. Marlins are also fished by commercial longline fishermen. In Hawai'i, the blue marlin is abundant during the summer months, the striped marlin mostly from fall to spring, and the shortbill spearfish during winter and the end of spring. The most popular of the several types of marlin are blue marlin or *kajiki*, striped marlin or *nairagi*, and shortbill spearfish or *hebi*.

BLUE MARLIN or _KAJIKI_ (*Makaira nigricans*)
Blue marlins are warm-water fish that can be distinguished from other marlin species by their heavier bill and rougher gray skin. Most of the fish marketed range from 80 to 300 pounds (36 to 136 kg), but they are known to get as large as 1,600 pounds (726 kg) in weight. The flesh varies in individual fish, ranging from red to light orange. When cooked it becomes firm yet flaky and turns to an appetizing creamy white.

SHORTBILL SPEARFISH or _HEBI_ (*Tetrapturus angustirostris*)
The shortbill spearfish is slender, and as its name implies, its bill is small. Its dorsal fin is also shorter. Shortbill spearfish caught in Hawaiian waters are usually between 20 and 60 pounds (9 to 27 kg) in weight. They are available year round in the islands with the peak being during the winter and spring. Most of the catch in Hawai'i is caught by commercial longline boats. The shortbill spearfish has an amber-colored flesh that is somewhat softer than that of the other marlin.

STRIPED MARLIN or _NAIRAGI_ (*Tetrapturus audax*)
Striped marlin, also a warm water fish, is mostly found in the Pacific and Indian Oceans. It is a migratory species that passes through the Hawaiian Islands annually. These fish range from 50 to 100 pounds (22.6 to 45 kg) and

are very rarely over 130 pounds (136 kg) in weight. The striped marlin has white to pale blue vertical stripes on the sides of its laterally compressed body; these stripes fade away soon after it is out of the water. The striped marlin has the thinnest bill of all the marlins. The flesh varies in color in individual fish, from orange to pink. Of all the marlin species, striped marlin is considered the finest for eating because of its tender flesh.

Moonfish or Opah (*Lampris guttatus*)

COMMON NAMES: Moonfish or *opah*: lookdown

SUBSTITUTION: Tuna, swordfish

QUALITY, FLAVOR, AND PREPARATION: *Opah* is a coarse-grained and fatty fish; the flesh color ranges from pink to orange and to a brilliant red in different parts of its body. Behind the head and along the backbone the flesh is orange, toward the belly the flesh is pink, and the fish cheeks are a deep red color; but almost all the flesh cooks to an off-white color. A small area of the flesh inside the breastplate is a brilliant red and turns to a deep brown when cooked. The fatty, coarse-grained flesh takes well to sauces and is best when stewed or braised. It is juicy with a rich flavor, and can also be steamed, baked or poached. It is available in fillet form.

CHARACTERISTICS AND HABITAT: Moonfish of the family Lampridae was known as the good-luck fish by old-time Hawaiian fishermen. Worldwide it is found in tropical to temperate waters and is one of the most colorful species available in Hawaiʻi. Thin and flat with a perfect round body, it has a gorgeous silvery gray skin on its upper body that shades to a rose red towards the belly. It is dotted with white spots, with the larger spots appearing more profusely around the belly. This beautiful fish has crimson fins and large eyes encircled with gold. It is a nonschooling, wandering species and is caught by longline fishermen year round with the peak being April to August. The moonfish landed in Hawaiʻi range from 60 to 200 pounds (27 to 90.7 kg). Moonfish was an underutilized species until recent times, but came to the forefront because of the rising demand for fresh fish in the islands.

Mullet, ʻAmaʻAma (*Mugil cephalus*)

COMMON NAMES: Gray mullet, striped mullet

SUBSTITUTION: Threadfin, any goatfish

QUALITY, FLAVOR, AND PREPARATION: The flesh of the mullet is firm and has a mild nutty flavor; it is moderately fatty. Drawn whole mullet may be roasted wrapped in foil or in cabbage or lettuce leaves or broiled or grilled. Many prefer to steam mullet Chinese style. Mullet is excellent smoked; the fish should be split or butterflied, spread open, and brined before smoking.

CHARACTERISTICS AND HABITAT: Mullet belong to the family Mugilidae, an important food that was abundant in the early times. During the time of the Hawaiian kings, mullet were specially reared in ponds for the royal table. They are bottom feeders and prefer to live along the shoreline areas in rather brackish water. The mullet has an oblong body covered with large scales and a head that is rounded in front. The body is shining silvery green or silvery brown, shading to white towards the belly. It is commonly fished when about 18 to 20 inches (45.7 to 50.8 cm).

Atlantic Salmon, Norwegian Salmon (*Salmo salar*)

COMMON NAMES: Scottish salmon, Eastern salmon

SUBSTITUTION: Pacific salmon

QUALITY, FLAVOR, AND PREPARATION: Atlantic salmon is at its best when it is around three years old and weighs 8 to 10 pounds (3.6 to 4.5 kg). It is also the best for smoking because of its high fat content. The fat helps the fish retain its moisture and flavor even after smoking. Salmon is available whole, pan dressed, and filleted in frozen or fresh state. Salmon is also available smoked and cured. Also see quality, flavor and preparation for Pacific salmon.

CHARACTERISTICS AND HABITAT: Atlantic salmon is in the Salmonidae family. It has a more streamlined body shape than other salmon species. The sides are a silver color; the back is a shade of bluish green with small black spots. It has white belly and a large mouth. The Atlantic salmon is andromous like its relatives the Pacific salmon, but it survives spawning to spawn again. The Atlantic salmon does not have the deep pink or red color associated with salmon. The flesh ranges from pale pink to pale orange, but it has a richer taste and a firmer texture than its Pacific relatives. Farm-raised Atlantic salmon have a deep red flesh; their fat content is much higher than the fat content of the wild salmon because of their high-protein seafood diets rich in fat. There is an abundance of farm-raised salmon throughout the year, notably from Norway and Chile.

Pacific Salmon

CHUM OR KETA (*Oncorhynchus keta*)
COHO OR SILVER SALMON (*Oncorhynchus kisutch*)
KING SALMON OR CHINOOK (*Oncorhynchus tschawytscha*)
PINK SALMON OR HUMPBACK (*Oncorhynchus gorbuscha*)
SOCKEYE OR BLUEBACK (*Oncorhynchus nerka*)

COMMON NAMES: Chum: *keta*, fall, dark; coho: *ginmasu*; king salmon: spring salmon; pink salmon: humpie, *gorbusch*; sockeye: blueback

SUBSTITUTION: Atlantic salmon, trout, butterfish

QUALITY, FLAVOR, AND PREPARATION: Many think that the color, texture, and flavor of wild salmon is superior to that of farmed salmon. Whether wild or farm raised, salmon in general have a unique flavor and color. The flesh color ranges from bright reddish orange to deep pink to pale pink, and the fat content ranges from high to low. The flesh color, fat content, and overall taste differ from one species to another. Salmon can be prepared in many ways. No matter what method is used to cook salmon, its high fat content helps to preserve its moisture when cooked. It is important, however, not to overcook. Take into account that the fish will continue to cook in its own internal heat (carry-over cooking) once it is removed from the heat and dished. Its fatty skin with a concentration of omega-3 of fatty acids is delicious when broiled or grilled skin on (scales removed) or when roasted whole, eviscerated with head and skin on with (scales removed). It is just as good poached and served hot or cold. Salmon has many fine scales that have to be removed before preparation starts. The salmon fillet has a row of pin bones, and care should be taken to remove them using tweezers or a pair of pliers (see Preparing Fish for Cooking). Salmon is available whole, pan dressed, filleted, steaked and chunked, in frozen or fresh state. It is also available brined, smoked, cured, and canned. The flesh of all fish in the salmonidae family is equally delicate, and recipes can be used interchangeably.

CHARACTERISTICS AND HABITAT: Pacific salmon is in the Salmonidae family. These well-proportioned fish have shiny silvery-black skins. The color and the beauty of this species earned them the name "king of fish." Salmon flourish in the temperate waters of both the northern and southern Pacific. The Pacific wild salmon are anadromous; they are born in fresh water but spend most of their life in the ocean before returning to fresh water to spawn. At maturity they have strong, well-proportioned bodies that enable them to swim from the ocean, fast and furiously up fresh-water streams, rivers, and waterfalls to spawn and die. In preparation for this strenuous journey upstream to spawn, they eat excessively to build up nutrients. Physiological changes take place at this time in their life cycle. Their flesh is deeper in color, rich in fat, and intense in flavor. As the salmon leave the ocean and enter the fast-flowing fresh-water rivers and streams, they are at their best. Their palatability is at the highest level; this is the right time to catch them. As the salmon migrate upstream, they do not feed, but sustain themselves with their own fat. The flesh becomes pale and dry and they become less desirable. Wild Pacific salmon are not easily available; however, they are successfully farm-raised now and abundant throughout the year.

CHUM or DOG (*Oncorhynchus keta*)

The chum salmon has silver or metallic dark blue sides with fine speckles on its back. All fins except the dorsal fin are edged with black. Because of its low fat content the flesh is pale pink and coarse textured when cooked. It is good for hot smoking. The average size of chum salmon is 10 to 15 pounds (4.5 to 6.8 kg), although they can grow up to 30 pounds (13.6 kg). They are caught commercially by trolling or nets close to river mouths. Chum are the least expensive of the salmon species. They are also extensively farm raised.

COHO or SILVER SALMON (*Oncorhynchus kisutch*)

The coho salmon has silvery sides with black spots on the back and upper lobe of the tail. It spends more time in fresh water, and when it does reach the ocean it remains close to the coast. Coho take lures easily and are a favorite sport fish. The average fish weight is around 10 to 12 pounds (4.5 to 5.4 kg). Some time ago wild coho salmon was common and was easily found in many markets. Today the numbers have dwindled in this commercially trolled fish. However, farm-raised coho salmon are easily available whole or, in the case of the smaller ones weighing 8 to 10 ounces (227 to 283 g), boned and butterflied. The deep pink flesh is comparatively low in fat; it is firm textured and mild flavored, and when cooked it faintly resembles the taste of farm-raised trout.

KING SALMON or CHINOOK (*Oncorhynchus tschawytscha*)

King salmon are the largest of the Pacific species, their average weight varying from 18 to 20 pounds (8 to 9 kg). The bulk of all salmon sold is king salmon. They have silver sides and a dark greenish blue back with black spots. Its flesh is tender, with the color ranging from a luscious coral red to pale pink. When cooked the flesh turns into large, succulent flakes with a rich flavor due to its high fat content. It is one of the fattier species and is also excellent for cold smoking. It is regarded as the best Pacific variety of salmon and is particularly sought after because of its rich flavor.

PINK SALMON or HUMPBACK (*Oncorhynchus gorbuscha*)

The pink salmon is silvery on its sides, with black spots on its back and tail. It is the smallest of the salmon species, averaging around 5 to 8 pounds (2.3 to 3.6 kg) though it can grow up to 14 pounds (6.4 kg). It has pale pink flesh and small flakes with a fine texture when cooked. The flavor is stronger than and distinct from that of other species. Pink salmon is delicious when roasted drawn, whole, or in a big chunk. Most of the catch is canned and frozen.

SOCKEYE or RED SALMON BLUEBACK (*Oncorhynchus nerka*)

The sockeye salmon has silver sides and a green back with fine speckles on it. The flesh is reddish orange, the deepest color of all the salmon species. Some time ago it was the preferred salmon for canning because of its fatty, firm flesh and its appealing deep color and delicate flavor. Highly prized in Japan, today this is where most of the catch is frozen and shipped to. Although sockeye can grow up to 15 pounds (6.8 kg), the average size is 10 pounds (4.5 kg). The fish is available all year round.

Scad or Akule (*Selar crumenophthalmus*)

COMMON NAMES: Bigeye scad, *halalu, paaʻa, aji*

SUBSTITUTION: *ʻŌpelu*, mackerel

QUALITY, FLAVOR, AND PREPARATION: Bigeye scad are available in fish markets in many countries around the world. This soft-fleshed fish must be eaten when very fresh. It is sold whole and should be drawn and dressed before preparation. It can also be butterflied and boned, then grilled, poached or baked. Scad can also be barbecued and are delicious stuffed and grilled or baked. Butterflied scad can also be marinated and smoked or air dried. The Philippine-style spicy smoked scad, available in markets now, make a delicious appetizer.

CHARACTERISTICS AND HABITAT: Bigeye scad are in the family Carangidae. They have a spindle-shaped body and resemble a mackerel although they are in the jack family. They are silvery blue-green on the upper third of the body and silvery white below with unmistakable large eyes being a prominent feature. This popular species is fast growing and is also the most abundant in the family. Some grow to be 15 inches (37 cm) in length but are usually caught at less than 10 inches (25.2 cm). They are schooling fish and inhabit the coastal waters around the islands. They are sometimes taken by hand line at night and hoop nets during the day, but mostly they are taken by surround nets or seines. Depending upon size, this species is known by various names in Hawaiʻi: *akule, halalu*, and *paaʻa*.

Hawaiian Sea Bass or Grouper (*Epinephelus quernus*)

COMMON NAMES: Sea bass or grouper: *hāpuʻupuʻu*, Hawaiian sea bass

SUBSTITUTION: Snapper, striped bass, black bass, halibut

QUALITY, FLAVOR, AND PREPARATION: The clear, white, delicate flesh is lean but moist and fairly dense. When cooked it has a firm texture and a luscious, slightly sweet taste. It takes well to steaming and is a favorite in Chinese eateries. Usually the smaller fish between 1 to 5 pounds (454 g to 2.3 kg) are sold head on, and these may be drawn and steamed as the Chinese do, to serve one or two persons. Larger fish are available in fillet form. Heads and bones are used for soups or soup stock. This versatile fish can also be poached, baked in a sauce, broiled, or grilled.

CHARACTERISTICS AND HABITAT: Hawaiian sea bass or grouper is of the Serranidae family, a near relative of black bass. This species of sea bass is found only in Hawaiʻi and is more common in the shallow waters at the northern end of the Hawaiian archipelago. This particular species has a very dark brownish black tough skin, usually with light spots. As with other members of the grouper family they are able to transform their color to mix in with their habitat. Hawaiian sea bass is a deep-water bottom fish; the smaller fish are caught off the main Hawaiian Islands and the larger ones are caught around the northwestern Hawaiian Islands. They attain a length of 3 feet (91.4 cm) and weigh up to 30 pounds (13.6 kg) and are caught by hook and line with the peak season being fall and winter months.

Smelt, Struhsaker's Deep-sea Smelt (*Glossanodon struhsakeri*)

COMMON NAMES: Deep-sea smelt, silversides

SUBSTITUTION: Large anchovies

QUALITY, FLAVOR, AND PREPARATION: Smelt are found in fresh or frozen form, whole, or gutted with or without the heads; they are available in fish markets in many countries throughout the world. The small ones can be easily gutted through the head. Using your thumb and forefinger, pull the gills and the guts will follow; twist the head and pull out all together and discard. Sometimes the smelts come with the roe; if you feel the roe inside the fish, gently squeeze the fish to push out the roe. Most people discard the roe, but many savor eating it along with the fish. The large smelts can be broiled or grilled or fried. The small ones are best tossed in seasoned flour, deep-fried, and served with a dipping sauce to serve as an appetizer. When cooked, smelts are soft textured with fine flakes and a sweet taste.

CHARACTERISTICS AND HABITAT: The Hawaiian deep-sea smelts are in the Argentinidae family and are closely related to the true smelts of the Osmeridae family. The name of this fish honors Dr. Paul Struhsaker, an ichthyologist of the National Marine Fisheries Service's Honolulu Laboratory. There are many species of smelt; some inhabit the Mediterranean, some the Atlantic off the coast of Canada, and the coast of Maine. The Hawaiian deep-sea smelt is a small, weak fish with a wedge-shaped head and a tapering body. Most are 3 to 5 inches (7.6 to 12.6 cm) in length. The iridescent light-colored body is marked by a wide darker strip that extends from head to tail. The habitat of this species is in the mid-water regions of the ocean; it is caught by deep-water trawling gear.

Gray Snapper or Uku (*Aprion virescens*)

COMMON NAME: Jobfish

SUBSTITUTION: Red snapper, pink snapper, sea bass, grouper

QUALITY, FLAVOR, AND PREPARATION: The gray snapper has clear, pale pink flesh that is moist and firm, firmer than that of other snappers. It cooks to an off-white color. It is also stronger in flavor than the other snappers. The fish harvested during the summer is high in fat content and is a good choice for **sashimi**. The gray snapper can be prepared like other snappers.

CHARACTERISTICS AND HABITAT: Gray snapper, of the Lutjanidae family, is gray blue in color and has a long head and long snout. It is a bottom fish found in the shallowest depths. Gray snapper are harvested year round, the peak being the summer season, whereas winter is the peak season for the deepwater Hawaiian snappers. Gray snapper weigh an average of 4 to 16 pounds (1.8 to 7.3 kg) and are found throughout Hawaiian Island waters. They are caught with vertical hook-and-line gear as well as by trolling.

Long-tail Red Snapper
or Onaga (*Etelis coruscans*)

COMMON NAMES: *Onaga:* Ruby snapper, long-tail red snapper, Pacific red snapper, *ulaʻula koae*

SUBSTITUTION: Pink snapper or gray snapper, grouper, halibut

QUALITY, FLAVOR, AND PREPARATION: Hawaiian red snapper has clear, soft, pale pink flesh and cooks to a white color. It is moist and has a delicate taste. Young fish are tender, but the larger ones over 3 pounds (1.4 kg) tend to be tough when cooked. Smaller fish are available head on; the larger ones are available whole and in fillet form, often with the skin on. The small fish less than 5 pounds (2.3 pounds) are drawn, with head on, and steamed, a popular preparation in Hawai'i. The fish fillet may be steamed, baked, sautéed, or grilled. It is especially good when cooked with the skin on, although care should be taken to remove all the scales before cooking. The fish heads are used for making soup and soup stock.

CHARACTERISTICS AND HABITAT: Hawaiian red snapper is one of Hawai'i's premium commercial fish, is better known by its Japanese name (*onaga*) than its Hawaiian name *'ula'ula*; it is in the family Lutjanidae. This deep-water bottom fish caught off the Hawaiian Islands has a beautiful form, a long tail, and a shiny, brilliant red skin. Restaurants often request this handsome whole fish for display. They range in size from 1 to 18 pounds (454 grams to 8.2 kg) and are caught with vertical hook-and-line gear in 600 to 1,000 feet (188 to 304 meters) of water. Hawaiian red snapper is harvested mainly during the fall and winter months, with the peak being reached during December in part because of the demand for *onaga* by the Asian communities in Hawai'i who use this fish in ceremonial dishes. Abundant during the winter months, these fish have a higher fat content than those caught during the warm summer months; the high fat content makes the fish ideal for **sashimi**, another reason for demand and high prices for this fish during winter. Many species of red fish are marketed as Pacific red snapper. Some are inferior species. Buyers should be aware of this and identify the true Hawaiian red snapper.

Pink Snapper
or 'Ōpakapaka (*Pristipomoides filamentosus*)

COMMON NAMES: Pink snapper, red jobfish, crimson jobfish

SUBSTITUTIONS: Gray snapper, red snapper, grouper, halibut

QUALITY, FLAVOR, AND PREPARATION: Hawaiian pink snapper is available whole or in fillet form with the skin on to enable buyers to identify the species. It has white to pale pink clear flesh that cooks to a firm yet moist texture and white color; these are desired qualities in a table fish. Small fish 1 to 2 pounds (454 to 907 g) in weight, drawn with head on, are best steamed or baked. This sweet-flavored fish is a choice fish for **sashimi** especially during the winter season when it is high in fat. It may be also sautéed, poached, grilled, or broiled. Fish heads are used for making soup and soup stocks.

CHARACTERISTICS AND HABITAT: Hawaiian pink snapper, in the family Lutjanidae is Hawai'i's premium commercial fish. Its popularity goes back to pre-World War II days, when it was one of the favorite common fishes served in restaurants. It is a deep-water bottom fish caught around the Hawaiian Islands. It has a pinkish brown skin, and it snaps aggressively with its sharp teeth when caught. Although this species is found in many tropical and subtropical ocean waters around the world, the largest are said to be in Hawaiian waters, where they get to be as big as 12 to 20 pounds (5.4 to 9 kg) and attain a length of 2.5 feet (76.2 cm). The average size of the fish caught is from 1 to 5 pounds (2.3 kg). They are caught using vertical hook-and-line gear. As in the case of Hawaiian red snapper, these snappers are caught year round with the peak harvest being during the winter season when the demand is high and the fish fetch high prices.

Short-tail Red Snapper
or 'Ehu (*Etelis carbunculus*)

COMMON NAMES: Red snapper, 'ula'ula

SUBSTITUTION: Red snapper, gray snapper, grouper, sea bass

QUALITY, FLAVOR, AND PREPARATION: Short-tail red snapper has pinkish white flesh that turns off-white when cooked; it has a delicate taste. To cook short-tail red snapper use the recipes for snapper in general. It is best to buy fish less than 3 pounds (1.4 kg) in weight if you plan to cook the fish whole because any fish over 3 pounds (1.4 kg) could turn out tough when cooked. These fish are occasionally implicated in ciguatera (see Understanding and Avoiding Seafood-related Illnesses) poisoning and should be drawn and thoroughly washed before cooking whole. This fish is also available in fillet form, fresh or frozen.

CHARACTERISTICS AND HABITAT: The bright red-skinned short-tail red snapper is in the Lutjanidae family and is similar in appearance to the long-tail red snapper. It reaches up to 12 to 15 pounds (5.4 to 6.8 kg), but is usually available from 1 to 6 pounds (454 grams to 2.7 kg). Its preferred habitat is the deep reefs in the 100-to-400-meters depth range; it is caught by hook and line. Red snappers reach their peak season during winter.

Swordfish or Shutome (*Xiphias gladius*)

COMMON NAMES: SWORDFISH: broadbill swordfish: broadbill, *shutome*, true
swordfish, *a'u ku*

SUBSTITUTIONS: Marlin, halibut, tuna, grouper

QUALITY, FLAVOR, AND PREPARATION: Swordfish is available whole or in fillet form
with or without the skin. The meat is sweet, with a slight seafood taste, and
has a firm meat-like texture. It has a medium-high fat content, rich when
cooked but hardly oily. The clear pink flesh is firm and holds its shape when
cooked; if overcooked it turns tough and dry. It is a good choice for steaks
and cubed for skewers. Swordfish can be broiled, stir-fried, poached, or
baked cloaked in a sauce.

CHARACTERISTICS AND HABITAT: Swordfish is in the family Xiphiidae. It has a
flattened sword projecting from its upper jaw and is easily distinguishable
from the marlin. This fish can reach 15 feet (4.5 m) in length, and it is known
to have attacked an occasional sailing vessel with its powerful sword. It is
an open ocean migratory fish and is tolerant to various water temperatures
ranging from tropical to temperate. Swordfish are harvested by commercial
longline fishermen, usually at night. They are abundant in Hawaiian waters
during the spring and early summer. Much of Hawai'i's catch is shipped to
the U.S. East Coast, where it fetches a premium price. The average harvested
weight ranges from 50 to 300 pounds (22.6 to 136 kg).

Pacific Threadfin, Moi (*Polydactylus sexfilis*)

COMMON NAMES: *Mana moi*—male; *moi*—female; *moi li'i*—juveniles; *pala moi*—
hermaphrodite

SUBSTITUTIONS: Red, pink, or gray snapper; trout; flounder

QUALITY, FLAVOR, AND PREPARATION: Pacific threadfin have a mild, delicate flavor
and a very tender texture. They are harvested when they are 12 to 15 ounces
(340 to 425 g) in weight. They can be prepared by any cooking method but
are best when the drawn fish is deep-fried after a dusting of cornstarch or
simply steamed Chinese style. When cooked the fish has a silken texture and
flakes easily.

CHARACTERISTICS AND HABITAT: *Moi* are shoreline fish in the family Polynemidae;
they are shoreline fishes. They reach up to 18 inches (46 cm). Their pectoral
fins have six long, slender filaments they use as feelers to trail over the

bottom—hence, the Latin name *sexfilis*. The body of the *moi* is yellowish white with silvery reflections, shading towards the almost white belly. In early Hawai'i they were bred and closely guarded in fish ponds and were reserved for royalty. Today they are highly sought after by shoreline fishermen and are among the fast-running shore game fishes. *Moi* are commercially raised in ponds and offshore cages.

Trout

BROOK TROUT (*Salvelinus fontinalis*)
BROWN TROUT (*Salmo trutta trutta*)
LAKE TROUT (*Salvelinus namaycush*)
RAINBOW TROUT (*Oncorhynchus mykiss*)

COMMON NAMES: Brook trout: eastern brook trout, brookies; brown trout: sea trout, salmon trout; lake trout: gray trout; rainbow trout: red-band trout

SUBSTITUTION: Salmon

QUALITY, FLAVOR, AND PREPARATION: Trout caught in the wild are superior to farmed varieties mainly because of their diet. They lead a rigorous fighting lifestyle that makes their flavor better than the flavor of the farm-raised trout that lead sluggish, easy lives.

The first thing to remember when buying trout is to look for freshness. Fresh trout should be handled as little as possible to avoid removing their slime, the natural coating on the flesh. Trout are easy to prepare for cooking. They have no scales and can be butterflied or filleted easily. They can be boned when cooked or raw without much effort. Trout have a mild and delicate taste and should not be drowned in strong sauces. Trout is best when it is simply pan-fried in butter, seasoned with lemon juice, and sprinkled with freshly chopped parsley. Trout can be grilled, broiled, poached, or baked. Large trout can be prepared in a manner suitable for salmon, either poached, stuffed and baked, or cured. Trout are available alive in tanks or whole, dressed, and butterflied frozen.

CHARACTERISTICS AND HABITAT: Trout belong to the salmon family Salmonidae and are members of the subfamily Salmoniae. Trout are usually found in cool, clear streams and lakes. Many of the species have anadromous strains, meaning they spend time in the sea before returning to their freshwater birthplace to spawn, but some spend their entire life in freshwater. They are distributed throughout North America, northern Asia, and Europe. As a group, trout are a somewhat bony fish. They are entirely without spines, but they have fins, including an adipose fin along the back near the tail. Because of their popularity, trout are often raised in fish farms. Trout that live in different environments have different colorations and patterns on the bodies, a camouflage that changes as the fish move to different habitats. Wild trout are said to have more vivid colors and patterns. The color of the flesh ranges from pale pink to deep pink, red, and orange. The lake trout is said to be one of the largest freshwater fish and can grow to be around 75 pounds (34 kg) although when farm raised the average weight is around 4 pounds (1.8 kg). Brook trout can reach 3 to 4 pounds (1.4 to 1.8 kg). Trout are marketed at the right size for individual servings: 8 to 12 ounces (227 to 340 g) for wild trout and 8 to 10 ounces (227 to 284 g) for farmed trout.

BROOK TROUT (*Salvelinus fontinalis*)

Brook trout are highly prized game fish. They live in the cool lakes and streams in the United States and Canada. The brook trout has a brownish green back with faint orange and reddish spots on the sides. The lower body fins are outlined in black with the edges tinted in white. Farmed brook trout has pale white flesh, while the wild trout has pale yellow luscious flesh. It is an excellent tasty fish especially if it comes from mountain streams.

BROWN TROUT (*Salmo trutta trutta*)

The brown trout is also a favorite with sport fishermen. This species was originally from Europe and Asia and was introduced to America by the first settlers. It is an excellent fish and common all over the United States and Canada. The brook trout is brown with large dark spots on its back and sides and has a white belly.

LAKE TROUT (*Salvelinus namaycush*)

Lake trout inhabit many of the deep-water large lakes in North America. They are said to be one of the largest freshwater fish, can grow to be around 75 pounds (34 kg), and live to about fifty years! The average weight is around 3 to 4 pounds (1.4 to 1.8 kg) when farmed. Their colors vary from pale green to dark green and brown and silver, with pale yellow spots. Their flesh is very fatty and appreciated by many and especially prized by fishermen. Large trout can be prepared in a manner suitable for salmon, either poached, stuffed and baked, or cured.

RAINBOW TROUT (*Oncorhynchus mykiss*)

The rainbow trout, the best known trout in the market, is a colorful freshwater fish. It has a metallic bluish green back, speckled silvery sides, and a distinguishable red strip along each side of its body. Rainbow trout has a life span of eleven years. Today rainbow trout is farmed in many parts of the world. Both wild and farm raised are easily available.

Tuna or 'Ahi

COMMON NAMES: Albacore or *tombo: ahipalaha*; bigeye: big head *'ahi, po'o-nui*; skipjack or *aku:* skipjack tuna, bonita; yellowfin or *'ahi: shibi*

SUBSTITUTIONS: Firm-fleshed fish such as swordfish, spearfish, mahimahi (dorado), mackerel

QUALITY, FLAVOR, AND PREPARATION: The best part of the tuna fish is the loin, which is mainly used for **sashimi**. Tuna is also available in steak form or as a fillet, generally without the skin; it may be broiled, baked, or sautéed. Tuna with a higher fat content and deeper red color are ideal for raw preparations and are also priced higher than those suitable for cooking. In its raw state the color of the fish ranges from a deep pink to a brilliant red. The meat is firm and dense and when cooked turns tender and flaky when tested. Tuna has a rich flavor and medium to high fat content. To preserve its moist quality, tuna is best when cooked lightly, rare to medium; the interior of the fish should still be pink in color. Tuna freezes well and may also be dried or smoked.

CHARACTERISTICS AND HABITAT: Tuna are an open ocean fish in the mackerel family Scombridae. In Hawai'i they are of high commercial value. Tuna accounted for 58 percent of the total catch taken by commercial fishermen in 2010. Although they are essentially fish of tropical and subtropical waters, some tuna caught off Hawaiian waters migrate long distances across the Pacific Ocean seasonally. Giant bluefin tuna (*Thunnus orientalis*), rather rare in Hawai'i, spawn in the Western Pacific near Japan and migrate over 6,000 miles (9 656 km) to the Eastern Pacific. Albacore tuna are found as far north as southern Alaska in the summer. Tuna are fast swimmers and take in large amounts of oxygen while swimming. In Hawai'i, the peak season for most tuna species is summer, but the largest landing of bigeye tuna occurs in the winter months from October to March. There are several varieties of tuna such as *aku* or skipjack tuna, bigeye or *'ahi*, yellowfin or *'ahi*, and *tombo* or albacore.

ALBACORE or TOMBO (*Thunnus alalunga*)

Tombo is the Japanese name for this fish caught in Hawaiian waters; elsewhere it is known as albacore. It is commonly found in temperate waters in all oceans. In the tropics, *tombo* is caught in deeper water by longline boats. Its flesh is light pink in color and fattier than all the other tuna. It has the mildest flavor of them all. Because of the soft texture of the flesh, it breaks up easily and thus is not a good choice for **sashimi**. *Tombo* is good broiled, but care should be taken not to overcook; basting while cooking will prevent the fish from drying out. *Tombo* is used for canning and is the only tuna species that can be canned as white meat in the United States.

BIGEYE or *'AHI* (*Thunnus obesus***)**

Bigeye is the most popular fish in the Hawaiian Islands. Bigeye and yellowfin caught in Hawaiian waters are both called *'ahi*. The bigeye is common in the tropical and subtropical Pacific, Atlantic, and Indian Oceans. Commercially they are caught in deeper, cooler water than yellowfin, by longline. Typically the smaller fish have long pectoral fins, the larger ones shorter pectoral fins.

The bigeye has a large head and big eyes but otherwise is similar in appearance to yellowfin. It has light-red flesh, rich and luscious, and when cooked turns a creamy white. Bigeye with a deeper red color and a higher fat content are used in raw preparations such as **sashimi** and sushi. They fetch higher prices.

SKIPJACK TUNA or *AKU* (*Katsuwonus pelamis***)**

Aku, the most common and the smallest among the major types of tuna caught in the vicinity of the Hawaiian Islands, range from 4 to 30 pounds (7.25 to 13.60 kg) in weight. Larger fish locally known as *otaru* move into Hawaiian waters during the peak season. This tuna has unmistakable longitudinal dark stripes on its silvery belly. These fish swim in schools and skip across the ocean waters, hence their name. In Hawai'i, one percent of the annual commercial catch is *aku*. *Aku* has a rich, red translucent flesh. Larger *aku* have the deepest brilliant red color and are the preferred choice of *aku* lovers for raw preparations such as **sashimi** and *poke*. The meat turns into an ivory color and the texture is firm when cooked. *Aku* has a bolder and more distinctive taste than the other tuna and thus is a traditional favorite among many of Hawai'i's ethnic groups.

YELLOWFIN or *'AHI* (*Thunnus albacares***)**

This warm-water fish, similar in appearance and habitat to the bigeye, is also known as *'ahi*. The common name yellowfin refers to the bright yellow tips of the second dorsal fin, the anal fin, and the dorsal and anal finlets. Large yellowfin tuna are commonly caught by longline fishermen; the small ones are fished with handline and bait. The flesh of the more mature fish is darker than that of other tuna, firm, and fatty. Yellowfin is a substitute for bigeye and is a common choice for raw preparations such as **sashimi** and *poke*.

Understanding and Avoiding
Seafood-related Illnesses

Anisakiasis is caused by infection with *Anisakis* worms: *Anisakis simplex* (herring worm) or *Pseudoterranova decipiens* (cod worm). The disease is caused mainly by consuming raw, pickled, or salted fishes that are infected with the larvae of the *Anisakis* worms. Humans are thought to be more at risk from eating wild fish, such as Pacific salmon, which are anadromous fish. Anisakiasis is a two-way threat: people may be infected with worms from eating underprocessed fish or suffer allergic reactions to chemicals left by the worms in the flesh of the fish. Abdominal pain, nausea, and vomiting may occur within hours of ingestion of the infective larvae. Occasionally the larvae pass into the bowel and cause severe eosinophilic problems. Fish known to carry parasitic larvae should be completely cooked to an internal temperature of 140°F (60°C) or more if not previously frozen; freezing to kill parasite larvae requires holding fish at -4°F (-20°C) for at least 7 days or at -31°F (-35°C) for at least 24 hours. Most fish known to carry harmful parasites are frozen or treated before sale and are safe to eat. Fish available in reputable stores are generally free of harmful parasites and safe to eat raw. Most countries require that all types of fish having potential risk of infection and intended for raw consumption be frozen before sale to kill parasites.

Ciguatera is a food-borne illness caused by eating certain reef fishes whose flesh is contaminated with toxins originally produced by the marine microorganism *Gambierdiscus toxicus*, which lives in tropical and subtropical waters. These dinoflagellates adhere to algae and seaweed where they are eaten and ingested by smaller reef fish, which accumulate the toxins. Larger fishes that consume the smaller toxic fishes further concentrate the toxin. Although many reef fishes carry the ciguatera poison, the most common are Jacks, grouper, and sea bass. To avoid ciguatera poisoning, you should clean and wash the fish very well before cooking. Avoid eating fish roe, liver, hearts, head, or guts because they have higher levels of poison. Remember that the poison cannot be destroyed by cooking, freezing, smoking, salting, or drying. General weakness, abdominal cramps, diarrhea, nausea, headache, sweating, dizziness, muscle and joint pains, and numbness around the mouth are symptoms of ciguatera, which can make you sick for days, weeks, or even months. None of the deep-sea fish such as *'ahi* and *aku* (tuna), *kajiki* (marlin) and *ono* (wahoo) have been found to carry ciguatera.

Diphyllobothriasis is an infection caused by the broad tapeworm or broad-fish tapeworm of the genus *Diphyllobothrium*. It is caused by consumption of raw or undercooked freshwater fish and other anadromous fish like the wild Pacific salmon infected with this large parasite. As stated above, wild salmon or any other fish species known to carry parasite larvae should not be eaten raw; they should be properly frozen or thoroughly cooked before eating. Symptoms of diphyllobothriasis are generally mild. They can include diarrhea, abdominal pain, vomiting, weight loss, fatigue, and constipation. In some cases the infection can continue for years without being detected. In some cases it can lead to severe vitamin B12 deficiency due to the parasite's absorbing most of the host's intake of B12.

Heterophysiasis is an intestinal infection caused by the larvae of the small intestinal trematode *Stellantchasmus falcatus*. The larvae may be present in mullet or other freshwater or brackish-water fish. Eating these fish raw or undercooked can cause this infection. Care should be taken to cook the fish thoroughly before consumption.

Ichthyoallyeinotoxism, or hallucinogenic fish poisoning, is caused by consuming certain species of reef and pelagic fishes found in parts of the tropics. It is unclear whether the toxins are produced by the fish themselves or by their diet as in the case of herbivorous fish that ingest certain potent algae. Certain types of goatfishes and mullet are said to have been implicated in cases of hallucinogenic fish poisoning. Collective common names for this toxic fish are "nightmare fish" and "dream fish." The effects of eating ichthyoallyeinotoxic fish are believed to be similar to those of LSD and may include vivid and terrifying auditory and visual hallucinations. Hallucinations may last for several days. Hallucinogenic fish cannot be detected by their appearance, and the poison is not destroyed by cooking. Therefore, although most types of goatfish and mullet are consumed around the world, caution must be taken before using them.

Mercury naturally occurs in the environment and can also be released into the air through industrial pollution. Mercury falls from the air and can accumulate in oceans and streams; over time it turns into the toxic form of mercury known as methylmercury in the water. Fish absorb methylmercury as they feed. Nearly all types of fish contain traces of methylmercury; it is found throughout fish tissue, including muscle tissue. Larger fish that have lived longer have the highest levels of methylmercury because it has had more time to build up in them. Risks from mercury in fish depend on the amount of fish eaten and the levels of mercury in the fish. Health problems that may result from eating contaminated fish range from small, hard-to-detect changes to birth defects and cancer. It is advisable to check the advisories issued by local health departments because mercury levels differ, and local authorities have the best information about local waters. It is advised that pregnant women, women who may become pregnant, nursing mothers, and young children avoid certain types of fish and eat fish that are lower in mercury.

"**Salmon poisoning disease**" is caused by *Nanophyetus salmincola*, an intestinal trematode. The parasite can be present in some freshwater salmonid fish like trout and wild Pacific salmon. This infection is related to consumption of raw or undercooked fish. Transmission of the parasite occurs upon ingestion of the infected fish. Dogs and cats are also vulnerable to the disease; they should never be fed raw or undercooked salmon. It is easily preventable by thoroughly freezing or cooking fish before consumption. Upon infection, humans are normally asymptomatic. If symptoms are present they are mistaken for other gastrointestinal problems. Symptoms include diarrhea, abdominal discomfort, nausea, weight loss, and fatigue.

Scombroid fish poisoning, also known as histamine poisoning, is a food-borne illness that results from eating inadequately preserved or spoiled fish with high levels of histamines. Fish should be stored at extremely low temperatures as soon as they are caught to prevent bacterial growth and stop the naturally present enzymes from forming histamine. Enzymes are inactive at freezing temperatures. Warm temperatures are conducive to spoilage. Scombroid fish poisoning is commonly associated with tuna, mackerel, sardines, anchovies, mahimahi, ono, swordfish, and related species that were inadequately refrigerated after being caught. When certain fishes, especially scombroid fish, start to decompose, histamine is formed rapidly. Freezing, cooking, smoking, curing, and canning do not destroy the toxins. Symptoms of scombroid poisoning consist of skin flushing, throbbing headache, burning sensation in the mouth, abdominal cramps, nausea, and diarrhea. Symptoms of poisoning can show within just a few minutes and up to two hours following consumption of toxic fish and can last for four to six hours or even up to two days.

Glossary

Bain-marie. A hot-water bath or a container used to keep cooked foods hot.

basmati rice. A generic name for a variety of long-grain rice grown along the foothills of the Himalayas in north India. This aromatic rice is considered the best rice in the world. Fine long grain rice may be substituted.

besan flour. Pale yellow in color, this flour is made by grinding the small yellow or pale-brown-skinned chickpea.

black mustard *(Brassica nigra).* The seeds of an annual herb in the cabbage family. Black mustard seeds are more pungent than the yellow variety.

cardamom *(Elettaria cardamomum).* A member of the ginger family. Its pale green or brown oval pods contain fifteen to twenty black seeds with a pungent, sweet, lemony fragrance. The seeds may be removed from the pods and ground for use. Partially crushed or bruised cardamom pods may be used in cooking rice dishes.

chili paste. A paste made from chili peppers, usually with oil, vinegar, garlic, and other flavorings. Many varieties of chili paste are available in Asian grocery stores. The most popular is the spicy, ground red-chili paste with vinegar and garlic known as *sambal olek.*

chili peppers. Tiny bird's-eye peppers 1 inch (2½ cm) or smaller and red or yellow in color. They are extremely hot. Generally the smaller the chili the hotter it is.

cinnamon *(Cinnamomum zeylanicum).* The inner bark of an evergreen tree native to Sri Lanka. It is rolled up and dried. Orangey-brown cinnamon sticks or quills have a sweet, distinctive flavor and fragrance. The bark of several cassia species, also referred to as false cinnamon, is also sold as cinnamon.

clarified butter. Purified butterfat, with water and milk solids removed. To clarify butter melt it in a heavy saucepan over moderate heat; skim the froth from the surface; carefully pour off the clear melted butter into a container, leaving the milky water at the bottom of the saucepan. One pound raw butter yields 12 ounces (340 g) clarified butter.

cloves (*Syzigium aromaticum*). The unopened dried flower buds of a tropical evergreen tree. They have a deep red brown color and a pungent, sharp, astringent flavor. On drying they turn chocolate brown in color.

coriander (*Coriandrum sativum*). Also known as cilantro. The tan seeds of the coriander plant are available whole or ground. This lemony-flavored spice seed is a major component of many Asian spice blends.

cumin (*Cuminum ciminum*). The dried fruit of the cumin plant. It is a small, crescent-shaped seed with an earthy flavor and aroma. Cumin is used raw or roasted and ground in many Asian spice blends.

curry leaves (*Murraya keonigii*). An important ingredient used in Sri Lankan, South Indian, Malaysian, and Fijian cooking. The fragrant small leaflets grow closely along a central axis and are referred to as a sprig of curry leaves. Pull the curry leaves off the axis and discard the axis, which is tough.

curry powder. A blend of spices. Different spices are used in varying proportions and ground to make curry powder. Curry powder is available commercially.

deglaze. Stir in a liquid such as stock or wine to a pan to loosen and dissolve the browned and caramelized food particles that are stuck to the bottom of the pan. The resulting mixture enriches the sauce.

fennel (*Foeniculum vulgari*). The oval, pale green-brown seed of the perennial fennel plant. It has a sweetish anise flavor and aroma. It is used in fragrant spice mixes of Asia and is also used as a mouth freshener.

fenugreek (*Trigonella foenum-graecum*). A small herbaceous legume. The brownish yellow seed is flat and oblong in shape. It is used as a spice in curries and has a bittersweet flavor. It goes well with fish but should be used with discretion. Fenugreek is also available in ground form.

fish sauce. A strong-smelling, salty, amber-colored clear liquid sauce made from anchovies, shrimp, or other small fish fermented in brine. The Thai version, which is milder and pale in color, is *nampla*; the stronger Vietnamese version is *nouc nam*; both are available in Asian grocery stores.

furikake. A Japanese ready-made blend of dried seasonings such as dried bonito flakes, ground and whole sesame seeds, crumbled dried seaweed, and salt.

garam masala. A mixture of highly aromatic roasted ground spices used in Indian cooking. This flavorful spice mix is available commercially.

goraka (*Garcinia cambogia*). Goraka is also known as fish tamarind, an acidic fruit native to Sri Lanka. It has a fluted skin, dividing the fruit into six to eight lobes. When dried, the lobes turn black in color. It has a tart flavor and is a preferred souring agent in Sri Lankan cuisine, especially in fish cookery.

hoisin. A Chinese sauce made from fermented soybean paste; it is both sweet and spicy.

Kaffir lime (*Citrus hystrix*). The fragrant, dark green Kaffir lime leaves are indispensable in Thai cooking; they have a piercing citrus aroma. They should be removed and discarded before a dish is served.

lemongrass (*Cymbopogon citratus*). A fragrant tropical grass with long, light-green stalks and grasslike leaves. The bulb and the tender inner stalks are used to impart a strong lemony flavor and aroma to Thai curries and other preparations.

mirin. Japanese rice wine. Mirin is sweet and syrupy and is used in sauces and marinades.

miso. A Japanese bean paste made from cooked, salted, and fermented soybeans and rice or barley. Miso comes in a variety of colors. Shiro miso is white in color, sweet and fine textured. Aka miso is red in color and has a saltier taste.

mizuna (*Brassica rapa* ssp. *nipposinica* var. *laciniata*). Japanese mustard. The dark green, feathery leaves are often used in mixed green salads; mature ones with the white succulent stems are excellent when fast wilted for a vegetable dish.

nonreactive. A term used to describe utensils used in cooking that are made of materials that do not react to acids and salts to form toxic substances or discolor food. Glass, enamel, ceramic, and stainless steel are some nonreactive materials.

nutmeg (*Myristica fragrans*). The fruit of the tree *Myristica fragrans*. It is encased in a dark, shiny, brittle shell which must be cracked and discarded; the kernel is then grated or ground for use as a spice.

ogo. A highly nutritious seaweed. Ranging in color from deep yellow to brown to a deep rose, it has a crunchy texture and a sweet sea flavor. It is used raw or blanched. It is available in Hawaiian markets.

palm sugar. A coarse, deep honey-colored sugar derived from boiling down the sap of the palm (*Careota urens*) or coconut palm (*Cocos nucifera*). A good substitute is dark brown sugar.

panko. A type of Japanese bread crumbs; you may substitute regular bread crumbs.

poi. A Hawaiian staple made from boiled taro root that is mashed to a smooth texture. It is fermented two to three days until sour and thick in texture. The sourness is a desired quality some look for in poi.

poppadom. Dried lentil wafers, mildly or highly spiced, available in packets in Asian grocery stores. They should be grilled or deep-fried before serving.

sachet. A cheesecloth bag filled with a blend of aromatic ingredients used to flavor stocks, sauces, soups, and stews. The sachet is removed and discarded, as indicated in each recipe.

saffron (*Crocus sativus*). The dried, yellow-orange stigma of the saffron crocus. This very expensive spice is used in food as a flavoring and coloring agent.

salted black beans. Black soybeans that have been fermented and heavily salted are a favorite Chinese ingredient. These are available commercially in cans or plastic bags; some are labeled preserved black beans. Black beans should be rinsed before use.

sashimi. A Japanese delicacy of thinly sliced fresh raw fish traditionally artistically presented and served with condiments such as Japanese horseradish and dipping sauces.

serrano chilies. A short, plump, green or orange red chili with a thick, crunchy texture and a very hot flavor.

shichimi. A Japanese mix of seven spices such as dried, powdered orange peel; poppy seeds, black sesame seeds, and white sesame seeds; chile powder; chili peppers; and powdered seaweed. Shichimi is also known as *shichimi togarashi* or *kichimi.*

shiso. Also known as perilla. This aromatic leaf, green or reddish purple in color, is close to mint and basil and is served as a garnish, especially with raw fish preparations.

shrimp paste. A pungent paste made from dried shrimp and often referred to as *blachan* or *trassi.* It is available commercially.

sriracha. A Thai condiment, sweet and spicy with a tang; it is a sauce that can be used like a chili paste.

tamarind (*Tamarindus indica*). A bushy tropical tree with cinnamon brown pods that have brittle shells. The pulp from the ripe pod has a sweet and sour flavor and is chocolate brown in color. When the pod is ripe, the pulp separates easily from its shell. Tamarind pulp is available commercially in block form. Bottled tamarind paste and juice are also available commercially. Asian grocery stores and health food stores usually carry these tamarind products.

Thai curry paste, red or green. A wet mix of spices and seasonings such as garlic, lemongrass, galangal, shrimp paste, etc.; commercially available in jars or cans. The green curry paste is made from hot green chilies and seasonings; the red is made from dried hot red chilies and seasonings.

turmeric (*Curcuma longa, C. domestica*). A tropical plant related to ginger; it has orange yellow rhizomes. These rhizomes are dried and ground to a fine powder. The spice has a strong flavor and is used as a yellow coloring agent in food. It should be used sparingly.

wasabi. A spicy green paste known as Japanese horseradish. It has a pungent and strong, biting flavor. It is available in powder or paste form. The fresh wasabi root should be peeled and grated to a smooth texture.

Index

About the Author

Kusuma Cooray, CCE, CHE, FCFA (CG), trained at Le Cordon Bleu; the National Bakery School, London; and École de Cuisine La Varenne, Paris. She obtained her technical training at Marks and Spencer Directors Dining Room, London, and Henri IV Restaurant, Chartres. She was awarded a scholarship by the School of Hotel Administration, Cornell University, and was also a guest lecturer there, where she shared her expertise in the cultures and cuisines of Southeast Asia.

Mrs. Cooray was corporate chef for tobacco heiress Doris Duke and later executive chef for the renowned Honolulu restaurant The Willows. She has won several awards, including the Burton trophy for Outstanding Student, National Bakery School, London; the Chaine des Rotisseurs Brillat Savarin Medal of Honor; and recently the Gold Star of Excellence, in recognition of her contributions toward the education of young chefs in Hawai'i and the Pacific. She is the author of *Burst of Flavor,* which focuses on highlighting spices and harmonizing East-West flavors.

Mrs. Cooray is currently professor at the Culinary Institute of the Pacific, University of Hawai'i. She serves as honorary consul for the Democratic Socialist Republic of Sri Lanka in Hawai'i and the Pacific.

Production notes for
Cooray / Ocean to Plate

Book design and composition by Mardee Melton,
in 10.5-point Warnock Pro, with display type in Inscription.

Printing and binding by Regent Publishing Services
Printed on 128 gsm glossy art